the **THIRD** edition

New Headway

Pre-Intermediate
Teacher's Book

D1325142

John and Liz Soars

Mike Sayer

OXFORD

UNIVERS

4 1 0267830 9

Contents

New Headway Pre-Intermediate – the THIRD edition

Introduction

New Headway Pre-Intermediate – the THIRD edition

What remains the same?

The basic *Headway* methodology is the same. Proven traditional approaches are used alongside those which have been developed and researched more recently.

Starter

Each unit begins with a *Starter* section, which is designed to be a warmer to the lesson. It is a short activity and always has direct relevance to the language to be introduced in the unit.

Grammar

Much of the grammatical syllabus is unchanged (but see *What are the differences? – Grammar*).

Grammar spot

Each grammar presentation contains a *Grammar spot*. This is a mix of explanation, questions, self-check, and pronunciation tasks to reinforce the grammar being taught. Each *Grammar spot* has a link to the fuller *Grammar Reference* section at the back of the book.

Practice

There is a wide variety of practice activities covering all the skills. There is great emphasis on personalized speaking.

Vocabulary

Vocabulary is not only integrated throughout, but also developed in its own section.

Skills work

Skills work is both integrated and balanced. All the texts for listening and reading come from authentic sources, and are simplified and adapted to suit the level.

Everyday English

This section focuses primarily on spoken English.

Tapescripts

There is a full bank of unseen tapescripts in a section at the end of the Student's Book.

What are the differences?

Grammar

The Student's Book now has twelve units, in response to feedback from teachers who said they did not have time to cover fourteen units in the academic year. However, the two main grammar areas which have been removed, the Past Perfect and reported speech, are both covered in *New Headway Intermediate, third edition.*

Grammar Reference practice exercises

The *Grammar Reference* has been extended to include short practice exercises on the language areas being studied in each unit. These can be used as the teacher wishes – for homework, or in addition to the *Practice* section in the unit.

Reading and listening texts

All the reading and listening texts are new, including those used in the presentation sections. We have taken this opportunity to find up-to-date texts and listening passages, chosen for their intrinsic interest and relevance to modern life.

Writing

The *Writing* section now appears separately at the back of the Student's Book. The syllabus consists of twelve complete writing lessons. These are cued from the most relevant page of the unit in the Student's Book, but can be used as and when the teacher wishes. The *Writing* section provides practice exercises and models for students to complete, adapt, and follow in order to produce a satisfying piece of writing.

Pairwork and extra material

This is now in a section at the back of the book, for ease of access for both students and teacher.

Music of English

We acknowledge that the patterns of stress and intonation in speech vary depending on accent, register, the message, sentence length, etc. Nevertheless, in this third edition of *New Headway Pre-Intermediate* we have decided to offer guidance to students in this area of their English pronunciation. We have done this in two ways:

- **Stress highlighting:** When beneficial to spoken tasks, we have indicated through highlighting where the main stress falls, to help students sound more natural. On many occasions there is a recorded model for students to listen and repeat. At times where there may be different possible stress patterns, we have chosen the one we think is the most sensible and useful model for students to follow.

- **Music of English boxes** focus on word and sentence stress, word linking, and intonation patterns in high-frequency everyday expressions. The accompanying recordings provide clear models for the students to listen and repeat.

What's in the Teacher's Book?

- **Full teaching notes**, answers, and suggestions about how to deal with likely problems. Reading texts are introduced with an *About the text* feature, which gives background information and suggests key vocabulary to pre-teach.

- **Tapescripts** in the main body of the teaching notes. Students also have tapescripts at the end of the Student's Book.

- *Don't forget!* **section** at the end of each unit, which refers to relevant exercises in the Workbook, the Grammar Reference section of the Student's Book, the Pronunciation Book, and the Word list in the Student's Book.

- **Photocopiable material and songs section** with teacher's notes.

- **Stop and check tests.** There are three *Stop and check* revision tests which cover Units 1–4, 5–8, and 9–12. These can either be set in class, or given for homework (preferably over a weekend) and then discussed in the next lesson. Students can work in small groups to try to agree on the correct answer, then you can go over it with the whole class, reminding students of the language items covered.

- **Progress tests.** There are two *Progress tests* which cover units 1–6 and 7–12.

What's in the Workbook?

The Workbook is an important component of the course, as it revises the grammatical input of the Student's Book. Some of the exercises can be found on the Student's Workbook CD/cassette, for use in class or at home. There are new reading and pronunciation sections, as well as a *Check it* section. This is a revision component, with a listening section which not only revises the content of each Student's Book unit, but also offers students valuable extra listening practice.

What are the other materials?

Tests

In addition to two versions (A and B) of each Unit Test, there are six new Review Tests and two separate Exit Tests. There is also a bank of optional Listening Tests.

DVD/Video

There is a *New Headway Pre-Intermediate* DVD/Video with Student's Book and Teacher's Book. The video is fresh and modern, and comprises six short episodes. Each episode consolidates and extends key language presented in the Student's Book. The accompanying Student's Book and Teacher's Book help to fully exploit video material.

Interactive Practice CD-ROM

This contains a variety of interactive tasks for revision and practice, and exploits materials from the video.

Headway online

There is a teacher's website with a comprehensive range of additional materials for teachers at www.oup.com/elt/teacher/headway. These materials further supplement and extend the Student's Book.

There is also a student's site with interactive practice exercises and games at www.oup.com/elt/headway.

Finally!

We try to guide students to an *understanding* of new language, rather than just having examples of it on the page. We attach great importance to practice activities, both controlled and free, personalized and impersonal. The skills work comes from a wide range of material – newspapers, magazines, biographies, short stories, radio programmes, songs – and features both British and American English.

We hope you and your students enjoy using the books, and have success with them, whether using *New Headway* for the first time, or having learned to trust its approach from previous use.

Introduction to the unit

You are probably beginning a new class with a group of students you don't know. Students might know each other, or they might not. Your main aim over the first few lessons together is to establish a good classroom atmosphere, where everyone feels comfortable. Hopefully you will all not only work hard, but have fun at the same time.

Another of your aims will be to check your students' language abilities. How good are they at using the tense system? Do they confuse the Present Simple and Continuous? Can they form questions in English? What's their vocabulary like? Is there a disparity in their skills abilities? Can they speak English better than write it? Do they panic when listening to a recording? All this information will allow you to get a feel for your students' abilities, and will also help you to plan your lessons.

The theme of this unit is getting to know people. *The Starter* and opening *Two Students* sections revise present and past tenses and question forms, and students are encouraged to ask questions to get to know each other in the *Practice* section.

The *Reading and speaking* section contains a text about how people meet on a blind date, and in the *Listening and speaking* section, four people describe their relationships with their best friends.

There are opportunities for students to roleplay polite conversations and practise social expressions.

Language aims

Grammar – tenses There is revision of the Present Simple and Continuous, the Past Simple, the *going to* future, the modal verb *can*, and the full verb *have*. (*Have* appears with the *do/does/did* forms. *Have got* and *have* are contrasted in Unit 2.) Students should be familiar with these tenses and verb forms, but they will no doubt still make many mistakes.

This unit provides general revision of these verb forms and their meanings, and gives you the opportunity to assess your new students' strengths and weaknesses. All the verb forms are dealt with in greater depth in later units of the course.

Question forms The secondary grammatical aim of Unit 1 is revision of question forms. These often present learners of English with problems.

Common mistakes:

Where you live?   *What you do last night?*
Where do he live?   *What did you last night?*
Do you can speak French?   *Where you went?*

Another problem for learners is voice range. English has a very wide voice range, and this is apparent in question formation.

Where do you live?

Do you like learning English?

Students often have a very flat intonation, and they need to be encouraged to make their voice rise and fall as necessary.

Vocabulary In the *Vocabulary and pronunciation* section, students are helped to use a bilingual dictionary effectively, both L1 to English and English to L1.

Everyday English Common social expressions are introduced and practised through dialogues.

Notes on the unit

STARTER (SB p6)

1 Ask students to work in pairs to match the questions with the answers.

Answers

Where were you born?	In Mexico.
What do you do?	I'm a teacher.
Are you married?	No, I'm single.
Why are you learning English?	Because I need it for my job.
When did you start learning English?	A year ago.
How often do you have English classes?	Three times a week.

2 Students ask and answer the questions in pairs.

TWO STUDENTS (SB p6)

Tenses and questions

ABOUT THE TEXT

The aim of the text is to test the students' ability to recognize and use basic tenses (Present Simple and Continuous, Past Simple and *going to* + infinitive).

Croatia is a small country on the Adriatic Sea in south central Europe. It borders Slovenia and Serbia, and was once part of the former Yugoslavia. Marija's first language is Croat. Her name is pronounced /mæˈriə/ /ˈkʊzmæ/.

Médecins sans Frontières is a France-based charity which works in developing countries.

1 Ask students to look at the two pictures, and describe the two people. Ask *Who are they? How old are they?*

Ask students to look at the photograph of Marija again, and think of a few questions they would like to ask her, for example *Where are you from?* Write a few suggestions on the board.

T 1.1 [CD 1: Track 2] Tell students to listen to Marija and read the text at the same time. Ask if they found the answers to any of their questions and check any words they didn't understand. Then ask students to work in pairs to complete the text with the verbs in the box.

Answers and tapescript

Marija Kuzma

Hello! My name's Marija Kuzma and I (1) **come** from Zagreb, the capital city of Croatia. I'm 20, and I (2) **'m studying** medicine at the University of Zagreb. The course (3) **lasts** six years and it's all in English! It's hard work, but I (4) **'m enjoying** it a lot. I (5) **live** at home with my mother, father, and grandmother. I can speak three foreign languages – English,

French, and Italian. I (6) **speak** Italian because my grandmother's from Italy, and she always (7) **spoke** to me in Italian when I was very young. I speak English because I (8) **went** to an English-speaking high school.

After I graduate, I (9) **'m going to work** for *Médecins sans Frontières* in West Africa, because I want to travel and help people.

In the feedback, ask students to tell you whether each verb has present, past, or future meaning, but don't get into detail about use at this stage.

2 Pre-teach/check *retired* (adj) and *to retire* (v). Ask students to look at the picture of Jim. Tell students that Jim is *retired* (he has stopped work because he is old). Ask them to work in pairs to complete the questions about Jim. Monitor and note the sort of problems your students have with question formation.

POSSIBLE PROBLEMS

- Students omit *does* and *did* in the Present and Past Simple. (*Where he live?*)
- They confuse the Present Continuous and the Present Simple (*What does he studying?*).
- They forget *is* in the *going to* question. (*What he going to do next year?*)

Answers

1 **Where does he** come from?
2 **Where does he** live?
3 **Who does he** live with?
4 **What did he** do before he retired?
5 When **did he** leave school?
6 What **is he** studying?
7 How many children **does he** have?
8 What **is he going to** do next year?

T 1.2 [CD 1: Track 3] Ask students to listen to Jim, then work in pairs to write the answers to the questions. Students then ask and answer the questions in pairs.

Answers and tapescript

1 He comes from the north of England, near Manchester.
2 He lives in a village (just outside the city).
3 He lives alone.
4 He worked in a paper factory.
5 He left school when he was 15.
6 He's studying Spanish.
7 Two (a son and a daughter).
8 He's going to visit his son and his Spanish wife in Spain.

T 1.2

Jim Allen

Hello. My name's Jim Allen and I come from the north of England, near Manchester. I live in a village just outside the city. I live alone now, because my wife died three years ago. But I'm near my daughter and her family, so that's OK. Until last year, I worked in a paper factory, but now I'm retired. I never liked my job much but now I'm really enjoying life! I'm a student again. I'm studying with the *University of the Third Age*. It helps retired people like me who want to study again, and it's really wonderful. You see, I left school when I was 15 and started work in the factory, because we needed the money. Now I'm studying Spanish. I love it. My son lives in Spain with his Spanish wife. Next year I'm going to visit them for six months, so I want my Spanish to be good!

3 **T 1.3** [CD 1: Track 4] Ask students to work in pairs to complete the questions. Students then listen to the recording and check the answers.

Answers and tapescript
I = Interviewer   J = Jim
1 I **Do you have** a job?
    J No, I don't. I'm retired. I'm a student now.
2 I Which university **do you go** to?
    J I don't go to university. I study at home.
3 I **Are you enjoying** the course?
    J Yes, I am. It's wonderful.
4 I What **are you doing** at the moment?
    J I'm writing an essay about *Don Quixote*.
5 I Why **did you** leave school at 15?
    J Because my family was poor. We needed the money.
6 I **Who are you going** to visit next year?
    J My son and his wife. They live in Spain now.

GRAMMAR SPOT (SB p7)

The *Grammar spot* in each unit aims to get students to think analytically about the language. Ask students to discuss the grammar questions in pairs before feeding back to the whole class, as this encourages peer teaching and builds students' confidence. If you are teaching a monolingual class, and your students find it easier or more rewarding to answer in L1, encourage them to do so.

1 If you didn't focus on this earlier, ask students to work in pairs to find examples of verb forms with present, past, and future meaning in the tapescripts about Marija and Jim. However, don't go into any detail about form and use of past and future tenses here, as they will be dealt with in later units.

Answers
Present tenses: e.g. *I come, I'm studying, The course lasts, I'm enjoying, I live*
Past tenses: e.g. *she always spoke to me, I was young, I went to*
Future tenses: *I'm going to work, I'm going to visit*

2 Ask students to discuss the two questions about present tenses in pairs or threes, then discuss their answers as a class.

Answers
The two tenses are the Present Simple and the Present Continuous.
They are formed differently. The third person of the Present Simple ends in –s. The Present Continuous is formed with the verb *to be* + –*ing*.
More importantly, they mean different things. The Present Simple is used to express an action which is always true, or true for a long time. The Present Continuous is used to express an activity happening now, or around now.

3 Ask students to work in pairs to match the question words and answers. Do the first as an example. This activity gets students to think about the meaning of the question words. In the feedback, you could get students to guess what the whole question might be. With weaker classes, you could extend this activity by getting students to ask and answer questions in pairs, using the question words.

Answers
What ...?	A sandwich. (e.g. *What did you have for lunch?*)
Who ...?	Jack. (*Who is that?*)
Where ...?	In New York. (*Where does Bill live?*)
When ...?	Last night. (*When did you see Maria?*)
Why ...?	Because I wanted to. (*Why did you do that?*)
How many ...?	Four. (*How many children do they have?*)
How much ...?	$5. (*How much did it cost?*)
How ...?	By bus. (*How do you get to school?*)
Whose ...?	It's mine. (*Whose bag is this?*)
Which ...?	The black one. (*Which jacket is yours?*)

Ask students to read Grammar Reference 1.1, 1.2, and 1.3 on SB p127 for homework.

PRACTICE (SB p8)

Talking about you

1 Ask students to work in small groups of three or four. Give them a few minutes to think about how to form the questions, then get them to take turns to ask and answer with other people in their group. It might be a good idea to do this as a mingle activity, where students stand up and move around to talk to different people, especially if students don't know each other very well. If your students do already know each other well, distribute pictures of famous people cut out of magazines, and they can assume these new identities.

Monitor as students are asking and answering questions, helping and correcting as necessary.

As a follow-up, get students to ask you the questions. Or, alternatively, give students three or four minutes in groups to think of some different questions to ask you. If they know you very well already, you could use a picture of someone else, e.g. a celebrity about whom you know a lot of personal details. Hold it up and say *This is me. Think of some questions to ask me.*

Correct any mistakes very carefully. You want to have genuine communication at this point, but you also want well-formed questions with good pronunciation.

2 **T 1.4** [CD 1: Track 5] Ask students to correct the questions and check their answers with a partner. Play the recording and check the answers in class. Ask students to tell you what tense each question is in.

> **Answers and tapescript**
> 1 Do you like listening **to** music? (Present Simple)
> 2 What sort of music **do** you like? (Present Simple)
> 3 Do you often **wear** jeans? (Present Simple)
> 4 What's your teacher wearing today? (Present Continuous)
> 5 Where **did** you go on your last holiday? (Past Simple)
> 6 What did you **do** yesterday evening? (Past Simple)
> 7 What **are** you doing this evening?
> (Present Continuous for future arrangements)
> 8 What are you going **to** do after this course?
> (*going to* + infinitive)

Read out each question, modelling good pronunciation. Alternatively, ask each question to an individual in the class, thus modelling pronunciation and getting students to think about how to respond. Divide students into small groups to ask and answer the questions. Monitor, help, and correct any errors.

An extension to this exercise is to ask students in pairs to change one word in each question to make new questions, for example *Do you like listening to the radio? What sort of films do you like?* Once they have reformulated questions, mix the pairs and get them to interview each other.

3 Ask students to write a paragraph about themselves, using the text about Marija as a model. You could set this as homework.

Check it

4 Students work in pairs to decide which is the correct verb form. As you get the answers, ask *Why?* each time to reinforce the rules about the Present Simple and Continuous, Past Simple, and the *going to* future.

> **Answers**
> 1 **comes** (because this is a fact which is always true)
> 2 **speaks** (same reason)
> 3 **is wearing** (because this is happening now)
> 4 **Do you like** (because this is always true, and *like* is a state verb)
> 5 **went** (because this is in the past)
> 6 **is going to study** (because this is in the future – an intention)

Exchanging information

5 In this information gap activity students must ask each other questions to find out about Dr Mary Steiner, a radio agony aunt.

Lead in by focusing students on the photograph of Dr Steiner and asking them questions about it, for example

Where's Dr Steiner? (in a radio studio)
What's she doing? (She's talking to listeners.)
What do radio agony aunts do? (They answer questions about personal problems on the radio.)
Who phones them and why? (Radio listeners, because they have a problem that is worrying them and they need answers and help.)

6 Divide the class into pairs, and ask each pair to decide who is A and who is B. Student A must turn to p143. Student B must turn to p146.

Give students four or five minutes to read through their information, then prepare questions using the question word prompts. Monitor and help them prepare. When they are ready, model the activity briefly by asking one or two questions, then let students ask and answer each other's questions to complete their information.

> **Answers (complete text)**
> Dr Mary Steiner lives in **Santa Barbara, California**. She's married and has **twin sons**. Her husband's name is **Dan** and he's a **surgeon**. They met **when they were both at college**. Both her sons went to **Harvard** University and studied **law**, and now they both work for **Miramax film studios in California**.
> Mary started working as a radio agony aunt **thirty years ago**, and does **five** programmes a week. Every day more than 60,000 people try to phone her. They have **money problems, relationship problems, work problems** – all sorts! The programme lasts **an hour**, and at the end Mary feels **really tired**. At the moment she's writing **a book about marriage**, because **she's worried about the number of divorces**. Her own parents divorced when she was **five**.
> She's going to retire **next year**. She wants to **spend more time travelling**.

ADDITIONAL MATERIAL

Workbook Unit 1
These exercises could be done in class to give further practice, for homework, or in a later class as revision.

Exercises 1–3 Tenses

Exercises 4–9 Question forms

Best friends

> **ABOUT THE LISTENING**
>
> This listening is made up of four short passages, in which four people describe their best friends. The fourth speaker, Brianna, is an American teenager. She uses American vocabulary items, notably *mom*, *downtown* (town centre), and *cool*. The tasks get students to listen for specific information.
>
> The word *friend* has many collocations. You may wish to lead in by eliciting a few from your students. For example: *good friend, best friend, old friend, close friend, great friend.*

1 Put students in pairs to discuss the questions.

2 **T 1.5** [CD 1: Track 6] Ask students to look at the photos and the chart. Drill the pronunciation of the names in the chart: Kirsty /ˈkɜːstɪ/ Azam /ˈæzæm/ Caleb /ˈkeɪleb/. Play the recording. Ask students to listen. Pause after each recording so that students have time to write their answers.

Let students check their answers in pairs before discussing them as a class.

Answers

Best friend	Whose friend?	When did they meet?	Why are they friends?
Kirsty	Shona	When we were 12.	We grew up together and know everything about each other. Kirsty knows me better than anyone else. I can always talk to her about my problems. She always listens and gives me good advice.
Sammy	Dominic	When I was four.	He's funny and he plays football.
Dave and Azam	Michael	At university.	Don't know! We were all very different.
Caleb	Brianna	When we were kids.	We grew up together. We always liked the same games. Now we're into the same music. He's like a brother to me.

3 **T 1.5** Read through the questions briefly as a class and point out difficult vocabulary: *share a hobby* (have the same hobby or interest), *He is like a brother* (he is the same as a brother).

Put students in pairs to discuss the questions. Then play the recording again.

Answers and tapescript

1 Shona and Kirsty
2 Brianna and Caleb (music), and Dominic and Sammy (football)
3 Michael, Dave, and Azam
4 Dominic and Sammy
5 Michael's
6 Dominic's
7 Shona's
8 Brianna's

T 1.5

Best friends

Shona

I have three or four good friends, but I think my best friend is Kirsty. We first met when we were 12. She started at my school, and the teacher asked me to look after her. We soon became friends. We looked quite funny together. She's very tall, and I'm quite small! Because we grew up together, we know everything about each other. So Kirsty knows me better than anyone else. I can always talk to her about my problems. She always listens and then gives me good advice! I hope I do the same for her. We are both married now, and we live quite near each other, but in different towns. We talk on the phone all the time, especially now, because we are both having a baby this summer!

Dominic

My best friend is called Sammy –er and he often comes to play at my house after school. A long time ago –er when I was four –er we went to Busy Bee Nursery School together. Me and Sammy are both six now. I like him 'cos he's funny and he plays football. I like going to play at his house, too. He's got a big garden, and a nice dog called King.

Michael

I have two very good friends from university called Dave and Azam. We stayed in the same house near the university. I don't know why we became friends. We were all very different. Dave was very quiet and always worked hard, and Azam was, well, a bit crazy! He never remembered his house keys. He climbed in through the window at least once a week. He loved cooking Indian food and having parties. We had parties all the time in our house.

Now, of course, life is very different. Dave is a writer and lives in France. He sends me long, funny emails every month. Azam is an international lawyer. He's working in Hong Kong at the moment. But we still meet once a year with our families. We usually meet at Dave's house in France and have a holiday together.

Brianna

My best friend is my neighbor, Caleb. He's 16. Our moms are good friends, and I call Caleb's mom Auntie Janine. We grew up together. When we were kids, we always liked the same games. Now we're into the same music. Weekends, we usually go on the Internet, or sometimes we go downtown to the music stores to listen to our favourite artists. Caleb's cool. He's like a brother to me.

Language work

4 Ask students to match the verbs with the words and phrases.

Answers	
become	friends
play	football, together
send	emails
give	advice
talk	on the phone
have	parties
grow up	together
go on	the Internet

WRITING (SB p102)

Describing friends – Correcting common mistakes

The aim of this writing section is to familiarize students with the common symbols used when marking written work. Once students have completed these activities, you can use the symbols to mark up any written work they hand in.

Using symbols, rather than simply correcting mistakes as the teacher, makes students think about the mistake they made and encourages them to correct themselves. If using symbols is new for your students, you might want to both correct and mark up mistakes with symbols once or twice before using the symbols alone.

1 Put students in pairs to look at the symbols and correct the mistakes. Monitor and help. In feedback, ask students whether these are mistakes that they typically make.

Answers
1 I'm enjoying the party.
2 My brother has a good job.
3 I have two younger brothers.
4 She's got some red shoes.
5 He arrived yesterday.
6 They aren't coming.
7 She's a doctor.
8 They went to Italy on holiday.

2 Divide the class into groups of four or five. Tell half the groups that they are Group As. Tell the other groups that they are Group Bs. Ask each group to mark up their mistakes with the symbols in exercise 1, but not to correct them.

Answers
A
1 I like Rome because ∧ is a beautiful city.
2 She studied <u>for three years psychology</u>. [WO]
3 There <u>aren't</u> any milk. [Gr]
4 He's <u>speaking</u> French, German, and Spanish. [T]
5 I watched TV <u>than</u> I went to bed. [WW]
6 Did you <u>by</u> any bread at the supermarket? [Sp]
B
1 I lost <u>my all</u> money. [WO]
2 What did you ∧ last night?
3 He always <u>wear</u> jeans. [Gr]
4 My town is <u>quite</u> at the weekend. [Sp]
5 I want <u>that I</u> pass the exam. [Gr]
6 They arrived <u>at</u> London. [Prep]

3 Ask students to stand up, walk round, and sit down next to someone from a different group. Ask them to correct each other's mistakes.

In feedback, ask whether the symbols helped the students to correct the mistakes.

Answers
A
1 I like Rome because **it** is a beautiful city.
2 She studied **psychology for three years**.
3 There **isn't** any milk.
4 **He speaks** French, German, and Spanish.
5 I watched TV **then** I went to bed.
6 Did you **buy** any bread at the supermarket?
B
1 I lost **all my** money.
2 What did you **do** last night?
3 He always **wears** jeans.
4 My town is **quiet** at the weekend.
5 I want **to pass** the exam.
6 They arrived **in** London.

4 Ask students to correct the piece of writing individually. Monitor and help. Let students check their corrections in pairs before discussing as a class.

Answers

My Best Friend

My best friend was my best man when I <u>got</u> married two <u>years</u> ago. <u>His</u> name is Mario and we met <u>at</u> university in Bologna. In fact, we met on our very first day <u>there</u>. Mario was <u>the</u> first person I spoke <u>to</u> and we discovered we were both studying Spanish and that we were both football fans. When we left university, we went <u>travelling together</u> for six <u>months</u>. We had a fantastic time touring <u>North</u> and <u>South America</u>. The <u>journey/trip</u> through Chile was amazing. When we were in Mexico, we met two sisters <u>from</u> London, Tamsin and Tanya. Now I'm married <u>to</u> Tanya, and next year Mario and Tamsin <u>are</u> going to get married. I like Mario because he <u>is</u> very funny and we <u>have</u> really good times together. He <u>lives</u> in a different town now, but we text or call <u>each other</u> <u>often</u>. I'm very lucky that he's my friend.

5 Ask students to write their own text about their best friend.

6 Ask students to exchange their text with a partner. Ask students to read each other's texts and mark mistakes with the correct symbols. Students should then correct their own work.

Ask a few students to read their texts aloud for the class.

If time is short, exercise 5 could be done for homework. Students then compare and correct their texts in the next class.

READING AND SPEAKING (SB p10)

A blind date

ABOUT THE TEXT

In this section, the skills of reading, listening, and speaking are integrated. Students read profiles of different people, and listen to two people describing their blind date and their first impressions of each other.

Blind dates are arranged meetings with people you don't know, to find out if you'd like to have a relationship with them. Point out that *blind date* = the event and also the person. The TV series called *Blind Date* was very popular for many years in the UK. Ask students if they have ever seen a similar programme in their own country. The article here is based on a real, regular column in London's popular newspaper, the *Evening Standard*.

Reading texts and vocabulary

Reading texts are an excellent source of new vocabulary because they introduce words in natural contexts which allow students to guess what words might mean. There are a number of different ways of dealing with the unknown vocabulary in this text and other texts in the Student's Book. Here are two suggestions:

- After they have read the text, ask students to underline some of the words they don't know (you could give a limit of 5–10 words) and then try to guess what they mean. You could get them to check with a partner before checking their guesses in a dictionary.
- If you know your students and their first language well, you could predict words they don't know, then give students synonyms or definitions and ask them to find matching words in the text, for example *Find a word that means friendly* (outgoing).

Discourage students from using dictionaries too much as they read. They may miss the basic meaning of the article if they spend too much time looking up words.

The vocabulary in this particular text is not demanding. However, a nice vocabulary follow-up to the reading is to elicit all the activity words in the text, write them on the board, get students to check them or mime them to show the meaning, and then get students to say which ones are important to them and important in a partner. Here is a complete list of activity words from the text: *reading, cycling, walking, skiing, snowboarding, going out, travelling, relaxing, camping, dancing, meeting friends, having barbecues, diving, visiting art galleries, wearing designer clothes, surfing, having a few beers, going to a football match, going clubbing.*

Arsenal = a leading English Premiership football team from North London.

Canary Wharf = London's business district

veggie = vegetarian

Star signs

Here is the pronunciation of the zodiac signs, and a few words to sum up some of their typical characteristics.

Aries /ˈeərɪːz/ *combative, argumentative, courageous*

Taurus /ˈtɔːrəs/ *sensible, loyal, hard-working, strong willed*

Gemini /ˈdʒemɪnaɪ/ *talkative, inquisitive, playful*

Cancer /ˈkænsə/ *sensitive, caring, moody*

Leo /ˈliːəʊ/ *dramatic, creative, attention-seeking*

Virgo /ˈvɜːgəʊ/ *careful, good at detail, efficient*

Libra /ˈliːbrə/ *diplomatic, charming, sociable*

Scorpio /ˈskɔːpiəʊ/ *serious, deep, controlling*

Sagittarius /ˌsædʒɪˈteərɪəs/ *adventurous, fun-loving, open-minded*

Capricorn /ˈkæprɪkɔːn/ *serious, ambitious, organized*

Aquarius /əˈkweərɪəs/ *independent, free-thinking, inventive*

Pisces /ˈpaɪsiːz/ *dreamy, imaginative, emotional*

1 Ask students to look at the star signs on p10. Check that the students know all the signs, and can pronounce them, (see the pronunciation guide in *About the text* above).

Divide students into groups of four or five to discuss the questions. You could extend the activity by asking students if they know what characteristics are typical for their sign, and whether they have them.

In feedback, ask one student from each group to say what everybody's star sign is. As a class, discuss whether it's interesting or necessary to know the star sign of boyfriends or girlfriends.

2 Ask students in pairs or small groups to look at the photos and headings in the newspaper article, and discuss the questions.

Answers
What is a blind date? A blind date is a meeting with someone you have never met before, in order to find out if you'd like to get to know them better and have a relationship.
What does the Evening Star do? It helps bring people together on blind dates.
Who are the people? A young man (Matt), who is looking for his perfect partner, and three young women that he can choose from.
What are their star signs? Matt's star sign is Capricorn, Miranda's is Scorpio, Beth's is Pisces, Holly's is Capricorn.

3 Give students a minute or two to read through the questions.

Ask students to read about Matt and answer the questions. Let them discuss their answers in pairs before discussing as a class.

Answers
1 He is a climate change scientist. He enjoys it (he says 'It's great for me') because it is what he studied at university.
2 He spent a lot of time at sea on scientific research ships.
3 It is much better for his social life, and he has a lot of friends.
4 He goes to the coast because he misses the sea.
5 He likes camping with friends, having barbecues, and diving or surfing.
6 He meets friends, has a few beers, goes to a football match, sometimes goes clubbing, and goes to an Indian restaurant at least once a week.
7 His perfect partner is outgoing, funny, and good to talk to. She dresses nicely, but isn't too worried about fashion. She enjoys having a good time in the city but it's important that she also likes travelling, sports, and country life.

4 Ask students to work with their partner to read about the three girls and discuss who Matt will choose and why.

Have a class discussion, asking each pair to explain their decision.

Answers
Students' own ideas.

Listening

5 **T 1.6** [CD 1: Track 7] Read out the questions, and make sure students are clear about the task. Then play the recording. Let students discuss their answers in pairs before having a class discussion.

Answers and tapescript
He chose Beth because he liked her eyes and because she seemed a bit different from the other London girls. Best of all he liked the fact that she couldn't think of anything that she hated. On the date, they went to an Indian restaurant, and talked about each other's jobs, cycling in London, and moving from the city to the country. They are going to meet again.

T 1.6
Blind Date
I = Interviewer   M = Matt
I   So, Matt, which lovely lady did you choose and why did you choose her?
M Well, they all looked lovely and at first I thought 'Oh I'll choose Holly, she sounds sporty and good fun'. But in the end I chose Beth. I chose her because I liked her eyes, and because she seemed a bit different from the other London girls. Best of all, I liked the fact that she couldn't think of anything that she hated.
I   So tell us about the date. What happened when you met?
M Well, I arrived first at the restaurant – an Indian restaurant, of course, and when Beth walked in –er I could see she was nice-looking, but she seemed quite nervous, –er, shy, and perhaps a bit embarrassed by being on a date with a stranger... but I liked that. We ordered our meals, and she tried to tell me why she was vegetarian. I felt a bit guilty because I ordered chicken curry, but it was OK, we laughed about it, and after that she started to relax and we began to really enjoy ourselves. I told her that she was very brave to cycle in London, because you know I can surf and swim in rough seas, but I really couldn't ride a bike in the London rush hour. But she said it's fine if you're careful. She was really interested in my job and my time at sea. We both agreed that one day we'd like to move out of London and live in the country – I'd like to be beside the sea, of course. Suddenly it was midnight and time to part. We're going to meet again next week. There's a lot more I'd like to know about Beth.

6 **T 1.7** [CD 1: Track 8] Again, read out the questions before playing the recording. In feedback, encourage students to say as much as they can about the people.

T 1.7

I = Interviewer   B = Beth

I And now Beth. What did you think of the date, Beth?

B Oh, I liked Matt a lot, the moment I saw him, but I felt so nervous. I was amazed he chose me and at first I just couldn't speak, but he was really kind. He asked me about my job and said how brave I was, cycling in London – it's not really brave – anyway, soon we were laughing like old friends. I think he's very good-looking. He has a really interesting job and he's very funny. I hope I'm interesting enough for him. Anyway, he's coming to see me at the bookshop next week and we're going to have lunch together. Who knows? I'd love to go camping with him one day.

Language work

Do the first question as an example, then ask students to write the other questions. Monitor and prompt. Ask pairs to compare their ideas with another pair before discussing as a class. You could build up a list of the best questions on the board.

Possible answers

Who is he/she?

What is he/she like? What does he/she look like? What does he/she like doing? What are we going to talk about? What am I going to say? What is his/her star sign?

Why did you choose him/her for me? Why do you think we are similar?

When are we going to meet?

Where are we going to meet? Where does he/she live? Where does he/she work?

How long have you known him/her? How will I recognize him/her?

What do you think?

Divide students into groups of four or five to discuss the questions. It is a good idea to make one student 'discussion leader'. It is their job to ask the questions, and make sure that everybody else contributes. Ask a different student to summarize their group's discussion for the class.

If you have a mixed class with people from different cultures, some of which may involve matchmaking or arranged marriages, take the opportunity here to let them tell the class about what happens in their culture. If anyone has been on a blind date (and is prepared to talk about it), encourage them to do so here.

Using a bilingual dictionary

Bilingual dictionaries are very useful when students are beginning to learn a language, but they need to be used with caution. They vary greatly in the amount of detail and accuracy of information. The better ones will separate out different meanings, and give plenty of example sentences. Problems arise especially when students look up a word in the L1 to English section and find perhaps three or four words in English to choose from. They need to look at the information very carefully to know which one is correct in context.

In these exercises, students are asked to look at a bilingual dictionary to see how much information it gives. They then practise using both halves of their own dictionary, first English to L1, then L1 to English.

1   Even if students are used to looking up words in dictionaries, it is worth revising the basic skills of dictionary use. Write a range of words starting with a different letter on the board and get students to say them in alphabetical order. Also elicit from the class the type of information you can find in a dictionary, e.g. pronunciation, part of speech (= the word type), example of use, other related words. In a bilingual dictionary, you also get the translation, of course.

Ask students to look at the dictionary extract. Get them to describe the order in which the information is given: the word itself, the phonetic symbols, the part of speech, the translation, etc.

2   Ask students to work in pairs and decide if the words shown are nouns, verbs, adjectives, adverbs, prepositions, or past tenses. Students then complete the exercise using the correct abbreviations.

Answers

computer	n
poor	a
speak	v
wonderful	a
in	prep
usually	adv
on	prep
came	pt
enjoy	v
quickly	adv
went	pt
factory	n

3   Ask students if they can think of any words in English with two meanings. Then focus them on the table and point out the two different meanings of *book*. Ask students in pairs to use dictionaries to look up the other words in the table and write sentences to show the two meanings of each word. Monitor and help.

T 1.8 [CD 1: Track 9] Ask students to compare their sentences with the sample answers on the recording.

Sample answers and tapescript

1 I'm reading a good book.
   I booked my flight online.
2 What kind of music do you like?
   My mother's a very kind person.
3 What does this mean?
   Some people are very mean. They don't like spending their money.
4 I live in a flat.
   Holland is a very flat country.
5 Can you swim?
   I'd like a can of coke.
6 Do you want to play football?
   We saw a play at the theatre.
7 The train's coming.
   Athletes have to train very hard.
8 The phone's ringing.
   What a lovely ring you're wearing!

4 If your students are unfamiliar with phonetic symbols, refer them to the chart on p159 of the SB. Ask them to check the pronunciation of each phoneme in the words by comparing them to the examples in the chart.

Ask students to read the words aloud, then write them down. In feedback, point out that English spelling is often not phonetic, and can be confusing. The same sound may have different spellings (*came* and *train*, for example, which both have the sound /eɪ/). Consequently, it is a good idea to refer to and use phonetic symbols.

Answers

1 wonderful	6 mean
2 computer	7 ring
3 flat	8 train
4 speak	9 quickly
5 came	10 factory

5 This final activity teaches students some useful everyday vocabulary, and then allows them to decide for themselves which words they would like to look up. You might decide to do it at the beginning of the next lesson as a quick revision of dictionary use.

Answers to everyday objects

laptop (computer), hairbrush, (a pack of) tissues, watch, wallet, chewing gum, mouse, mouse mat, ruler, sunglasses, pen, diary (NOT *an agenda* – *an agenda* is a list of things to be discussed at a meeting), scissors, pencil, pencil sharpener, rubber

SUGGESTION

Instead of getting students to look around the room, bring in as many everyday objects as you can. When students have found the word for an object in their dictionaries, put it on the floor. Carry on until all (or most) of the objects are on the floor. Point to an object and ask for the word to be repeated. Correct any mistakes. Ask a student to come out to the front and point at an object and say its name.

What follows is a memory game. Remove one object from the floor. Students must remember what the object was, so that when you point to the empty space on the floor, they can still tell you the word. Carry on removing objects until about a third remain on the floor. After that, it becomes very difficult to remember exactly what was where!

ADDITIONAL MATERIAL

Workbook Unit 1

Exercise 11 Pronunciation – Phonetic symbols

EVERYDAY ENGLISH (SB p13)

Social expressions 1

1 **T 1.9** [CD 1: Track 10] Focus attention on the stress highlighting. Play the recording. Ask students to listen and say which words are stressed. Play the recording again and ask students to repeat. In the feedback, ask why.

Answers and tapescript

In the first expression *are* is stressed because this is the word that carries most meaning. The speaker is asking about the other person's state.
In the second expression *you* is stressed. It is similar to the speaker saying, *And you?*
This is an example of shifting stress. Stress can shift depending on which word carries most meaning.

T 1.9
Hi, Anna. How are you?
I'm fine thanks. How are you?

MUSIC OF ENGLISH – stress and intonation

The *Music of English* boxes give students some guidance on getting the stress and intonation right for these key high-frequency expressions.

T 1.10 **T 1.11** [CD 1: Tracks 11/12] Play the recordings. Ask students to listen and repeat. Or you could model the examples yourself for different students to repeat.

Tapescripts

T 1.10
Thank you very much indeed.
I'm sorry. I can't come tonight.
Can you help me with this exercise?

T 1.11
Good morning!
Excuse me!
Can I help you?

2 Ask students to look at the pictures. Ask *Where do you think the people are? What's the relationship between them?* Ask students what they think the people are saying to each other.

3 Ask students to match the expressions and responses. Do one as an example. This exercise is more difficult than it at first appears. Some students will finish it very quickly, but will probably have made several mistakes. Monitor closely, look at their work and say how many they have right and wrong, without saying which ones, and ask them to look again.

Ask students to tell you which expressions go with the photos, and in what situations the other dialogues are taking place. This will also answer the question as to which expressions are more formal.

T 1.12 [CD 1: Track 13] Students listen to the recording to check the answers.

Answers and tapescript
1 'Good morning!' 'Good morning! Lovely day again.'
   (*Photo 1* Formal and informal: said, for example, at work, or in the street.)
2 'See you tomorrow!' 'Yeah! About nine in the coffee bar.'
   (Informal – could be students talking.)
3 'How do you do?' 'How do you do? Pleased to meet you.'
   (*Photo 2* Formal. Said when you meet somebody for the first time, especially in a business situation.)
4 'Thank you very much indeed.' 'Not at all. Don't mention it.'
   (Formal. Informally, we might say *That's OK*.)
5 'Excuse me!' 'Yes. Can I help you?'
   (Formal. In a shop, for example, to get someone's attention.)
6 'I'm sorry. I can't come tonight.' 'Never mind. Perhaps another time.'
   (Informal apology.)
7 'Can you help me with this exercise?' 'Of course I can. No problem.'
   (*Photo 5* Student to teacher in a classroom – informal)
8 'Can I help you?' 'No, thank you. I'm just looking.' (In a shop – quite formal.)
9 'Bye!' 'Bye! See you later.' (Informal)
10 'Bye! Have a good weekend!' 'Thanks! Same to you.'
    (*Photo 3* Informal – said on a Friday afternoon or evening.)
11 'Sorry I'm late.' 'It doesn't matter. You're here now.'
    (Informal)
12 'Cheers!' 'Cheers!' (*Photo 4* Informal – when you're having an alcoholic drink.)

Refer students to the stress shading. Play the recording again and get students to repeat each expression as a class. Alternatively, you could model the expressions getting individuals in the class to repeat, focusing on correct stress and intonation, which is very important here.

4 Ask students to work in pairs to test whether they can use the expressions.

5 Students work in pairs again to prepare two short dialogues. Introduce this activity by building up a dialogue as a model on the board first, and getting students to think where their dialogue is to take place before they start writing. Monitor and help.

Listen to a few of the dialogues, and feed back on any errors, focusing on students' intonation.

Don't forget!

Workbook Unit 1

Exercise 10 Reading – If you can't master English, try Globish

Exercise 12 Vocabulary – Words with more than one meaning

Exercises 13–14 Check it

Grammar Reference
Look at the exercises on SB p127 as a class, or set for homework. The answers are on TB p155.

Word list
Remind your students of the Word list for this unit on SB p152. They could translate the words, learn them at home, or transfer some of the words to their vocabulary notebook.

Pronunciation Book Unit 1

Video/DVD Episode 1

2

Present tenses • *have/have got*
Collocation – daily life
Making conversation 1

The way we live

Introduction to the unit

The theme of this unit is the way we live. In the opening section students read about the contrasting lifestyles of a Canadian hotel owner and a Chinese factory worker. The *Practice* section provides the opportunity to practise present tenses and *have/have got* in the context of lifestyles. The texts in the *Reading and speaking* section describe the lifestyles of two people who live and work in two different countries. The *Vocabulary and speaking* section has collocations of nouns and verbs around the topic of daily life, and the *Listening and speaking* section contains a radio programme in which four night workers talk about their jobs.

There are opportunities throughout the unit for students to talk about their own way of life and about their own country.

Language aims

Grammar – Present tenses Present tenses are revised in terms of form and use, with particular attention given to forming Present Simple questions and short answers using the auxiliary *do/does*. It is assumed that students will have a certain familiarity with both the Present Simple and the Present Continuous, although of course mistakes will still be made.

have/have got The verb *have* for possession is used as part of the practice for the Present Simple. However, it is also contrasted with *have got* for possession in both form and use.

Students at this level are often familiar with *have got* from their beginners and elementary courses, but they are a little confused about its relation to the full verb *to have*, both in its form, particularly in questions and negatives, and in its use. In fact, they are often interchangeable, but generally speaking *have got* is more informal.

Vocabulary The first vocabulary activity is a matching exercise which gets students to collocate verbs with noun phrases, and the second is an exercise which gets them to order these phrases under the topic headings of different rooms. The lexical area is 'Daily life', chosen because it fits well with the theme of the unit, allowing students to talk about what they do in their homes.

There is a personalized practice activity in which students are asked to describe their favourite room to their partner.

Everyday English This provides practice in making conversation. It introduces and practises phrases students can use to start a conversation and keep it going.

Notes on the unit

STARTER (SB p14)

As a lead-in, and to revise vocabulary, mime a few typical morning activities. For example, mime *eating breakfast*, *having a shower*, *brushing your teeth*, etc. Elicit words and write them on the board.

Ask students to complete the sentence starters by themselves, then put them in pairs or threes to tell people about their typical mornings. Monitor and note how accurately students are using the Present Simple and frequency adverbs, but you don't need to correct or explain at this stage.

TWO DIFFERENT LIVES (SB p14)

Present tenses and *have/have got*

> **ABOUT THE TEXT**
>
> This is a jumbled text exercise. Students read two different texts of four short paragraphs, which have been jumbled up. The students' first reading task is to read the paragraphs quickly for gist, and put them in the correct order, using clues in the vocabulary and context. The texts also contextualize the Present Simple and Continuous, and uses of *have* and *have got*.
>
> *Quebec City* is the capital of Quebec province. It is on the St Lawrence River in eastern Canada. 95% of the population speak French as their first language. However, many also speak English. *Guangdong province* is in southern China. It is a region of rapidly expanding industry and enterprise.
>
> The vocabulary in the texts should not be demanding. However, there are two sets of words you may wish to pre-teach.
>
> Work words: *factory, dormitory* (a large room where many people sleep), *employ, worker, overtime* (extra time at work), *monthly wage*.
>
> Winter sports words: *skiing, snowmobiling* (a snowmobile is a small vehicle that travels on snow or ice), *dog-sledding* (in which a team of dogs pull a *sled* – or *sledge* in British English).
>
> One way of pre-teaching these words is to write them on the board and ask students to make sentences, using the words. For example, *a worker works in a factory/ sleeps in a dormitory.*

1 Tell students to look at the pictures and ask the questions. Elicit as much information as you can.

> **Answers**
> Anne-Marie Boucher and her husband, Pascal. Near Quebec City, Canada.
> Lien Xiaohong and her colleagues, in a factory and in a computer class. In Guandong province, China.

2 **T 2.1** [CD 1: Track 14] Ask students to read the paragraphs and match them to the correct person. To get students started, you could read paragraph *a* as a class, and discuss which person it is talking about. Let students check their answers in pairs. Then play the recording so that students can compare their answers.

> **Answers and tapescript**
> Anne-Marie Boucher: b, e, f, h
> Lien Xiaohong: a, c, d, g
>
> **T 2.1**
> Anne-Marie Boucher has a small family hotel with her husband, Pascal, near Quebec City, Canada.
> It's situated on the coast outside the town, and near two national parks. She says, 'Our hotel has got wonderful views of the St Lawrence River and the Isle of Orleans.'
> She has visitors from all over the world. She says, 'We speak French, English, and a little Italian, which is very useful! Our guests keep us busy both summer and winter, so we've always got lots to do.'
> They don't have much free time. 'But I like it that way,' she says. 'And I love meeting new guests.' In winter it's very cold, –10° C. Their guests go skiing or snowmobiling in Mont Sainte-Anne Park.
> It's January now, and she is enjoying her favourite sport, dog-sledding. She's got twelve dogs, and she's racing them across the snow. She says 'I'm working the dogs very hard at the moment. Next year I want to race in a dogsled competition. It's really exciting.'
> Lien Xiaohong is 22. She lives and works in a toy factory in Guangdong province, China.
> She lives in a room with 14 other women in the factory dormitory, seven hundred miles from her family. The factory where she works employs 15,000 workers, nearly all of them women in their twenties.
> She works from 8 a.m. to 7 p.m. She has just an hour for lunch. She says, 'I work five and a half days a week, but I usually do overtime in summer. It's very tiring. When I'm not working or studying, I sleep.'
> Her monthly wage is about $65, enough to send a little back home to her family, and to pay for computer classes and English classes in town. She says, 'I haven't got any money left to buy things for me.'
> It's the evening now, and she is having a computer lesson in a private school. 'There are two skills that are essential these days,' she says. 'English and computers. One day I want to be my own boss.'

3 Put students in pairs to discuss the questions. Then have a short whole-class feedback and discussion.

Possible answers

1 Anne-Marie has a small family hotel and Lien works in a toy factory.
2 *Anne-Marie*: The good things are the wonderful location and views from the hotel, being busy and having lots to do, meeting new guests, and dog-sledding. The temperature in winter, –10°C, is not so good.
Lien: The good thing is that she earns enough to send money to her family and pay for classes, and she has the opportunity to study English and computing. The not so good things are that she lives a long way from her family, works long, tiring hours, and doesn't have enough money to buy things for herself.
3 Arguably, Anne-Marie.
4 Anne-Marie speaks French, English, and a little Italian. Lien speaks Chinese and a little English.
5 Anne-Marie is dog-sledding and Lien is having a computer lesson.
6 Anne-Marie wants to race in a dog-sled competition. Lien wants to be her own boss.

GRAMMAR SPOT (SB p15)

Focus the attention of the whole class on these questions so that your students are clear about the grammatical aims of the lesson.

Answers

1 The tenses used are the Present Simple (for example, *She lives in a room, She works from 8 a.m. to 7 p.m., They don't have much free time.*) and the Present Continuous (for example, *When I'm not working or studying, ... she is having a computer lesson.*)
2 *He works in a bank* and *She has a hotel* refer to all time. *He's working hard for his exams* and *She's having a computer lesson* refer to now.
3 *Anne-Marie Boucher <u>has</u> a small family hotel...*
'*Our hotel <u>has got</u> wonderful views...*' (paragraph b)
She <u>has</u> just an hour for lunch. (paragraph c)
'*I <u>haven't got</u> any money...*' (paragraph d)
She <u>has</u> visitors from all over the world. (paragraph e)
'*...we<u>'ve</u> always <u>got</u> lots to do.*' (paragraph e)
They <u>don't have</u> much free time. (paragraph f)
...she <u>is having</u> a computer lesson. (paragraph g)
She<u>'s got</u> twelve dogs. (paragraph h)

Have got is more informal.
Refer students to Grammar Reference 2.1–2.4 on p128.

4 The aim here is to provide written controlled practice of the question forms of the Present Simple and Continuous, and *have/have got*.

Do the first as an example. Then ask students to work individually before checking their answers with a partner.

T 2.2 [CD 1: Track 15] Play the recording so that students can check their answers.

You could extend this activity by getting students to practise asking each other the questions, and giving true answers.

Do you have a job, Maria?
Yes, I do. I'm a manager.

Answers and tapescript

1 'Do **you like your** job, Lien?'
'No, I don't like it much. My hands hurt all the time.'
2 'What **are you doing** at the moment?'
'I'm having a computer lesson.'
3 '**Have you got** any brothers or sisters?'
'I've got a brother. He lives with my parents in Hunan province.'
4 'Where **do you go on holiday**, Anne Marie?'
'Well, we don't usually go on holiday, so we're lucky to live in this beautiful place.'
5 'Why **are you working** the dogs so hard at the moment?'
'Because I want to race in a competition next year.'
6 'How many **dogs have you got**?'
'I've got twelve. They don't live in the hotel, of course.'

PRACTICE (SB p16)

This section aims to provide controlled oral and written practice of the grammar.

Talking about you

1 Note that the forms of *have* and *have got* are different. *Have* behaves like a full verb in the Present Simple with the auxiliary *do/does* in questions, negatives, and short answers. *Have got* uses *has/have* as the auxiliary in questions, negatives, and short answers.

T 2.3 [CD 1: Track 16] Play the recording and ask students to repeat the different forms, paying attention to the pronunciation, particularly the stress and falling intonation in the answers.

Do you have a car?   *Yes, I do.*

Tapescript

Do you have a car?	Yes, I do.	No, I don't.
Have you got a car?	Yes, I have.	No, I haven't.
I don't have a car.	I haven't got a car.	

2 Ask students to work in pairs. Tell them to use the prompts to ask and answer questions. Model the activity with a confident student.

This practice is personalized but still controlled. It is important that you go round the class to help and correct where necessary.

Tell students to take it in turns, first to ask and then to answer the questions. They can choose whether they use *have* or *have got* in the question, but the answer must match.

POSSIBLE PROBLEMS
- Students omit the auxiliary *do/does* and/or *got*:

  *Have you a car?

  *I haven't a computer.
- They mix the two forms:

  *I don't have got a computer.

  Have you got a car? *Yes, I do.
- They are reluctant to use the more natural short answers:

  Have you got a car? *Yes, I've got a car. (rather than just *Yes, I have.*)

  Do you have a computer? *No, I don't have a computer. (rather than just *No, I don't.*)

A nice way to end the activity and draw the full class together again is to ask one or two members of the class to tell the others about their partner. This also provides practice of the third person after the first and second person practice in the pairwork.

Teacher *Thomas, tell us about Maria.*

Thomas *Maria has a camera and a DVD player but she doesn't have a computer or a bicycle, etc.*

Exchanging information

3 **T 2.4** [CD 1: Track 17] Ask students to look at the photo of Miguel and complete the chart by listening to the recording.

Answers and tapescript

Name and age	Miguel, 21
Town and country	Valencia, Spain
Family	Parents (mother and father); two brothers
Occupation	Waiter (in parents' restaurant)
Free time/holiday	Sailing/visiting brother in Madrid
Present activity	Studying English at a language school in Oxford

T 2.4

I = Interviewer   M = Miguel
I   Thank you for agreeing to do this interview, Miguel.
M   No problem.
I   First of all, where exactly do you come from?
M   I'm from Valencia in Spain.

I   And where do you live in Valencia?
M   I live with my parents. They've got a restaurant in the old town centre.
I   Have you got any brothers or sisters?
M   I've got two brothers. They're both older than me, and they don't live at home.
I   And what do you do?
M   I work in my parents' restaurant. I'm a waiter.
I   And what do you like doing in your free time?
M   I love sailing. We've got a small boat in the marina.
I   Where do you go on holiday?
M   I usually go to stay with my brother, Rolando. He lives in Madrid.
I   And what are you doing here in Oxford?
M   I'm studying English at a language school here.
I   Oh, really? Well, your English is very good!
M   Thank you! And thank you for the practice!

4 This exercise is a controlled information gap activity which brings together practice of the Present Simple and *have/have got*. It also reminds students of the difference between the uses of the Present Simple and Present Continuous.

Tell students to look at the photos of Chantal, and Mario and Rita. Ask *What can you tell me about the people?* Elicit guesses from the pictures.

Put students in pairs. Tell them to work together to prepare questions to ask each other about the people, in order to complete the categories in the chart about Miguel. This should preferably be done orally, but some weaker students might feel happier doing it in writing too.

Possible answers

Where does she come from? / Where do they come from?

Is she married? / Are they married?

Does she have any children? / Do they have any children?

Has she got any brothers or sisters?

How many children/sisters/brothers has she got / do they have?

What does she do? / What do they do?

What does she do in her free time? / What do they do in their free time?

Where does she go on holiday? / Where do they go on holiday?

What's she doing at the moment? / What are they doing at the moment?

Divide the pairs into As and Bs, and tell them to find their charts in the back of the Student's Book. Student A must turn to p144. Student B must turn to p147. Tell students to ask and answer the questions to complete their missing information. Model the first couple of questions with a confident student to get them started.

While students are asking and answering questions to complete their charts, you should go round the pairs to help and check.

When the charts are completed, ask one or two individuals to tell the whole class about the person they have asked questions about.

T 2.5 [CD 1: Track 18] Ask the students to listen and compare their answers.

> **Answers and tapescript**
> **Chantal**
> 'Where does Chantal come from?' 'Marseilles, in France.'
> 'Is she married?' 'No, she isn't.'
> 'Does she have any brothers and sisters?' 'Yes, she has one brother.'
> 'Has she got any children?' 'No, she hasn't.'
> 'What does she do?' 'She's a fashion buyer.'
> 'What does she do in her free time?' 'She goes to the gym.'
> 'Where does she go on holiday?' 'She goes to her holiday home in Biarritz.'
> 'What's she doing at the moment?' 'She's buying clothes in Milan.'
> **Mario and Rita**
> 'Where do they come from?' 'Siena, in Italy.'
> 'Are they married?' 'Yes, they are.'
> 'Do they have any children?' 'Yes, one daughter.'
> 'Have they got any grandchildren?' 'Yes, they've got one grandson.'
> 'What do they do?' 'He's retired and she's a housewife.'
> 'What do they do in their free time?' 'They go to the opera.'
> 'What are they doing at the moment?' 'They're preparing to go to the USA.'

Check it

5   The aim of this activity is to check that students have grasped the differences between the Present Simple and the Present Continuous, and *have* and *have got*, in terms of form and meaning. Ask students to work individually or in pairs. Putting students in pairs to do this exercise enables them to help and teach each other.

> **Answers**
> 1 Where do you go on holiday?
> 2 Do you have any children?
> 3 I come from Germany.
> 4 Everyone is dancing.
> 5 I don't have a mobile.
> 6 but he doesn't wear a uniform.
> 7 'He's sitting by the window.'
> 8 I like black coffee.

Go through the answers as a class. Ask students why they have reached their decisions, and in this way you will revise the rules. Alternatively, you may wish to set this activity for homework.

ADDITIONAL MATERIAL

Workbook Unit 2
These exercises could be done in class to give further practice, for homework, or in a later class as revision.

Exercises 1–5 Present Simple

Exercises 6–8 Present Simple or Continuous?

Exercises 9–10 *have/have got*

VOCABULARY AND SPEAKING (SB p17)

Daily life

1   Begin by telling students to look at the first box of verbs and nouns. Ask them if they can match any verb with a noun. If necessary, do one or two as an example. Tell them to work in pairs to match verbs and nouns in the rest of the boxes. You could circulate and help at this stage, but don't be tempted to give the answers.

T 2.6 [CD 1: Track 19] When students have finished, play the recording so that they can listen, check, and repeat their answers.

> **Answers and tapescript**
>
> | | |
> |---|---|
> | have breakfast | make a cup of coffee |
> | wash your hair | relax in front of the TV |
> | watch the news on TV | listen to music |
> | text your friends | do your homework |
> | have a shower | cook a meal |
> | clear up the mess | go to the toilet |
> | do the washing-up | put on make-up |
> | send an email | read magazines |

Go through the answers with the whole class and deal with any problems with meaning and pronunciation.

2   Tell students to match the activities from exercise 1 with the correct room. You could elicit one or two examples under the heading *Kitchen* to start them off. Ask students to work in pairs and to write the phrases in the boxes. Circulate and help. When students have finished, go through the answers as a class.

> **Sample answers**
> **Kitchen**: have breakfast, make a cup of coffee, do the washing-up, cook a meal
> **Bathroom**: wash your hair, have a shower, go to the toilet, put on make-up
> **Living room**: watch the news on TV, relax in front of the TV, read magazines
> **Bedroom**: text your friends, listen to music, do your homework, clear up the mess

Ask students to discuss their answers, and to tell their partners about their everyday life, for example *I don't read magazines in the living room, I read them in my bedroom.*

3 **T 2.7** [CD 1: Track 20] Ask students to complete the sentences with the correct words. Let them check their answers in pairs before playing the recording.

Answers and tapescript
1 I never **have** breakfast on weekdays, only at weekends.
2 I have a hot **shower** every morning and every evening.
3 My sister washes her **hair** at least four times a week.
4 She didn't have time to **put on** any make-up this morning.
5 My brother never reads books or newspapers, he only reads music **magazines**.
6 I don't often do the **washing-up** because we've got a dishwasher.
7 I'm going to **make** a cup of coffee. Does anybody want one?
8 My dad always **watches** the ten o'clock news on TV.
9 My mum says I text my **friends** too much.
10 *You* made this mess, so *you* **clear** it up!
11 Can I **send** an email from your computer?
12 How can you listen to **music** while you're working?
13 I'm always so tired after work, I just want to **relax** in front of the TV.
14 I cooked a **meal** for ten people last night.
15 I didn't forget to *do* my homework, I forgot to *bring* it.
16 Can you wait a minute? I need to **go** to the toilet.

Get students to practise saying the sentences.

4 The aim of exercises 4 and 5 is to practise the vocabulary in a personalized way.

Model the activity by telling students which is your favourite room and telling them two or three things you do in that room using the vocabulary from exercise 1. Then get students to look at the example in the book. Give them a few minutes to choose their favourite room and think about what they are going to say.

5 Put students in pairs or groups. Ask them to describe their favourite room to their partner or group, without saying which room it is. Their partner or group guesses the room. The main aim here is fluency, but you could circulate and make sure students are using the vocabulary accurately.

Alternatively, you could set this as a written homework and your students could describe the room to each other at the beginning of the next lesson.

EXTRA IDEA
Remember to encourage students to keep a vocabulary notebook and remind them to add words to this whenever they do a vocabulary exercise such as this one. Suggest that they record words in groups, as shown on this page. They can also refer to the *Word list* for each unit at the back of the SB.

WRITING (SB p103)

An email – Linking words *but, although, however, so,* and *because*

The aim of this writing section is to practise linking words in an informal email.

1 Read the introduction as a class. Then brainstorm a few ideas and put them on the board to get students started. Give students four or five minutes to write some notes, and let them compare with a partner if they get stuck. Tell students that they will need the notes later in the lesson.

but, although, and *however*

2 Put students in pairs to compare the sentences. In feedback, elicit students' ideas and discuss the rules as a class.

Answers
But, although and *however* all express contrast.
Although and *however* are more formal than *but*, and are often used in formal writing.
But joins two clauses. It must go before the second clause.
Although joins two clauses. It can go at the start of the sentence, in which case a comma separates the clauses. (It can also go in the middle of the sentence, in which case it is preceded by a comma.) *Although* expresses a surprising contrast.
However joins two sentences, and introduces the second sentence. It is preceded by a full stop and followed by a comma.

3 Ask students to join the sentences with the linking words. Let them discuss their answers in pairs.

Answers
1 He's a good friend **but** we don't meet often.
   Although he's a good friend, we don't meet often.
   (He's a good friend, **although** we don't meet often.)
   He's a good friend. **However**, we don't meet often.
2 She isn't English **but** she speaks English very well.
   Although she isn't English, she speaks English very well.
   (She speaks English very well, **although** she isn't English.)
   She isn't English. **However**, she speaks English very well.
3 It rained a lot **but** we enjoyed the holiday.
   Although it rained a lot, we enjoyed the holiday.
   (We enjoyed the holiday, **although** it rained a lot.)
   It rained a lot. **However**, we enjoyed the holiday.

so and *because*

4 Ask students in pairs to match the sentences and patterns. In feedback, discuss the rules of use as a class.

Answers
1 b 2 a
so introduces a result or consequence
because introduces a reason

5 Ask students to join the sentences with the linking words. Let them discuss their answers in pairs.

> **Answers**
> 1 She went home **because** she was tired.
>   She was tired, **so** she went home.
> 2 We didn't enjoy our holiday **because** the weather was bad.
>   The weather was bad, **so** we didn't enjoy our holiday.
> 3 He worked hard, **so** he passed all his exams.
>   He passed all his exams **because** he worked hard.
> 4 I enjoy history lessons **because** I like the teacher.
>   I like the teacher, **so** I enjoy history lessons.
> 5 It started to rain, **so** we stopped playing tennis.
>   We stopped playing tennis **because** it started to rain.

6 Ask students to read the email quickly and answer the questions.

> **Answers**
> Rebecca is writing to Martha. She is replying to Martha's email. Martha has recently written to her after ten years.
> Rebecca tells Martha about her marriage and divorce, her two children, her farmhouse in Wales, and her marriage to Hugo King.

Ask students to complete the email with the correct linking words. Let them check their answers in pairs.

> **Answers**
> | | | | |
> |---|---|---|---|
> | 1 | although | 7 | because |
> | 2 | so | 8 | but |
> | 3 | so | 9 | because |
> | 4 | However | 10 | although |
> | 5 | because | 11 | but |
> | 6 | although | 12 | so |

7 Put students in pairs to compare notes. They can then write their emails in class, with you monitoring and helping, or as homework.

When the students have finished, ask them to exchange emails with a partner. You could ask the partner to mark up mistakes in the email with correction symbols.

> **EXTRA IDEA**
> If you have a computer room in your school, pair students up and get them to write and send the emails to each other electronically.

ADDITIONAL MATERIAL

Workbook Unit 2

Exercise 11 *have* + noun = activity

Tales of two cities

> **ABOUT THE TEXTS**
> This is a fluency activity, in the form of a jigsaw reading. The class divides into two groups and each group reads a different article about someone who lives and works in two different cities.
>
> After the reading, students from the different groups get together to swap information about the person in their article. The selection of the articles means that students will need to use (naturally and without noticing it) some of the grammar taught in this unit – Present Simple and *have/have got*.
>
> *Manchester* is an industrial town in the north-west of England, famous for its football teams (United and City), its music scene, and its weather. However, it is also an exciting place to live, with a vibrant arts scene and lots of bars and restaurants. *Brooklyn* is a borough of New York, across the East River from Manhattan. It too is an increasingly fashionable place to live. *Cambridge*, in eastern England, and *Nuremberg*, in southern Germany, are both historical university cities.
>
> The title, *Tales* (stories) *of two cities*, is a play on words. There is a famous novel, *A Tale of Two Cities*, by Charles Dickens.
>
> The vocabulary in the text is not very demanding, and it is good to encourage students not to worry about unknown words as they read. However, you may wish to get students to find and guess the meaning of the following phrases once they have read and discussed both texts, (i.e. after exercise 5).
>
> *miss* (a person or place) = feel sad because you are not with that person or in that place
> *act the part* = play the role (here, play the role of 'being English')
> *sip a glass of wine* = drink in small amounts
> *drink a pint of beer* = In the UK, a pint is equal to 0.57 litres – beer is still measured in pints in the UK, even though other measurements are metric
> *a trendy bar* = a fashionable and modern bar
> *a local pub* = a traditional pub which is close to where you live
> *share a rooftop flat* = live with other people in a flat at the top of a high-rise building with access to the roof
> *live in a city-centre loft* = a loft is also a room or flat at the top of a block of flats

1 Put students in pairs or small groups to discuss the questions. In feedback, encourage students to share their ideas with the class.

2 Ask students to look at the photos on the page. Ask *What can you see? What do you think the texts are about?* Ask students to read the introduction quickly, or read the introduction out as they listen and read. Ask *Why is it easier for people to have different lives these days?* (Because cheap travel and communication technology have made the world smaller and smaller, so that we can work and live almost anywhere.)

3 Divide the class into two groups for the jigsaw activity at this point. A good way to do this is to divide the class into groups of three or four, then tell half the groups to read text A, and half to read text B.

Ask the groups to read their text and discuss the questions. Monitor and make sure the groups have accurate and complete answers to their questions.

Answers
Claire
1 Manchester and Brooklyn, New York
2 She is a gallery owner.
3 She flies once a month, and spends a month in each place.
4 She has a rooftop flat in New York and a city-centre loft in Manchester.
5 He travels a lot in his job, too.
6 She dresses differently in New York – and wears her hair up. She also acts more 'English'. In New York, she goes to trendy bars. In Manchester, she goes to local pubs.
7 She misses New York manicures.
8 Americans love the English accent.
Joss
1 Cambridge and Nuremburg
2 He is a snowboard designer.
3 Every two weeks. Sometimes he drives but he usually flies.
4 He has a farmhouse in both countries.
5 She travels a lot, too.
6 In Cambridge, he lives with his partner. In Nuremberg, he lives with his colleague. In Nuremberg, he eats more meat, drinks more beer, and watches TV.
7 He doesn't like flying – it's exhausting and he has always got a cold.
8 Germans always want to practise their English with him.

4 Tell students to stand up, then find and sit down with a student who has read the other text. Students have to tell each other about the person in their article. Monitor and prompt.

5 Once students have finished describing their person's lifestyle, get them to discuss the questions. Feedback by asking a few of, but not necessarily all of, the questions in exercises 3 and 5.

Answers
1 They both live in two different places, they both fly often, they both like beer.
2 Joss travels every two weeks, whereas Claire travels once a month. But Claire travels a longer distance.
3 Students' own opinions.

What do you think?

This activity is to round off the lesson and make the discussion more personal to students.

They could form groups or pairs again to get some ideas, but there probably won't be much time for a long discussion.

LISTENING AND SPEAKING (SB p20)

A 24/7 society

> **ABOUT THE LISTENING**
> The main aim of this activity is to develop your students' ability to listen for gist and for specific information. However, the context also revises and extends students' ability to use the Present Simple with frequency adverbs. Try not to over-correct students, as a key aim should be general fluency.
> A *nighthawk* is a *hawk* (=bird of prey) that hunts at night. The word is also used to describe a person who likes to stay up late at night.

1 Ask students to look at the picture. Ask *Who painted it?* (Edward Hopper). Put students in small groups to discuss the questions.

Answers
1 Edward Hopper. *Nighthawks*.
2 Night.
3 In a coffee bar. Students' own ideas.

2 Put students in pairs or small groups to discuss the questions. In feedback, find out if any students (or people in their family) have worked nights.

Possible answers
24/7 means 24 hours a day, 7 days a week. So, a 24/7 society is one where nothing stops or closes.
Typical night jobs: factory shift worker, nurse, security guard, nightwatchman, emergency workers such as firefighters, ambulance drivers, and police officers.

3 **T 2.8** [CD 1: Track 21] Play the recording. Ask students to listen and complete the chart. Let students listen again and check their answers in pairs.

Answers and tapescript

Jerry

Place of work: BMW car factory

Hours: 12 hours a night, four times a week

Why working nights? He can earn more working at nights. Also, the robots work at nights, so people need to work to finish each car.

Problems: You have to be very careful between one o'clock and three o'clock in the morning, because that's when accidents happen.

Jackie

Place of work: Hairdresser's (Hairwear)

Hours: Friday nights only

Why working nights? Because customers want the hairdresser's to be open at night.

Problems: Most of the customers fall asleep under the hairdryer.

Doreen

Place of work: Co-op bank – telephone banking

Hours: Sunday to Wednesday, 10pm to 7am

Why working nights? She enjoys it. The work is more relaxed because customers aren't in a hurry.

Problems: It's bad for you. You need to look after your health or you get ill.

Dan

Place of work: Local supermarket

Hours: Midnight to 6am

Why working nights? For the money.

Problems: It's difficult to change from working days to working nights. It isn't easy to see his friends or girlfriend. Sometimes he sleeps all weekend.

T 2.8

A 24/7 society

P = Presenter   I = Interviewer   Je = Jerry

Ja = Jackie   Do = Doreen   Da = Dan

P Good morning, and welcome to today's lifestyle programme *A 24/7 society*. Over eight million people now work at night. What do they do, and why do they do it? Our reporter, Richard Morris, finds out.

I Well, it's 8pm on a Thursday night, and I'm in a BMW car factory, where they make the Mini. The night workers are arriving now. With me is Jerry Horne. Jerry, tell me, what hours do you work?

Je I work 12 hours a night, four times a week.

I And do you like it?

Je Well, it was difficult at first, but it's OK now. And the money's good. I can earn much more working at night.

I Why do people work at night here?

Je Because the robots do! The robots make a lot of each car, but we finish them. And the Mini is very popular, so we need to make 200,000 a year!

I That's amazing! Are there any problems working at night?

Je Well, the main problem is that you need to be very careful between the hours of 1 o'clock and 3 o'clock in the morning. That's when accidents happen.

I Right. Thanks, Jerry. And have a good night!
...

I It's 10.30pm, and a lot of people are going to bed now. But I'm in a hairdresser's called Hairwear with Jackie Wilson, the manager. Jackie, is this the country's first 24-hour hairdresser's?

Ja Yes, it probably is! We're only open for 24 hours on a Friday night at the moment. But I think that will change in the future, because people want it. And I think it's a good idea.

I What sort of people come in?

Ja All sorts! Young mothers come in when their husbands get home. A lot of people come in before they go to a night club. A politician comes in after work at midnight. And of course, other night workers come in after work between 2 o'clock and 6 o'clock in the morning. It helps them relax before they go to bed.

I Yes, I'm sure. Any problems?

Ja Not really. The main problem is that most of the customers fall asleep under the hairdryer!
...

I It's now 1 o'clock in the morning and I'm in the Co-op bank. I'm sitting next to Doreen. At night this telephone banking centre only has six workers. Doreen, what hours do you work?

Do I work from Sunday to Wednesday from 10pm to 7am.

I Aha. And what do you think of the job?

Do I love it! We're like a family at night. We're all good friends, and the work is more relaxed. Customers aren't in a hurry at 2 o'clock in the morning!

I Are there any disadvantages?

Do Well, it's bad for you! You need to look after your health. If you don't, you get ill. But it's OK for me – I could never sleep at night, anyway!
...

I Well, it's 4 o'clock in the morning, and I'm feeling very sleepy! I'm in the local supermarket with Dan. So, Dan, when did you start work?

Da At midnight. And I finish in two hours' time at 6 o'clock. But some weeks I work during the day. The difficult thing is changing from day working to night working.

I Any other problems?

Da Well, often it isn't easy to see my friends or my girlfriend. They're going out and I'm going to work! And at weekends, sometimes I sleep all day. My girlfriend doesn't like that much!

I So why do you do it?

Da For the money, really. And I don't mind working at night.

I Thanks, Dan. So there you are. These are just some of the many people who have a different sort of lifestyle. Well, I'm off to bed now. Good night!

What do you think?

The aim of this activity is to provide some free speaking in which students are encouraged to express their own opinion. It could be done as a class. Alternatively, you could divide students into small groups to discuss the questions, then take a few comments from each group at the end.

Making conversation 1

The aim of this section is to get students to think about the techniques involved in starting and keeping a conversation going, and to introduce and practise some phrases which might help them.

1 **T 2.9** [CD 1: Track 22] You could lead in by eliciting from students ways of having a successful conversation and listing these suggestions on the board. Alternatively, ask students to tell you what problems they have when having a conversation in English, and list the problems on the board.

Focus students on the instructions in the Student's Book and ask students to listen and say which dialogue is more successful and why.

Answers and tapescript

The second dialogue is more successful because Marco asks questions, shows interest, and adds comments of his own.

T 2.9

1 J = James N = Nicole
J Hello. What's your name?
N Nicole.
J I'm ... James. I'm a teacher. And – er, where are you from?
N Paris. I come from Paris.
J How lovely. Paris is so beautiful.
N Yes, I like it.
J Er ... What ... what do you do –er in Paris?
N I'm a student.
J Mm. And ... how do you find living in London, Nicole?
N It's OK.
J Are you having a good time?
N Yes.
J Can I get you a coffee?
N No.
J Er ... Are you missing your family at all?
N No.
J Have you got any brothers or sisters?
N Yes. I've got a brother.
J Er ... Oh! Er ... what does he do?
N He's a student, too.
J Oh well, I've got a class now. Goodbye, Nicole.
N Bye.

2 C = Catherine M = Marco
C Hello. What's your name?
M I'm Marco. And what's your name?
C Catherine.
M What a pretty name. In Italy, we say Caterina.
C Oh, that's lovely! So, you're from Italy, Marco. Where exactly are you from?
M I come from 'Roma' – or as you say in English, Rome.
C Oh, yes of course, 'Roma'! That sounds so nice.

M That's right. And you, Catherine, where do you come from?
C I'm from Dublin, in Ireland.
M Oh, I'd love to visit Ireland one day.
C You must. It's really beautiful. And what do you do in Rome, Marco?
M I'm a student. I'm studying to be an architect.
C Oh, really?
M Yes. I want to design beautiful, modern buildings for my beautiful, old city.
C How interesting! I just love Rome.
M Do you know Rome?
C Not really. I once had a weekend there and I just loved it.
M Ah, you must visit again.
C I'd love to. And how do you find London? Are you enjoying it here?
M Oh yes, I am, very much indeed. I'm making a lot of good friends and even the food's not bad.
C But not as good as Italian food!
M Aaah! What can I say? Caterina – er Catherine, can I get you a coffee?
C Yes, please. I'd love one. There's still ten minutes before class.
M OK. Why don't we s........

---

2 As a class, discuss the list of things that help a conversation. See if students can add to the list. Ask students to read the dialogues in the tapescript on p117 in pairs, and compare them, finding examples of how Marco keeps the conversation going. Get feedback from the class.

MUSIC OF ENGLISH – HIGHS AND LOWS

English is a language with a very broad intonation pattern. Point out that flat intonation can make the speaker sound bored, disinterested, or even rude.

1 **T 2.10** [CD 1: Track 23] Play the recording. Ask students to notice how much more musical Marco's intonation is.

Tapescript
N Paris. I come from Paris.
M I come from 'Roma', or as you say in English, Rome.

2 **T 2.11** [CD 1: Track 24] Play the recording. Ask students to listen and repeat the lines, imitating the intonation pattern.

Tapescript
M And you, Catherine, where do you come from?
C I'm from Dublin, in Ireland.
M Oh, I'd love to visit Ireland one day.
C You must. It's really beautiful.

---

3 Put students in pairs to practise Catherine and Marco's conversation on p117 of the Student's Book.

4 Ask students to work in pairs to match a line in **A** with a reply in **B** and a comment in **C**. Do the first one as an example and check vocabulary if necessary before students start. Monitor and help.

T 2.12 [CD 1: Track 25] Students listen to the recording to check answers and focus on pronunciation.

Answers and tapescript

1 **A** What lovely weather we're having!
  B Yes, wonderful, isn't it? Just like summer!
2 **A** What terrible weather!
  B I know. Really awful, isn't it? I just hope this rain stops soon.
3 **A** How are you today?
  B I'm very well, thanks. How about you?
4 **A** Did you have a nice evening?
  B Yes. Excellent, thanks. We all went to that new night club in King Street.
5 **A** How do you find living in Chicago?
  B I'm enjoying it a lot. It was a bit strange at first, but I love it now.
6 **A** Did you have a good journey?
  B Yes, no problems. The plane was a bit late, but it didn't matter.
7 **A** Did you watch the football yesterday?
  B No, I missed it. Was it a good game?
8 **A** What a lovely jacket you're wearing!
  B Thank you. I'm glad you like it. I got it in the sale for only £40.
9 **A** If you have any problems, just ask me.
  B Thank you very much. That's really kind of you.

Point out the musical intonation pattern of some of the phrases and remind students that you can sound bored and uninterested if you don't vary your tone when speaking.

Ask students to practise the dialogues in pairs using the stress shading to help with stress and intonation. Monitor closely and encourage students to put some feeling into their intonation.

5 The aim here is to provide some light-hearted practice in keeping a conversation going. Ask students to work individually to prepare questions based on the three subjects in the Student's Book. Monitor and help.

When students are ready, tell them to have conversations in pairs. Monitor and prompt, making sure students are attempting a good intonation pattern.

You could easily turn this into a mingle activity. Ask students to walk round the class and start different short conversations with different people.

Don't forget!

Workbook Unit 2

Exercise 12 Pronunciation – *-s* at the end of a word

Exercises 13–14 Check it

Grammar Reference
Look at the exercises on SB p128 as a class, or set for homework. The answers are on TB p155.

Word list
Remind your students of the Word list for this unit on SB p152. They could translate the words, learn them at home, or transfer some of the words to their vocabulary notebook.

Pronunciation Book Unit 2

Past tenses
Adverbs
Time expressions

What happened next?

Introduction to the unit

The theme of this unit is telling stories. The Past Simple and Past Continuous tenses are revised and practised in the context of newspaper stories, one about a dog 'mystery' and one about an art thief. In the *Listening and reading* section, students are asked to listen to and read extracts from a James Bond story, *The Man with the Golden Gun*.

Students have the opportunity to practise past tenses by means of personalized pairwork activities, writing a news report, and telling stories round the class.

Language aims

Grammar – Past Simple Students will already have a certain familiarity with the Past Simple, and may be able to use it quite accurately on a basic level.

POSSIBLE PROBLEMS

*   Many regular verbs will be known, but you can expect problems with the pronunciation of *-ed* at the end, for example:

happened	*/hæpəned/	instead of	/hæpənd/
looked	*/lʊked/	instead of	/lʊkt/

    Students will also know some irregular verbs, such as *came, went, saw, met,* and *took,* but there are still quite a few more to learn! Remind students that there is a list of irregular verbs on p158 of the Student's Book. You could ask them to learn five new irregular verbs every week. Do a little test on them from time to time.

*   The use of *did* causes problems. Students forget to use it, for example:

    *What time you get up?   **Where you went last night?*

    *I no see you yesterday.   **You have a good time at the party?*

*   Learners try to form a past tense of *have* with *got,* which is uncommon in English.

    *I had got a cold last week.

Past Continuous The Past Continuous could well be new to students at this level. In this unit it is contrasted with the Past Simple, and in this context, the difference between the two tenses is clear. However, the fundamental use of the Past Continuous to describe background events and temporary situations in the past is quite a difficult one to grasp. Learners find it hard to see the difference between sentences such as

It rained yesterday.   *It was raining when I got up.*
I wore my best suit to the wedding.   *She was wearing a beautiful red dress.*

The Past Continuous is not dealt with in great depth in this unit. At this stage, it is enough to lay a foundation, so that students will learn to recognize the tense as they see it in context, and gradually begin to produce it.

Vocabulary The Vocabulary section looks at adverbs, both adverbs of manner that end in *-ly,* and other adverbs. In particular, it concentrates on the position of adverbs in sentences.

Everyday English The *Everyday English* section deals with time expressions – saying dates and using the correct preposition with expressions. *The Music of English* looks at linking.

Notes on the unit

STARTER (SB p22)

In this Starter activity students' knowledge of basic irregular past tenses is checked.

Ask students to work in pairs to write the infinitives, then feed back as a class, drilling any past tenses that students find difficult to pronounce. If necessary, refer students to the list of irregular verbs on SB p158.

Answers			
1	be	7	do
2	be	8	get
3	go	9	have
4	see	10	make
5	think	11	come
6	put	12	say

WHAT A MYSTERY! (SB p22)

Past Simple

> **ABOUT THE TEXT**
>
> Regular and irregular forms of the Past Simple are contextualized in this short, humorous text based on a newspaper story.
>
> *Battersea Dogs' Home* is Britain's largest, oldest, and most famous dogs' home. It is a sanctuary for stray, abandoned, or abused dogs. Some students may recognize that *Who let the dogs out? Woof! Woof!* was the chorus of a dance hit by *The Baha Men*, which is used to introduce the recording.
>
> Vocabulary you may wish to pre-teach or get students to guess from context:
>
> *woof!* = the noise dogs make
> *staff* = people who work in an office, factory, etc.
> *cage* = a metal box for animals
> *ghosts haunt* (a place) = ghosts (spirits of dead people) appear in (a place)
> *make a mess* = make a place very untidy
> *lurcher* = a type of dog

1 Ask students to read the opening paragraph of the newspaper story, then discuss the questions as a class. Encourage lots of speculation, but don't give away the story at this stage.

2 **T 3.1** [CD 1: Track 26] Play the recording. Ask students to read and listen to the article. Let them discuss the answers to the questions in 1 in pairs before discussing as a class.

Answers and tapescript

The 'dark figure' is a dog (a lurcher) called Red.
He opened the other doors to release his 'friends'.
He went to the kitchen to steal food.
The story takes place in Battersea Dogs' Home.

T 3.1

Who let the dogs out? Woof! Woof!

Last month, strange things began to happen at London's Battersea Dogs' Home. Every morning, when the staff arrived, they saw that a lot of the dogs were out of their cages. It was a mystery. 'It happened so many times,' said Amy Watson, one of the staff. 'We even thought that perhaps it was the ghost of Mary Tealby.' They say that Mary Tealby, who started the Home in 1860, comes back at night to haunt it. So they put cameras in all the cages and filmed what happened.

Next day the staff watched the film. They were amazed at what they saw. Red, a four-year-old lurcher, used his teeth to open the door of his cage. Then he did the same for his friends in the next cages. All the dogs got out and had a great time. Amy told us, 'They ate lots of food, had lots of fun and games, and made lots of mess!'

Reporters from Japan, Germany, and America came to film Red, and 400 people phoned because they wanted to give him a home. Red's a famous film star now. 'He's a real celebrity!' said Amy.

You could follow up by asking students if they have (or know of) any pets with 'special skills'.

3 Let students discuss the past forms in pairs before discussing as a class.

Answers

looked	started
ran	watched
opened	used
began	told
arrived	ate

looked, arrived, opened, watched, started and *used* (which all add *-d* or *-ed* to the infinitive) are regular past forms.

4 **T 3.2** [CD 1: Track 27] Tell students that they are going to listen to some sentences about the story which are incorrect. They must listen and correct the mistakes. Read the example very carefully, and point out that they have to make two sentences, one negative and one positive. Play the recording. Pause after each sentence (there is already a pause on the audio) and see if anyone in the class can produce the sentences. Play each line twice if necessary, and give students time to write the answers if they need to. Then ask them to say the sentences, and repeat the model on the recording. Refer students to the stress shading on the example, and insist on good pronunciation. This requires a wide voice range to express surprise and strong stress to show contrast.

Answers and tapescript

1 It happened every morning.
  It didn't happen every morning. It happened every night.
2 Red locked all the doors.
  He didn't lock all the doors. He opened them.
3 Amy Watson started the home.
  Amy Watson didn't start the home. Mary Tealby started it.
4 They saw a man on the film.
  They didn't see a man on the film. They saw a dog.
5 He opened the doors with his nose.
  He didn't open the doors with his nose. He opened them with his teeth.
6 Reporters came to film Amy.
  Reporters didn't come to film Amy. They came to film Red.

5 Ask students to work in pairs to complete the questions. Monitor and help.

T 3.3 [CD 1: Track 28] Play the recording so that students can check their answers. Then put students in pairs to practise asking and answering the questions. Insist on correctly formed questions, and make sure the question starts with the voice high.

What did Red do?

You could extend this task by writing the question words, (*What?/Why?/How often?* etc.), in order on the board, then getting students to ask and answer, using the prompts, and remembering the questions and answers.

Answers and tapescript

1 What **did Red do**?
  He opened all the cage doors.
2 Why **did he open** the doors?
  Because he wanted to go to the kitchen.
3 How often **did he do it**?
  Many times.
4 Who **did Amy think** it was?
  The ghost of Mary Tealby.
5 What **did** they **put** in the cages?
  Cameras.
6 How **did he open** the doors?
  With his teeth.
7 **Did they have** a good time?
  Yes, they did. They had a great time.
8 Why **did 400 people** phone the dogs' home?
  Because they wanted to give Red a home.

GRAMMAR SPOT (SB p23)

1 Ask students to work in pairs or threes to answer the grammar questions.

Answers

1 The Past Simple. The question is formed with *did* + infinitive (students will probably use the term infinitive instead of base form).
  The negative is formed with *didn't* + infinitive.

Spelling

2 Ask students to work in pairs or threes to write the regular Past Simple forms and answer the grammar questions.

Answers and tapescript

a looked	c arrived
played	used
wanted	decided
b tried	d stopped
studied	planned

Regular past tenses are formed by adding *-ed*.
If the verb ends in consonant + *y*, change the *-y* to *-ied*.
We double the final consonant when the verb ends consonant – vowel – consonant.

Pronunciation

3 **T 3.4** [CD 1: Track 29] Play the recording. Ask students to listen and make their lists.

Tapescript See answers to 2.

T 3.5 [CD 1: Track 30] Play the recording. Students listen and check their answers, then listen again and repeat.

Answers and tapescript

/t/	/d/	/ɪd/
looked	played	wanted
stopped	tried	studied
	arrived	decided
	used	
	planned	

Refer students to the list of irregular verbs on p158, and Grammar Reference 3.1 on p129.

Making connections

The aim of this activity is to give students further accuracy practice in producing past forms, and to check their ability to use the linking words *so*, *because*, *and*, and *but*.

> **POSSIBLE PROBLEMS**
> Students may not be sure about how to use the linking words, particularly *so*. You may wish to check students' ability to use them before starting the exercise by asking check questions. For example:
> Which word makes a contrast? … *but* …
> Which word adds extra information? … *and* …
> Which word shows a consequence? … *so* …
> Which says why you did something? … *because* …

1 Focus students on the box and the example, then ask students to work in pairs to produce as many sentences as they can. This could be done as a written exercise or, if you think your students can manage it, it could be done as an oral exercise in pairs. Monitor, help, and correct, paying particular attention to the pronunciation of past forms.

   T 3.6 [CD 1: Track 31] Students listen and compare their answers.

> **Sample answers and tapescript**
> 1 The phone rang, so I answered it.
> 2 I felt ill, so I went to bed.
> 3 I made a sandwich because I was hungry.
> 4 I had a shower and washed my hair.
> 5 I lost my passport, but I found it later.
> 6 I called the police because I heard a strange noise.
> 7 The printer broke, so I mended it.
> 8 I forgot her birthday, so I said sorry.
> 9 I took my driving test and I passed it!
> 10 I told a joke but nobody laughed.

Talking about you

The aim here is to round off the lesson with a personalized free-speaking activity using the Past Simple.

2 Ask students to work in pairs to talk about what they did last night, last weekend, etc. Monitor the groups carefully. As you go round the groups, you could write down some mistakes (not too many!), and after you have conducted the feedback you could write them on the board for the class to correct.

ADDITIONAL MATERIAL

Workbook Unit 3
These exercises could be done in class to give further practice, for homework, or in a later class as revision.

Exercises 1–7 Past Simple

Past Simple and Continuous

> **ABOUT THE TEXT**
> The text is a newspaper story about an art thief who stole priceless paintings and hung them in his bedroom. The phrases using the Past Continuous have been taken out and students must decide where they go in the story. The idea is to show students that the main events of a story are expressed by the Past Simple – the stories make sense without the phrases containing the Past Continuous. The Past Continuous phrases give background information and description.
> *Alsace* is a region of eastern France which borders Germany. Its major city is Strasbourg.
> You may wish to pre-teach, or get students to find and explain from context, the following set of words.
> Art: *art thief, painting/work of art, museum/art gallery, priceless* (very valuable and impossible to replace), *it's worth $2 billion dollars* (It has a value of …)

1 Put students in pairs to check the meanings in their dictionaries and find past forms. In feedback, check the students' understanding by miming some or all of the words, and asking students to tell you which word you are miming.

> **Answers**
> | | |
> |---|---|
> | filled | destroyed |
> | stole /stəʊl/ | took |
> | hid | cut |
> | threw /θruː/ | thought /θɔːt/ |
> | spent | |
>
> *filled* and *destroyed* are regular.

2 Tell students they are going to read an article about a crime. Ask them to look at the photos and headline and guess what it might be about. Students then read the article quickly to see if they were right. In the feedback, check any difficult vocabulary.

   Ask students to work in pairs to put the past forms from exercise 1 in the gaps.

> **Answers**
> | | |
> |---|---|
> | 1 stole | 6 cut |
> | 2 hid | 7 threw |
> | 3 filled | 8 destroyed |
> | 4 thought | 9 spent |
> | 5 took | |

3 Ask students to discuss the questions with their partner, then briefly as a class.

Answers

1 239 paintings.   3 Because she destroyed a
2 No   lot of paintings.

4 **T 3.7** [CD 1: Track 32] Ask students to put the lines in the story, in the spaces marked (…), then check with a partner. As an example, ask students first to tell you which line goes in the first space. Elicit a range of answers from the class, then play the recording to check.

Answers and tapescript
b, c, e, a, d

T 3.7 **The thief, his mother, and $2 billion**
Stephane Breitwieser, 33, from Alsace, in France, is the greatest art thief in Europe. For over six years, **while he was working as a lorry driver**, he stole 239 paintings from museums in France, Austria, and Denmark. He went into the museums **just as they were closing** and hid the paintings under his coat. Nobody looked at him **because he was wearing a security guard's uniform**. Back in his apartment, **where he was living with his mother**, he filled his bedroom with priceless works of art. His mother, Mireille, 53, thought all the paintings were copies. One day **while they were having supper**, the police arrived, and they took Stephane to the police station. Mireille was so angry with her son that she went to his room, took some paintings from the walls, and cut them into small pieces. Others she took and threw into the canal. Altogether she destroyed art worth two billion dollars! Both mother and son spent many years in prison.

GRAMMAR SPOT

Ask students to work through the questions individually or in pairs. With weaker students, read through the notes with the whole class.

Answers

1 The tense used is the Past Continuous. The Past Continuous is used to give background information and description. (The Past Simple is used to tell the story.) This is demonstrated by the fact that these lines can be taken out of the story without seriously affecting comprehension.

2 We form questions by inverting the subject with *was* or *were*.
   He was working. – Was he working?
   We form negatives by adding *not* or *n't* after *was* or *were*. We usually use the short form *n't* when speaking.
   He was working. – He wasn't working.

3 In the first sentence, she made coffee after they arrived, possibly as a result of their arrival.

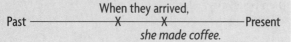

          When they arrived,
Past ————————X————X————Present
              she made coffee.

In the second sentence, she started making coffee before they arrived and the making of the coffee was still in progress when they arrived.

          When they arrived,
Past ————————X————————Present
   |--------------------------|
          she was making coffee.

Pronunciation

T 3.8 [CD 1: Track 33] Play the recording and get students to repeat chorally and individually. Focus attention on the weak form /ə/ in *was* /wəz/ and *were* /wə/. The *r* in *were* is silent unless it is followed by a vowel sound, e.g. *were eating* /wəriːtɪŋ/. If appropriate, point out that in negatives and short answers *was* and *were* are stressed and so have strong vowel sounds: /wɑz/ and /wɜː/.

If students need more practice, get them to read out the lines from exercise 4, paying attention to the weak forms in *was* /wəz/ and *were* /wə/.

Tapescript
He was working.
Where was he living?
They were having supper.
What were they doing?

Refer students to Grammar Reference 3.2 and 3.3 on SB p129.

5 In pairs, students take turns to read aloud parts of the story. Monitor and check for weak forms /wəz/ and /wə/ in the Past Continuous.

PHOTOCOPIABLE MATERIAL: EXTRA IDEA
Song **After T 3.8** [CD 1: Track 34]
***Don't you want me?*, TB p129**
This is intended as an informal and fun activity, which you may like to include at the end of a lesson. Photocopy the sheet on TB p129 and give a copy to each student. Work through the activities, allowing students to work in pairs wherever possible and encouraging plenty of discussion. You could do the final exercise with the whole class to round off the activity. The answers to the activities are on TB p150.

PRACTICE (SB p25)

EXTRA IDEA
Before going on to the *Practice* exercises, you might decide that your students would like some more information about the Past Continuous tense. In Unit 3 of the Workbook, exercise 8 is a mechanical drill to practise forming the Past Continuous. Once they have done it, your students might feel more confident about doing the following exercises.

Discussing grammar

1 Students work in pairs to decide which is the correct verb form and underline it.

> **Answers**
> | | |
> |---|---|
> | 1 saw | 4 did you break, was skiing, hit |
> | 2 was shopping, lost | 5 arrived, was having |
> | 3 stopped, was driving | 6 Did you have |

2 Students work in pairs to put the verbs in the correct form.

> **Answers**
> 1 was going, met
> 2 didn't want, was raining
> 3 rang, was leaving
> 4 picked
> 5 said, were watching

fortunately/unfortunately

The aim of the following exercises is to introduce the words *fortunately* and *unfortunately* and then to give students lots of practice in using the Past Simple tense by means of a fun whole-class activity.

3 Focus students on the story and model it, paying particular attention to your intonation, rising on *fortunately*, falling on *unfortunately*.

fortunately   *unfortunately*

Gesture to a student to continue the story by adding the next sentence, beginning *Fortunately*. Then gesture to another student to continue, and so on around the class. You could correct any errors at the end.

4 Put students in a circle if possible, and start one of the stories by reading out the first sentence. As the story goes around the class, note down any errors to feed back at the end. Alternatively, put students in groups to do the activity and monitor the groups.

Exchanging information

5 Ask students to read the headline and look at the photo. Ask them what kind of person they think Hugo Fenton-Jones is (you could point out that double-barrelled names like *Fenton-Jones* are associated with upper class families). Ask them what they think he bought and what a *spending spree* is (an uncontrolled episode of excessive shopping).

6 Put students in A and B pairs. Read the instructions as a class, then ask students to find their newspaper story on p143 (for student A) and p146 (for student B) of the Student's Book.

Give students three or four minutes to read their information and prepare questions. Monitor and help. When the pairs are ready, model the activity briefly with a reliable student, then give a clear start signal. Monitor and listen for errors, particularly with question formation, as they do the activity.

> **Answers** (complete text)
> Teenager Hugo Fenton-Jones stole **his father's credit card** while his father was working **in the garden**. He then went to **Paris** and stayed in the **Ritz** Hotel. His room was **£500** a night. While he was shopping in the **Champs-Élysées**, he bought **clothes, jewellery, and perfume**.
> He phoned two English friends because **he wanted them to come to Paris**. They were eating breakfast **in the Ritz** when Hugo's father, James, phoned. His credit card company wanted to know **why he was spending so much money**. They thought James was staying in the Ritz.
> Hugo went **home to London**, where **his father** was waiting for him. 'He isn't speaking to me at the moment,' said Hugo yesterday. 'He's a bit angry with me.'

ADDITIONAL MATERIAL

Workbook Unit 3

Exercises 8 and 9 Past Continuous

Exercise 10 Past Simple or Continuous?

LISTENING AND READING (SB p26)

The name's Bond, James Bond

> **ABOUT THE TEXT**
> This is an adapted extract from the popular James Bond spy story, *The Man with the Golden Gun*. Students have to listen and read for specific information, then retell the story, using picture clues. The text and activities recycle the Past Simple and Past Continuous tenses.
>
> James Bond, 007, was the creation of English writer Ian Fleming. He wrote the first James Bond novel, *Casino Royale*, in 1953. *The Man with the Golden Gun* was made into a movie in 1974, starring Roger Moore as 007. In the story, Bond tracks down a mysterious international hit man called Scaramanga, who kills his victims with a trademark golden gun and bullet.
>
> (See Student's Book p149 for a summary of the story. Students refer to this after doing exercise 7 on p27. You might want to read the summary yourself before starting the *Listening and reading* section of the unit.)
>
> The text contains quite a lot of new vocabulary, but students should be able to understand a lot of it from context. Some of the more difficult verbs are included in exercise 8, but you might want to pre-teach/check

the vocabulary first, especially with weaker students. Use the pictures in the Student's Book and mime to check the more difficult vocabulary: *his heart was thumping* (beating hard because he was nervous), *relief, pillow, creep, curse, whisper, bang shut, lead* (v). *HQ* = headquarters, *KGB* = the secret service of the former Soviet Union.

1 Ask students to work in pairs or small groups to write down things they know about James Bond. In feedback, encourage ideas by asking questions, for example *What happens in a typical James Bond movie?* (fights, car chases, special effects, beautiful women), and *What sort of person is Bond?* (cool, handsome, masculine).

2 Ask students to look at the film posters and say which of the films they have seen. Put students in pairs to write a list of other James Bond films. Be prepared to help with the names in English if students know the names of the films in their own language.

Answers

The posters show: *You Only Live Twice* (starring Sean Connery), *Octopussy* (starring Roger Moore), *Golden Eye* (starring Pierce Brosnan) and *Casino Royale* (starring the latest James Bond, Daniel Craig).

Other James Bond films include: *Dr No, From Russia with Love, Goldfinger, Thunderball, Live and Let Die, The Man with the Golden Gun, The Spy who Loved Me, Licence to Kill, Moonraker, The Living Daylights, The World is not Enough, Die Another Day, A View to a Kill, Tomorrow Never Dies, For your Eyes Only.*

Ask students to think about the names of the films in their own language. Ask if they are similar to the wording in English, or even a direct translation, or if they have a completely new title.

3 Get students to cover the text of the story. Focus attention on the pictures. Use this stage as an opportunity to pre-teach/review key words like *pillow, gun, curtain,* and *put your hands up.* (Also see note about vocabulary in the *About the text* box.) Ask students to work in pairs or small groups to describe what is happening in the story. Elicit a few ideas from the class but do not accept or reject them at this stage.

4 **T 3.9** [CD 1: Track 35] Give students time to read through the questions. Play the recording and get students to listen without following the text in their books (the audio script is slightly different from the text in the Student's Book). Encourage students to refer to the pictures to help them follow the recording. Put students in pairs to answer as many questions as they can. Play the recording again to allow students to complete their answers. Remind students to use past

tenses in their answers. Encourage them to speculate, as there may be more than one interpretation of what they have heard. Ask students if they had guessed correctly about the story when they did exercise 3.

Answers and tapescript

1 James Bond, Mary Goodnight, and Scaramanga. They're in a hotel room and the bathroom connected to it.
2 She climbed through the window that James Bond left open before he went to sleep.
3 She wanted to warn him about an important message from HQ. A KGB man was looking for Bond.
4 They talked in the bathroom, on the side of the bath.
5 Scaramanga told James and Mary to come out of the bathroom with their hands up. He was holding his golden gun and pointing it at Bond.

T 3.9
The man with the golden gun
N = Narrator   B = Bond   M = Mary
  S = Scaramanga
N James Bond got back to his hotel room at midnight. The windows were closed and the air-conditioning was on. Bond switched it off and opened the windows. His heart was thumping in his chest. He breathed in the air with relief, then he had a shower and went to bed.
  At 3.30 Bond suddenly woke up. There was a noise. It was coming from the window. Something was moving behind the curtain.
B Mary Goodnight! What the hell are you doing here?
M Quick, James! Help me in!
B Oh, my g . . . !
M I'm terribly sorry, James!
B Sh! Sh! Sshh!
B What the hell are you doing here? What's the matter?
M James, I was so worried. A 'Most Immediate' message came from HQ this evening. A top KGB man, using the name Hendriks, is staying in this hotel. He knows you're here. He's looking for you!
B I know, Hendriks is here all right. So is a gunman called Scaramanga. Mary, did HQ say if they have a description of me?
M No, they don't. They just have your name, Secret Agent James Bond.
B Thanks, Mary. Now, I must get you out of here. Don't worry about me, just tell HQ that you gave me the message, OK?
M OK, James. Please take care, James.
B Sure, sure. Now, come on!
S This is not your lucky day, Mr Bond. Come here both of you and put your hands up!
N Scaramanga walked to the door and turned on the lights. His golden gun was pointing directly at James Bond.

5 Tell students that they are now going to read the story from *The Man with the Golden Gun.* Ask the students to work in pairs or small groups to find the lines in the text that match the pictures. Review answers as a class.

Answers
1 James Bond got back to his hotel room at midnight. The windows were closed and the air conditioning was on. Bond switched it off and opened the windows.
2 Suddenly, he woke up. He listened. There was a noise. It was coming from the window. James Bond took his gun from under his pillow...
3 (James Bond) crept slowly along the wall toward the window.
4 Bond pulled it (the curtain) back with one quick movement. Golden hair shone in the moonlight. 'Mary Goodnight!' Bond cursed. 'What the hell are you doing here?' 'Quick, James! Help me in!' Mary whispered urgently.
5 Bond put down his gun and tried to pull her through the open window. At the last moment the window banged shut with a noise like a gunshot.
6 He quickly led her across the room to the bathroom. First he turned on the light, then the shower. They sat down together on the side of the bath.
7 Mary Goodnight stood up and looked into his eyes. 'Please take care, James.'
8 Scaramanga walked to the door and turned on the lights. His golden gun was pointing straight at James Bond.

6 Do the first sentence as an example, then ask students to work in pairs to correct the false sentences. Correct students' misuse of past tenses when you go through the answers in feedback.

Answers
1 True
2 False. He was dreaming about three black-coated men with red eyes and angry white teeth.
3 False. A noise behind the curtains woke him.
4 False. He angrily asked her why she was there.
5 False. The window banged shut with a noise like a gunshot.
6 True
7 True
8 False. He wanted to help her get out, but before he could, Scaramanga arrived.

What do you think?

7 Give students time to read through the questions and possible answers. Deal with any vocabulary queries students may have. Put students into groups of three or four to discuss the questions. Encourage students to use what they know about the character of James Bond and what often happens in Bond films to help them with questions 3 and 4.

Refer students to the summary of the story on p149 of the Student's Book to check their ideas.

Language work

8 Students work in pairs to write the past forms of the verbs, referring back to the text if necessary.

Answers (I) = irregular

got (I)	whispered	breathed
put (I)	woke up (I)	tried
took (I)	led (I)	crept (I)
gave (I)	shone (I)	stood up (I)

Telling the story

9 Students should now be ready to retell the story in some detail. Let them first do this in pairs to practise. Monitor them carefully, correcting the most important mistakes. This exercise is midway between a fluency and an accuracy-based activity. You want students to speak at length, but you also want the past tense usage to be correct.

When students are ready, ask one or two of them to tell the story to the rest of the class, allowing other students to interrupt with any key events that have been missed. You could begin the next class by asking a different student to retell the story. It only takes a few minutes and it is a good way to revise the key vocabulary and past tenses.

PHOTOCOPIABLE MATERIAL: EXTRA IDEA
Ian Fleming TB p130–131
This is an information gap activity based on a short biography of Ian Fleming's life.

Before the lesson, make one copy of the worksheet for each pair of students. Cut the worksheets in half. Teacher's notes and answers to this activity are on TB p150.

VOCABULARY AND SPEAKING (SB p28)

Adverbs

The aim here is to revise the use of adverbs, focusing in particular on exactly where adverbs go in a sentence.

Here is a way of leading in to this lesson: Write some adjectives on the board, for example, *careful, slow, quick, lazy, gentle, quiet, noisy, angry, happy*. Get students to tell you how to change the adjectives to adverbs. Then tell students to mime things, using the adverbs. For example, say *Speak quietly, Brush your hair gently, Stand up slowly*. Students must act out your instructions. You could then ask individuals to come to the front of the class and act out an action and adverb. The rest of the class must guess which adverb they are miming.

1 Ask students to work in pairs to match verbs in **A** with adverbs in **B**. Do one as an example. Let students check their answers by referring back to the text.

> **Answers**
> dream peacefully
> creep quietly/slowly
> wake up suddenly/slowly
> get out of bed quietly/suddenly/slowly
> whisper quietly/urgently
> breathe quietly/heavily/peacefully/slowly

2 Ask students to work in pairs to find examples of the adverbs in the text.

> **Answers**
> back (line 1), still (line 4), here (line 32), again (line 27), first (line 25), together (line 26), just (line 36), straight (line 49)

VOCABULARY SPOT

Position of adverbs

1 and 2 Read through the rules and examples as a class. You could add that nothing should ever separate the verb and its object in English if possible.

3 Put students in pairs to rewrite the sentences.

> **Answers**
> 1 First tidy your room...
> 2 Can't change.
> 3 ... Unfortunately, it started to rain.

---

3 Ask students to rewrite the sentences. Let them check their answers in pairs before discussing as a class. There is sometimes more than one possible answer, but the one used in the recording is the most suitable.

T 3.10 [CD 1: Track 36] Play the recording. Ask students to listen and check their answers. Then put them in pairs to practise saying the sentences.

Answers and tapescript
1 I was dreaming **peacefully** when **suddenly** a loud noise woke me up (**suddenly**).
2 My Grandma is **nearly** 75 and she **still** goes swimming **regularly**.
3 I (**quietly**) unlocked the door **quietly** and went **outside** into the night.
4 She whispered **softly** in his ear (**softly**), 'Do you **really** love me?' '**Of course** I do,' he replied.
5 I was **just** relaxing with a **really** good book when someone knocked **loudly** on the door (**loudly**).
6 **First** break the eggs into a bowl and **then** mix them **together** with the flour.
7 I (**quickly**) got up **quickly** and crept **downstairs** to the front door.
8 I work **hard** and I do my homework **carefully**, but I **still** don't get good marks.

An adverb poem

4 **T 3.11** [CD 1: Track 37] Play the recording. Ask students to listen and read. Put students in pairs to think of a title. Then ask them to take it in turns to read the poem aloud.

> **Answers and tapescript**
> Possible titles: The end of love / A broken heart
>
> **T 3.11**
> **An adverb poem**
> I ran into your arms so happily,
> You looked at me guiltily,
> You spoke to me quite softly,
> I turned and walked away sadly.
> Gradually I learned to smile again.

5 Check that the students understand the adverbs. Then ask them to write a poem with their partner. Ask pairs to read out their poem with feeling, to the class.

WRITING (SB p104)

Telling a story – Position of adverbs and adjectives

The aim of this writing section is to write a narrative in the past using adverbs and adjectives.

1 Put students in pairs to rewrite the sentences with the adjectives and adverbs in the correct place.

> **Answers**
> 1 A **large** dog **suddenly** jumped up at me.
> 2 Thank you for your **kind** invitation. **Unfortunately**, I can't come.
> 3 I got out of bed and went **downstairs** to make a **nice** cup of tea.
> 4 We had a **lovely** meal and **then** went to the theatre.

5 I was sitting at home **last Thursday evening** when something **very strange** happened.
6 He's got three **older** sisters and I've got three sisters **too**.
7 There was a **good** documentary on TV last night. I enjoyed it **very much**.
8 I worked **really hard** all **last** week.

In feedback, ask students what rules for adjectives and adverbs they can work out from the sentences.

Answers
Adjectives go before nouns: ...a *large* dog...
Adverbs of manner go after verbs: ...I worked really *hard*...
Adverbs of degree go before adjectives: ...*very* strange...
Some adverbs can go at the start or end of sentences:
Unfortunately, I can't come.. / I can't come, *unfortunately*.
Some adverbs go at the end of sentences or clauses: ..., *too*. /
...*very much*.

2 Put students in pairs. Ask them to describe the pictures and guess the story. In feedback, pre-teach key words in the pictures: *mirror, portrait, hurry, refuse*.

Ask students to write the story in pairs, using the word prompts. Monitor and help. Make sure students are using adverbs and adjectives. When students have finished, ask one or two pairs to tell the class their story.

Ask students to compare their stories with the version on p149 of the Student's Book.

3 You could repeat the procedure as in exercise 2 in a later lesson, or you could set this writing task for homework.

4 Ask students to compare their stories in pairs. Ask one or two to tell the class their story. Ask students to compare their stories with the version on p150 of the Student's Book.

EVERYDAY ENGLISH (SB p29)

Time expressions

Lead in to the lesson by asking a few general questions around the class. Ask *What's the date today? When is your birthday? When is Christmas?* Note how well students form and pronounce dates in their answers, but don't correct or present how to say dates at this stage.

1 **T 3.12** [CD 1: Track 38] Focus attention on the conversation in exercise 1. Play the recording and get students to follow in their books. Elicit the two ways of saying dates (*October the 11th and the 11th of October*).

Put students in pairs to practise the conversation. Tell them to practise it at least twice, changing roles each time. Monitor and check students' pronunciation.

T 3.12
A Did you send Oliver a birthday card?
B I had no idea it was his birthday. When was it?
A On October the 11th.
B The 11th of October! That's a week ago. I'll phone him this evening and apologize.

2 Write the first date on the board: June 2. Elicit the two ways of saying it:

the second of June   *June the 2nd*

POSSIBLE PROBLEMS
- Students forget the definite article *the*.
  **I came here on second of June.*
- Students might not remember all the ordinal numbers, especially *first, second, third*, and *twenty-first, twenty-second*, etc. Be prepared to drill these as a class if students have problems. The pronunciation of some ordinals is difficult because of consonant clusters: *fifth, sixth, twelfth*, etc.
- Students often get years wrong, sometimes because of interference from their own language. You may need to remind them that we usually divide the numbers into two sets of two, e.g. 1980 – *nineteen eighty*; we use *oh* not *zero* in dates, e.g. 1906 – *nineteen oh six*; dates for the first decade of the new millennium are usually read like ordinary numbers, e.g. 2002 – *two thousand and two*.
- Point out that in American English the month, not the day, is usually written first, e.g. 8/21/07 – *August twenty-first two thousand seven*. Note that it is normal in American English to omit *the* and *and* in dates like these.

Elicit more pairs of dates from the class. Students practise saying the dates in pairs. Give them time to concentrate on getting the form right before playing the recording.

T 3.13 [CD 1: Track 39] Play the recording, pausing after each pair of dates. Ask students to listen and check. Be prepared to drill the two ways of saying the dates if students have problems.

T 3.13
the second of June / June the second
the thirty-first of August / August the thirty-first
the fourth of July / July the fourth
the first of May / May the first
the seventeenth of September / September the seventeenth
the seventh of January eighteen sixty-eight / January the seventh eighteen sixty-eight
the twenty-eighth of December nineteen oh one / December the twenty-eighth nineteen oh one

the fourteenth of February nineteen eighty / February the
fourteenth nineteen eighty
the fifth of November two thousand and two / November the
fifth two thousand and two
the fifth of April two thousand and ten / April the fifth two
thousand and ten

3 Students work in pairs to complete the time expressions.
Monitor to find out how well students do the exercise,
then check the answers.

Answers
at six o'clock, **on** Saturday, **in** 1989, **on** Monday morning,
– last night, **in** April, **at** the weekend,* – yesterday evening
in the evening, **in** summer, **on** January 18, – two weeks ago
* **on** the weekend in US English

Tell students that we use *at* with times, e.g. at *six o'clock*.
Put students into pairs and ask them to work out the
rules for the use of *in* and *on*, and when to use no
preposition. List the rules on the board.

Rules
at   times, at the weekend
in   months, years, seasons, parts of the day
on   days, dates, on Monday morning, etc.
no prepositions   last night, yesterday evening, etc., two weeks
ago, etc.

Say exactly when you were born. Then get a student to
read out the example in the Student's Book. Elicit a few
more examples from the class. Put students in pairs and
get them to continue asking and answering the question.
Monitor and check for accurate use of the prepositions
and for the ways of saying the dates. Be prepared to drill
the correct forms again as necessary.

MUSIC OF ENGLISH – WORD LINKING

1 **T 3.14** [CD 1: Track 40] Read through the *Music of
English* box as a class. Play the recording and get
students to repeat.

If students have problems understanding or producing
word linking, write a phrase on the board and show
how it breaks down into smaller units by using
phonemic script:

/æ/ /tɪ/ /le/ /vənə/ /klɑk/   at eleven o'clock

Point out that the *h* in *four hours* ago is silent and so
needs a consonant–vowel link:

/fɔːrauəzəgəʊ/

If students seem to find word linking difficult, try to
show them how it makes it easier to run the words
together, especially in normal conversation.

T 3.14
this evening
this afternoon
at eleven o'clock
in August
last autumn
twenty-eight years old
four hours ago
first of all

4 **T 3.15** [CD 1: Track 41] Give students time to read
through the gapped conversation. Play the recording and
get students to complete the conversation with the time
expressions. Check the answers.

Play the recording again and get students to mark the
linking. Pause the recording at the end of each line to
give students time to mark their answers. Play the
recording again if students have problems. Then check
the answers.

Notice that a /w/ sound links *so* and *am*, and that the /t/
in *don't* and the /k/ in *like* are not pronounced.

Answers and tapescript
A What star sign‿are you?
B I'm‿Aries.
A Hey, so‿am‿I! When's your birthday?
B The 11th‿of‿April.
A I don't believe‿it! Same‿as me. Which year?
B 1990.
A That's‿amazing! We're like twins!

Play the recording again and get students to follow in
their books and listen out for the linked words. Briefly
review the pronunciation of the star signs with the class
(see Teacher's Book p12). With weaker classes, elicit new
wording for the conversation with the whole class first,
replacing the star sign, date, and year. Give students time
to practise the conversations in pairs, changing roles at
least once. Monitor and check for the correct formation
of dates and years, and for signs that students are trying
to link the words. Don't insist on perfect pronunciation!

5 **T 3.16** [CD 1: Track 42] Play the recording through
once to let students understand the general content of
each conversation. Ask *What are the conversations about?*
and elicit the answers (1 the date of Easter this year, 2 the
date of the next meeting, 3 the date and time of a flight).

Play the recording again, pausing at the end of each line
to give students time to write down the time expressions.
With weaker classes, elicit the answers for conversation 1
with the whole class.

Answers and tapescript

1 Easter; this year; early; Easter Sunday; on the 27th or the 28th of March
2 next month; Wednesday the 16th of June; at 2.30
3 Tuesday, May the 7th at 7.40 a.m.; Tuesday the seventh of May at 6.40

T 3.16

1 **A** When's Easter this year?
  B It's early, I think. Easter Sunday's on the 27th or the 28th of March.
  A Yes, you're right. Look, it's the 27th. That is early!

2 **A** Judy, can you tell me when the next meeting is?
  B Let me see. Ah, yes. It's next month. Wednesday the 16th of June.
  A What time?
  B It starts at 2.30.
  A So, Wednesday, the 16th at 2.30?
  B That's right.
  A Thanks.

3 **A** Miss Lomax, I've scheduled your flight for Tuesday, May the 7th at 7.40 a.m.
  B Let me put that in my computer diary. So ... that's Tuesday the seventh of May at 6.40?
  A No, 7.40 a.m., Miss Lomax.
  B Oh. yeah. Thanks, Sally.

6 Refer students to SB p118 and tapescript 3.16. Put students in pairs and let them choose one of the three conversations. If a lot of students choose the same one, you may have to adapt their choice to ensure they cover all three conversations. If you have time in class, let students rehearse the lines until they have learnt them by heart. Monitor to help with pronunciation. Ask students to act out their conversation to the class. If you are short of time, get students to learn the lines at home and act out the conversations at the beginning of the next class.

Don't forget!

Workbook Unit 3

Exercise 11 Adverbs

Exercises 12–13 Check it

Grammar Reference
Look at the exercises on SB p129–130 as a class, or set for homework. The answers are on TB p155.

Word list
Remind your students of the Word list for this unit on SB p153. They could translate the words, learn them at home, or transfer some of the words to their vocabulary notebook.

Pronunciation Book Unit 3

much/many • some/any
a few, a little, a lot of • Articles
Shopping • Prices

The market place

Introduction to the unit

The theme of this unit is market places. In the opening section, expressions of quantity are introduced in the context of a couple discussing their supermarket shopping list. In a separate presentation section, a text about eBay, the global online market place, there is some work on the use of articles in English. The *Reading and speaking* is about three famous market places around the world, and the *Vocabulary, listening, and speaking* consists of four dialogues set in different shops.

Language aims

Grammar – Expressions of quantity It is assumed that students will have some knowledge of expressions of quantity, but that mistakes will still be common.

The point is also made that the rules about the use of *something/anything*, etc. are the same as for *some* and *any*. These are also practised.

Articles It is expected that students will not have actually studied articles in English to any great extent. However, they will probably be aware that the use of articles varies between languages. There are many languages that don't use articles, e.g. Japanese, Arabic, and many Slavic languages (Russian, Czech, etc), and speakers of these languages will find their use particularly difficult. Don't expect your students to have a deep understanding of article usage at the end of this unit. There are too many rules and exceptions.

Vocabulary Vocabulary is introduced around the topic of things we buy, in a brainstorming activity before the main listening texts.

Everyday English Prices and the functional language of shopping are chosen to fit the theme of the unit. These are practised in a variety of everyday shopping situations.

Notes on the unit

STARTER (SB p30)

The aim of the alphabet game is to see how well your students understand the idea of count and uncount nouns. It also brings out a lot of vocabulary, revises past tenses from the previous unit, and it is fun.

Focus students on the examples in the book, then model the first sentence. Nominate a student to read the second sentence and so on until they have got the idea. If you have a small class get them to sit in a circle to do this activity. Insist on good stress and a good rhythm.

•   •   •   •

Yesterday I went shopping and I bought an apple and some bread.

Don't let this activity go on too long. As you get towards halfway through the alphabet, students' memories will be tested. Be prepared to give lots of prompts, so you can get on to the main part of the lesson.

AT THE SUPERMARKET (SB p30)

How much/How many?

You could personalize the lead-in by writing *shopping list* on the board and eliciting from students what they or their family usually buy every week.

1 Set the scene by reading the introduction and asking students to look at the photographs of Nick and Sarah. Ask *Where are they? What are they doing? What is the relationship between them?*

Focus students on the shopping list and check any unknown words. You may also wish to check the meaning of *a pint of milk* and *a dozen eggs*. (1.76 pints /paɪnts/ = 1 litre, dozen /dʌzən/ = 12) Milk is sold in litres now in Britain, but people still tend to refer to a half litre of milk as a pint!

T 4.1 [CD 1: Track 43] Ask students to read and listen to the conversation between Nick and Sarah. Point out the use of *How much?* and *How many?*

Tapescript
N = Nick S = Sarah
N It just says 'milk' here. How much milk do we need?
S Two pints.
N And eggs? How many eggs?
S A dozen.
N And what about potatoes? How many potatoes?
S A kilo's enough.

GRAMMAR SPOT (SB p30)

Put students in pairs to discuss the questions in the *Grammar Spot*.

Answers
We can't count milk but we can count eggs.
We say *How much* when the noun is uncountable.
We say *How many* when the noun is countable, (one, two, three, etc.).

In the feedback, you could check students' understanding by asking individuals check questions with other nouns.

Sergio, can we count cheese?

Maria, can we count sausages?

Alternatively, you could write different foods at random on the board, then ask students to categorise them according to whether they are count or uncount nouns. For example:

Count	Uncount
eggs	milk
potatoes	butter
tomatoes	cheese

sausages	Coke
crisps	wine
	bread

Point out that plural count nouns usually end with -s or -es.

Refer students to Grammar Reference 4.1 on p131.

2 Ask students to match the expressions in the box with the items on the shopping list.

Answers

a large tube (of)	toothpaste
six rolls (of)	toilet paper
just one brown loaf (of)	bread
four or five big ones	tomatoes
a bottle of red	wine
200g of Cheddar	cheese

3 Put students in pairs to continue the conversation. Monitor and correct. Encourage good pronunciation of the questions, particularly the intonation.

4 **T 4.2** [CD 1: Track 44] Students read and listen to the rest of the conversation between Nick and Sarah and complete it. Ask a few questions afterwards to check that students have followed the conversation, and to see how well they can use expressions like *a few*, *a little*, and *not many*.

For example
How much orange juice have they got?
How many vegetables have they got?

Answers and tapescript
N = Nick S = Sarah
N Is that everything?
S Let's have a look. We've got some **apples**, but there aren't any bananas. And we've got some **tea**, but there isn't any coffee.
N OK, bananas and coffee. What about orange juice? Is there any orange juice left?
S Let's see. There's a little, but not much.
N Orange juice, then. And vegetables? Have we got many vegetables?
S Well, we've got some broccoli and a few **carrots**, but there aren't many onions.
N Right, onions ...
S Oh, and don't forget – your nephews are coming tomorrow! We need something for them.
N OK, lots of crisps and **ice-cream**. Anything else?
S I don't think so. But for goodness sake, don't forget the nappies. Oh, and a big bunch of **flowers** for me!

1 Ask students to work in pairs to find eight count nouns and five uncount nouns in the conversation in exercise 4.

> **Answers**
> Count nouns: apples, bananas, vegetables, carrots, onions, crisps, nappies, flowers
> Uncount nouns: tea, coffee, orange juice, broccoli, ice-cream

2 The aim of this activity is for students to discover for themselves from context the sometimes confusing rules of use involved with count and uncount nouns. This exercise is not easy. Be prepared to give lots of help.

Students work in pairs to complete the table by finding examples of use in the conversation in exercise 4.

> **Answers**
>
> | We use ... | with CNs | with UNs | in positive sentences |
> |---|---|---|---|
> | some | ✓ | ✓ | ✓ |
> | any | ✓ | ✓ | ✗ |
> | much | ✗ | ✓ | ✗ |
> | many | ✓ | ✗ | ✗ |
> | a lot/lots of | ✓ | ✓ | ✓ |
> | a few | ✓ | ✗ | ✓ |
> | a little | ✗ | ✓ | ✓ |
>
> | We use ... | in questions | in negative sentences |
> |---|---|---|
> | some | ✓ | ✗ |
> | any | ✓ | ✓ |
> | much | ✓ | ✓ |
> | many | ✓ | ✓ |
> | a lot / lots of | ✓ | ✓ |

You might want to check students' ability to use this language by doing exercises 1 to 3 in the *Practice* section at this stage.

3 Focus students on the table and ask them to find three examples of these words in the conversation. The use of the phrases is checked in exercise 6 of the following *Practice* section.

> **Answers**
> Is that everything?
> We need something for them.
> Anything else?

Refer students to Grammar Reference 4.1 on p131.

Discussing grammar

1–3 Ask students to do the five sentences in exercise 1 on their own, then check with a partner. Do the same for 2 and 3, then go through all the answers together as a class. Point out that in exercise 2 *a lot of/lots of* could be used in all the sentences except for number 5, and check students understand that it can only be replaced by *many* and *much* in questions and negatives.

> **Answers**
> 1 1 any 2 any 3 some 4 some 5 any
> 2 1 much 2 many 3 much 4 many 5 many
> 3 1 a few 2 a lot of 3 a little 4 a lot of 5 a few
>   6 a little

Find the differences

4 Ask students to look at the photograph and say what they can see. Focus on the items on the shelf – this is vocabulary preparation for the picture difference activity that they are going to do.

> **Answers**
> deodorant, shampoo, shaving foam (cans of), hairbrush, toilet paper, toothpaste, toothbrushes, soap, towels, nappies

Elicit the other vocabulary that students will need for the picture activity, i.e. make-up, perfume/aftershave.

Drill all the vocabulary for pronunciation. Make sure the students know the plural endings of *hairbrushes*, *toothbrushes*, and *nappies*.

Ask the students which ones they think are countable and which ones uncountable.

> **Answers**
>
> | Countable | Uncountable |
> |---|---|
> | towels | soap |
> | nappies | toothpaste |
> | toothbrushes | shampoo |
> | hairbrushes | toilet paper |
> | | shaving foam |
> | | make-up |
> | | deodorant |
> | | perfume/aftershave |
>
> **NB** Some of the uncountable items become countable if the container is added – a bar/bars of soap, a tube/tubes of toothpaste, a roll/rolls of toilet paper, a can/cans of shaving foam, a bottle/bottles of shampoo/perfume/aftershave.

5 Divide students into pairs. Tell them to decide who is A, and who is B. As look at the picture of the bathroom on p144. Bs look at the picture of the bathroom on p147. Tell students they have different pictures, and they have to find out what their partner has in their bathroom and

how many/much. Refer the students to the questions on their page and model one or two first.

Is there any make-up in your picture?

Once students have got the idea they can ask and answer questions in their pairs. Monitor closely and listen for errors and examples of good language use. Correct errors in a brief feedback.

Sample answers

	Picture A	Picture B
towels	a few / not many	a lot / lots
soap	a lot / lots / some	none
nappies	a lot / lots	a few / one or two/ not many
toothbrushes	a lot / lots	a lot / lots
toothpaste	a little / not much	a lot / lots
shampoo	some / a little / not much	none
toilet paper	a lot / lots	a little / not much
shaving foam	a lot / lots	none
make-up	none	a lot / lots
deodorant	none	some
perfume/ aftershave	a little / some / not much	a lot / lots
hairbrushes	a lot / lots / some / three	one

something/someone/somewhere

6 Do the first question as an example. Students work in pairs to complete the rest.

T 4.3 [CD 1: Track 45] Students listen and check their answers.

Answers and tapescript

1 'Did you meet **anyone** nice at the party?'
  'Yes. I met **someone** who knows you!'
2 'Ouch! There's **something** in my eye!'
  'Let me look. No, I can't see **anything**.'
3 'Let's go **somewhere** hot for our holidays.'
  'Yes, but we can't go **anywhere** that's too expensive.'
4 'I'm so unhappy. **Nobody** loves me.'
  'I know **someone** who loves you. Me.'
5 'I've lost my glasses. I've looked **everywhere**, but I can't find them.'
6 'Did you buy **anything** at the shops?'
  'No, **nothing**. I didn't have any money.'
7 'I'm bored. I want **something** interesting to read, or **someone** interesting to talk to, or **somewhere** interesting to go.'
8 'It was a great party. **Everyone** loved it.'

ADDITIONAL MATERIAL

Workbook Unit 4
These exercises could be done in class to give further practice, for homework, or in a later class as revision.

Exercise 1 Shops – John's shopping trip

Exercises 2–3 Count and uncount nouns

Exercises 4–8 Expressions of quantity

THE AMAZING WORLD OF eBay (SB p32)

Articles

ABOUT THE TEXT
Students read the short text about eBay for specific understanding. They then research the text for contextualized examples of how articles are used.

eBay is an online market place. Basically, people advertise things they want to sell on the website, and subscribers bid for the things. The highest bid, at a pre-set closing time, wins. A *Learjet* is a make of small jet aeroplane, often bought by the super-rich for their own personal use.

The only difficult words you may wish to pre-teach are the things you can buy on eBay: *stamps, jewellery, art, clothing, jet*. Use the pictures to teach them.

1 Ask the whole class the questions. Encourage students who have used the website to share their experiences with the class.

2 Ask students to look at the photos, and check that they know what the objects shown are. Ask students to read the text and answer the questions. Let them check their answers in pairs.

Answers
1 Learjet = $4.9 million; football = £18,500
2 125 million
3 Pierre Omidyar
4 In 1995. He wanted to create a website for everybody to buy and sell things.

1 Ask students to read the text again more carefully and find all the definite and indefinite articles.

Answers
Where can you buy **a** football kicked by David Beckham, or **an** old Learjet? On eBay, of course – **the** world's first global online market place. **The** football sold for £18,500, and someone paid $4.9 million for **the** jet! Every day on eBay, there are 34 million things for sale, and 125 million buyers and sellers. You can buy everything – stamps, jewellery, art, clothing, old cars, and anything strange and interesting. All you need is **a** computer and **a** little time.
Pierre Omidyar, **a** French-Iranian computer scientist, invented eBay in California in 1995. He wanted to create **a** website for everybody to buy and sell things, not just big businesses. He started **the** website as **a** hobby, but now it is **the** biggest 'business' in **the** world!

2 Point out that there is no article in front of eBay. Ask students to find other nouns in the text where there is no article.

Answers
David Beckham, eBay, things, buyers and sellers, stamps, jewellery, art, clothing, old cars, California, 1995, big businesses

Before they turn to the Grammar Reference section you could ask them a few general questions about articles.

Sample questions
Can you give any rules about the use of articles in English with examples from the text?
Do you know of any differences between the use of articles in English and in your own language?

At this stage you could ask students to turn to Grammar Reference 4.2 on p131 and find rules for some of the examples in the text. Some rules are given below.

Answers
(The words are in the order they appear in the text.)
a football/a Learjet (because they are referred to for the first time)
the world's first... (we usually use *the* with a superlative because it is the only one)
stamps, jewellery, art ... (general categories, not talking about any particular stamps, jewellery, etc.)
a little time (an expression of quantity)
a computer scientist (we use *a* with jobs)
California (no article with countries or states)
The biggest business in the world (we usually use *the* with a superlative because it is the only one – and there is only *one* world)

1 Ask students to complete the sentences. Let them check their answers in pairs before discussing them as a class. In feedback, discuss why an article is or isn't used (reasons are shown in brackets).

Answers
1 I bought <u>an</u> unusual football on <u>x</u> eBay. <u>x</u> David Beckham kicked it in <u>the</u> 2004 European Cup Final! (**an** = referred to for first time; **no article** = no article in front of names; **the** = a unique event)
2 There was <u>an</u> old Learjet for sale. <u>A</u> famous film star paid <u>a</u> lot of money for it. (**an** = referred to for first time; **A** = referred to for first time; **a** = part of expression of quantity)
3 <u>The</u> film star who bought <u>the</u> Learjet collects <u>x</u> aeroplanes. (**The/the** = speaker and listener know them already; **no article** = plural countable nouns in general)
4 eBay is <u>a</u> very clever idea. It's <u>the</u> biggest market in <u>the</u> world. (**a** = referred to for first time; **the** = with superlative; **the** = 'world' is unique)
5 I don't go out to <u>x</u> work. I work at <u>x</u> home on my computer (**no article** = with set expressions *to work* and *at home*)
6 I do all my shopping on <u>the</u> Internet. What <u>a</u> great way to shop! (**the** = 'Internet' is unique; **a** = a *what* exclamation, and there are other great ways to shop)

I bought it on eBay!

2 ▶ **T 4.4** **[CD 1: Track 46]** Play the recording. Ask students to listen and complete the chart. Ask students to compare their answers in pairs, then play the recording again to check.

Answers and tapescript

	Linda	Megan	Charlie
What did she/he buy?	cooker	shoes	car (Volvo)
How much did it cost?	£100	£2	£1,000
Does she/he like using eBay?	Yes	Yes	Not now
Does she/he use eBay often?	Yes	Yes	Yes, but he's not going to for a while

T 4.4
I bought it on eBay!
Linda
The first time I used eBay I bought a cooker! It's for the kitchen in my new house. I was amazed, because it was so easy. And it was cheap, too! I bought an expensive Italian cooker for only £100, and I went to get it yesterday. It looks fantastic in my new kitchen. I think eBay's a brilliant idea. I'm going to buy a fridge next!

Megan
Oooh! Don't talk to me about eBay! It's a real problem for me – I like it too much. Parcels arrive every day, usually with shoes. I just love buying shoes on eBay. Yesterday a beautiful pair of green sandals arrived. They only cost £2. Can you believe it? My

boyfriend says he gets worried every time he sees the postman – but you can't have too many shoes, can you?

Charlie
I can't believe it! I'm so stupid! I bought a car on eBay, and it was a big mistake. I've bought plenty of other things on eBay, and it usually works very well. And I heard that a car sells every two minutes on eBay, and the sellers are usually very good. So I paid £1,000 for an old Volvo, and I went to get it last week. But on the way home the car stopped. A mechanic told me it was worth less than half the price I paid. Now I don't know what to do. But I'm not going to use eBay again for a while.

Discussing grammar

Ask students to work in pairs to do these two exercises.

3   Ask students to identify the mistake in each sentence and discuss why it is wrong. Let them refer to the Grammar Reference if necessary.

> **Answers**
> 1   He's **a** postman, so he has breakfast at 4 a.m. (a job)
> 2   **Love** is more important than money. (in general)
> 3   I come to school **by bus**. (no article with *by* + form of transport)
> 4   I'm reading **a** good book at the moment. (referring to a thing for the first time)
> 5   'Where's Jack?' 'In **the** kitchen.' (we know which one)
> 6   I live in **the** centre of town, near the hospital. (there's only one)
> 7   My parents bought **a** lovely house in the country. (referring to a thing for the first time)
> 8   I don't eat **bread** because I don't like it. (in general)

4   The aim of this activity is to focus on the contrast between no article for talking about things in general, and the definite article for talking about specific things. Refer students to the examples and discuss why the article is or isn't used.

I think ice-cream is delicious. (no article because we are talking about ice-cream in general)

The ice-cream in this café is delicious. (definite article because we are talking about one specific type of ice-cream)

Ask students to work in pairs to write the sentences for the remaining words. Let them refer to the Grammar Reference if necessary.

> **Sample answers**
> I haven't got any money./Here's the money I owe you.
> Chocolate is wonderful./Who's eaten all the chocolate?
> Cats are beautiful./Can you open the door and let the cats out?

ADDITIONAL MATERIAL

Workbook Unit 4
Exercises 9–11 Articles

READING AND SPEAKING (SB p34)

Markets around the world

> **ABOUT THE TEXT**
> This is a jigsaw reading activity. Students work in three groups to read three different texts, answer specific information questions, then share their information with students from other groups.
>
> The texts are about three markets: one in Bangkok, in Thailand in south-east Asia, which is a floating market on canals, and sells local food and traditional clothing; one on a Sunday morning in a small town in Provence, a region in southern France, which sells local French food and antiques; and one in Marrakech, in Morocco, in northern Africa, called a *souk*, which sells spices, clothes and carpets.
>
> You may wish to pre-teach vocabulary around the topic of markets: *market, stall, sellers, to bargain, packed, busy, noisy*. After reading, you may need to explain some of the things that can be bought in the markets:
> *olives* = small black or green fruit, from which oil is extracted
> *antiques* = very old objects
> *lace* = a light delicate cloth
> *bunches of flowers* = groups of cut flowers
> *herbs* = plants used to flavour food
> *lavender* = nice-smelling purple flowers
> *silk* = thin smooth cloth made by silkworms
> *rugs/carpets* = a thick, soft cover on the floor – carpets cover the whole floor, rugs are smaller and cover a part of the floor

1   Ask students to look at the pictures of the markets. Ask *Where are they? What do they sell?* (See *About the text* above.)

Put students in pairs to discuss the questions. Demonstrate *to bargain* by trying to buy something from one of the students and arguing about the price he/she suggests.

> **Answers**
> 1   A shopping centre is a modern, covered building, full of different shops. The shops are high street or international names, and sell global brands.
>   A market is often open air (unless it is a covered market), and made up of small stalls. They usually sell local products.

2   Ask students to read the introduction, then discuss the question as a class.

> **Answers**
> Because they sell goods that are different, and made and grown locally.

3 Divide students into groups. If you have a small class, e.g. 12, divide them into three groups of 4. If you have a large class, e.g. 30, divide them into six groups of five, two groups reading text **A**, two groups reading text **B**, etc.

Make sure each group knows which text to read.

4 Ask students to read through the questions, then tell them to research their text and find answers. Encourage students to discuss the answers in their groups. Do not check answers at this stage.

5 Tell students to stand up, walk round, and sit down with two students who have read a different text. Manage this proactively, making sure everybody finds partners. Once students are in threes, tell them to share their answers.

In feedback, get one student from each three to summarize findings for each question.

Answers

Bangkok
1 On the canals around the town of Damonen Saduak.
2 Every day from 6.30 a.m.
3 Tropical fruit and vegetables, fresh coconut juice, and local food. Hot soup.
4 Traditional hats, silk dresses, flowered shirts.
5 There are old ladies with huge hats, and food sellers with cookers on their boats.
6 Colourful, noisy, fascinating.
7 Continue along the canal to the canal villages.
8 Bangkok is a city of contrasts – tall glass buildings and the 100-year-old canals.

Provence
1 In a small town called Isle-sur-la-Sorgue, in southern France.
2 Every Sunday, from early morning until 1 o'clock.
3 Olives, cheese, roast chicken, herbs, olive bread, tomatoes, ham, melons.
4 Antique French furniture, antique lace and cloth, flowers, soap, lavender, sun hats, beach towels, local rosé wine.
5 The sellers call out in the singing accent of the south. The antique and flower sellers fill the pavements with their goods.
6 Truly amazing, packed, noisy, busy, beautiful, brightly coloured.
7 Find a cool place next to the river for a picnic.
8 It's a sleepy little town, with narrow streets and many bridges – like Venice.

Marrakech
1 Behind the main square in Marrakech, Jemaa el Fna.
2 From early morning until lunchtime, and again in the evening.
3 Spices and meat.
4 Clothing, gold, silver, carpets, and rugs.
5 Mr Youssaf invites you to sit down and gives you tea, and talks for hours about his rugs.
6 Narrow, busy, aromatic, noisy, colourful, beautiful.

---

7 Return to the main square and watch the snakes (and count your money).
8 It looks like a Hollywood film set. A city of ancient, sand-coloured buildings and palm trees in the middle of the desert.

What do you think?

This is a personalized fluency discussion which aims to revise vocabulary and get students talking.

Ask students to discuss the questions in their groups of three.

WRITING (SB p106)

A postcard – Synonyms in writing

The aim of this writing section is to write a postcard to a friend using a range of synonymous adjectives.

1 Ask students to look at the photograph on the postcard. Ask *What can you see? What famous places can you visit in New York?*

Ask students to read the postcard, and answer the questions.

Answers

Richard and Sandy are enjoying their holiday in New York. It's nice! Their friend went to the South of France.
The problem with the style of writing is that they over-use 'nice' as an adjective.

---

2 Ask students to work in pairs to complete the sentences with better adjectives. Monitor and help.

Answers
1 great/good/wonderful/brilliant
2 great/good/wonderful/amazing/warm and sunny/beautiful
3 great/good/wonderful/luxurious/spectacular/beautiful (*hotel*)
   an interesting/a wonderful/an exciting/a beautiful (*part of town*)
4 great/good/wonderful/spectacular/amazing/brilliant/beautiful
5 great/wonderful/spectacular/amazing/brilliant/beautiful
6 a great/an interesting/a wonderful/a spectacular/ an amazing/a brilliant/an exciting
7 a great/an interesting/a good/a wonderful/a spectacular/ an amazing/a brilliant/an exciting
8 wonderful/brilliant/beautiful
9 good/wonderful
10 great/interesting/good/wonderful/spectacular/amazing/ brilliant/beautiful

---

3 Ask students to take turns to read the postcard aloud with different adjectives. Ask them where the best place to use *nice* is.

Answers

Nice is best used in ... *having a nice time* or *Did you have a nice time ...?*

Sample answer

Dear Sam,
Here we are in New York having a great time. The weather is very warm and sunny. We're staying in quite a luxurious hotel in an interesting part of town, Lower Manhattan. We have spectacular views of the Chrysler and Empire State Buildings from our bedroom window. We think all the skyscrapers are amazing. Yesterday we went on a really exciting helicopter tour of the city and then in the evening we saw a brilliant show on Broadway. Today we are going shopping for clothes in Bloomingdales. I want to buy some beautiful designer jeans. They are much cheaper here. Did you have a nice time in the South of France? We hear that the markets there are wonderful.
See you soon,
Love,
Richard and Sandy

4   Ask students to write one or two brief notes under the headings in the Student's Book. Let them compare their ideas with a partner.

Ask students to write a postcard, using a range of synonymous adjectives. They could write their postcards to someone else in the class, and you could then 'deliver' them.

ADDITIONAL MATERIAL

Workbook Unit 4

Exercise 12   Vocabulary – Clothes

VOCABULARY, LISTENING, AND SPEAKING (SB p36)

Shopping

1   Focus attention on the photos. Elicit where the people are in each one (*in a chemist's, in a café, in a post office, and in a clothes shop*).

Ask students what they can buy or do in a chemist's. Write some of their ideas on the board, then put them in pairs or threes to do the rest of the exercise. Give students a time limit so that they do this quite quickly, then feed back with the whole class. (Note that the answers below are for these types of shop in the UK – it may be different in the students' own countries).

Sample answers

a chemist's	buy medicine, aspirin, soap, etc.; get a prescription; get photos developed
a café	buy a coffee or tea; eat a sandwich or cakes; drink beer or wine; read a paper; talk to friends; look at the menu; pay the bill
a post office	buy stamps; send a parcel; buy cards and stationery; pay bills; exchange money or traveller's cheques
a clothes shop	buy a shirt, jumper, etc.; try on clothes; look in a mirror; go in a changing room

2   Put students in pairs to complete the table. If students have access to dictionaries, allow students to use them to check any new words. If not, be prepared to explain any new items with simple board drawings or definitions.

T 4.5   [CD 1: Track 47] Play the recording. Students listen, check their answers, and repeat. Write *tissues* on the board and elicit where the main stress is (see *Answers* below). Play the recording again and get students to mark the main stress on the rest of the words. Ask students to practise saying the words. Be prepared to drill the pronunciation of some of the more difficult words, e.g. *tissues* /'tɪʃuːz/, *foam* /fəʊm/, *doughnut* /'dəʊnʌt/, *sandwich* /'sænwɪdʒ/.

Answers and tapescript

a chemist's	tissues; deodorant; aspirin; shaving foam
a café	an espresso; a doughnut; a toasted sandwich; a sparkling mineral water
a post office	a parcel; envelopes; scales; a book of stamps
a clothes shop	a T-shirt; a tie; a belt; a leather jacket

3   **T 4.6**   [CD 1: Track 48] The aim of this first listening activity is to improve students' ability to listen for gist, using contextual and lexical clues to work out the situation. Read through the questions together, then play the recording. Pause after each conversation and ask students to discuss their answers in pairs before getting feedback.

Answers and tapescript
Conversation 1
1   a café
2   a coffee and a doughnut
3   Yes
4   an espresso coffee and some carrot cake

Conversation 2
1   a chemist's
2   something for a bad cold and a sore throat
3   Yes
4   aspirin and tissues

Conversation 3 (first part)
1 a clothes shop
2 nothing – just looking
3 No
4 Nothing

Conversation 3 (second part)
1 a clothes shop
2 a black jacket
3 Yes
4 a black jacket

Conversation 4
1 a post office
2 to send a parcel
3 Yes
4 stamps to send the parcel; a book of first class stamps

T 4.6

1 A Good morning. Can I have a coffee, please?
  B Espresso?
  A Yes, please. Oh, and a doughnut, please.
  B I'm afraid there aren't any left. We've got some delicious carrot cake, and chocolate cake.
  A OK. Carrot cake, then.
  B Here you are. Is that all?
  A Yes, thanks.

2 A Hello. I wonder if you could help me? I've got a bad cold and a sore throat. Can you give me something for it?
  B Yes, of course. Are you allergic to aspirin?
  A No, I'm not.
  B OK. You can take these three times a day.
  A Thank you. Could I have some tissues as well, please?
  B Sure. Anything else?
  A No, that's all, thanks.

3 A Good morning. Can I help you?
  B I'm just looking, thanks.
  A No problem.
  ...
  A And you sir? Can I help you?
  C Yes, please. I'm looking for a jacket like this, but in black, not brown. Do you have one?
  A I'll just have a look. What size are you?
  C Medium.
  A Ah, yes. You're in luck. This is the last one. Here you are.
  C That's great. Can I try it on?
  A Of course. The changing rooms are over there.
  C Mmm. I really like it.
  A It suits you.
  C OK. I'll take it.

4 A Hello. I'd like to send this parcel to France, please.
  B Put it on the scales, please. ... That's £4.10.
  A Will it get there by Monday?
  B Well, it will if you send it special delivery but that's £3.85 extra.
  A Oh, OK then. And a book of first class stamps, please.
  B Certainly. That'll be £10.95 altogether.

MUSIC OF ENGLISH – SOUNDING POLITE

1 **T 4.7** [CD 1: Track 49] Ask students to read the questions through to themselves. Explain that they will hear each one twice and they have to say which speaker sounds more polite. Play the recording and elicit the answer.

Answers and tapescript
The second speaker is more polite. The wider the intonation pattern, the more polite you sound.

T 4.7
Good morning! Can I have a coffee?

2 **T 4.8** [CD 1: Track 50] Students listen to the polite requests.
Play the recording again and get students to repeat chorally and individually. It can be helpful to exaggerate the intonation and use hand gestures to show whether the intonation rises or falls. Encourage students to start the intonation high so that they can achieve the voice range used when sounding polite. Also point out the small fall–rise in intonation at the end of each question.

Tapescript
Could I have some tissues as well, please?
I wonder if you could help me?
Can I try it on?

Shopping in your town

4 Give your answers to the questions in this exercise as an example. Then discuss the questions with the whole class. Encourage a range of opinions from the students, including what they *don't* like shopping for.

5 The aim of this activity is to provide some fluency-based practice for students. It is also an opportunity for you to find out whether students can use quantifiers like *some, any, a few*, etc. appropriately in a fluency task.

Put students in groups of three or four. Give them time to make a list of shops/places in their area, including a list of what they sell. Elicit a range of answers, checking the pronunciation as necessary.

Sample answers
supermarket – food and household items
baker's – bread and cakes
butcher's – meat
grocer's – food and household items
greengrocer's – fruit and vegetables
chemist's – medicines and toiletries
newsagent's – newspapers and magazines
clothes shop – clothes and accessories
bookshop – books
music shop – CDs and DVDs

post office – stamps and stationery
market – fruit and vegetables; clothes; household items
gift shop – presents and cards

Focus attention on the example sentences in the Student's Book. Elicit a few more sentences from one group, e.g. *There aren't many gift shops. There's only one clothes shop. It sells nice jeans and T-shirts.* Students continue talking about the shops in their groups. Monitor and check for accurate use of the quantifiers. Make a note of any common errors, but wait until the next lesson to feed back on them in order to keep the focus on fluency.

6   Ask students to look back at their lists from exercise 5 and tick three shops/places that they use regularly. Ask them to put a cross next to the ones they never use. Ask students to discuss their shopping habits in their groups before reporting back to the whole class.

EVERYDAY ENGLISH (SB p37)

Prices

1   Ask students to look at the prices in the boxes. Drill them round the class for pronunciation.

LANGUAGE NOTE

Note that English tends to omit *and* and *pence* or *cents* with prices;

£6.40 = six pounds forty NOT six pounds ~~and~~ forty ~~pence~~

Pence and *p* are both acceptable

50p = fifty p, or fifty pence

Euro is pronounced /ˈjuːrəʊ/

---

2   Put students in pairs or threes to discuss the questions. Monitor and prompt students to correct any errors when forming or pronouncing prices.

If you have a multinational class, you could make this activity interesting by finding out which country has the cheapest/most expensive petrol, cigarettes, etc.

3   **T 4.9** [CD 1: Track 51] Play the recording. Students listen and write what the conversations are about, and which numbers they hear. Put them in pairs to check their answers. Then have a whole class feedback on where each dialogue takes place.

Answers and tapescript
1   Buying stamps in a post office; 12, £3.64
2   Buying a jumper in a clothes shop; £34.50
3   Buying bread in a supermarket or baker's; 3, 6, £1.82
4   Buying sparkling mineral water in a shop; 2, €2.30
5   Returning borrowed money to a friend; $20, $30, $30.40
6   Talking about a house; £2 million
7   Asking about the price of a car; $10,000
8   Asking about a cheque; $160

T 4.9
1   A   A book of twelve first class stamps, please.
    B   Three pounds sixty four, please.
2   A   How much is this jumper?
    B   Thirty-four pounds fifty.
3   A   A white loaf and three rolls, please.
    B   A brown loaf and six rolls –er that'll be …
    A   Er, no, I said a *white* loaf and *three* rolls
    B   Sorry. That'll be one pound eighty-two.
4   A   Two bottles of sparkling mineral water, please.
    B   That's two euros thirty.
5   A   Here's the twenty dollars I owe you.
    B   Not twenty dollars. Thirty dollars.
    A   Thirty dollars! I'm sure it was twenty.
    B   No, thirty. Thirty dollars and 40 cents to be exact.
6   A   What a fantastic house!
    B   Darling! It cost two million pounds!
7   A   How much was your car?
    B   Ten thousand dollars.
8   A   How much was the cheque for?
    B   A hundred and sixty dollars.

4   Give students a couple of minutes to read through the dialogues and missing lines. Check difficult vocabulary: *commission* (the money a bank charges when it changes money); *cash a cheque* (give you money in exchange for a cheque); *sterling* (British money).

Put students in pairs to complete the conversations. Monitor and prompt.

5   **T 4.10** [CD 1: Track 52] Play the recording. Ask students to listen and check their answers.

Give students a few minutes to practise the conversations in their pairs. Go round and help with their pronunciation. You could ask one or two pairs to act out some conversations in front of the class.

Answers and tapescript
1   A   Hello. I'm looking for this month's edition of *Vogue*?
    B   Over there. Middle shelf. Next to *Marie Claire* and *Cosmopolitan*.
    A   Thanks. **How much is it?**
    B   £2.60.
    A   Here you are.
    B   **Right, that's £2.40 change.**
    A   Just a minute! I gave you a £10 note, not a £5 note.
    B   **I am sorry. That's £7.40, then.**
2   A   I'd like to change these dollars into sterling, please.
    B   Right. How much is here?
    A $200.
    B   **That's £150, plus £2 commission.**
    A   OK, thanks. **And can I cash a traveller's cheque for $100?**
    B   Certainly. Have you got your passport?
    A   Yes, here it is.

3 A Hello. How much is it to get in?

B £8 for an adult, £4.50 for children under 12.

A OK. Two adults and three children, please.

B Then it's cheaper if you have a family ticket. **That's £24.50, please.**

A Thank you very much.

Don't forget!

Workbook Unit 4

Exercise 13 Vocabulary – Spelling of plural nouns

Exercise 14 Reading – Kid's bedrooms are their kingdoms

Exercise 15 Pronunciation – Weak and strong stress

Exercises 16–17 Check it

Grammar Reference

Look at the exercises on SB p131–132 as a class, or set for homework. The answers are on TB p155.

Word list

Remind your students of the Word list for this unit on SB p153. They could translate the words, learn them at home, or transfer some of the words to their vocabulary notebook.

Pronunciation Book Unit 4

5

Verb patterns • Future forms
-ed/-ing adjectives
How are you feeling?

What do you want to do?

Introduction to the unit

In the opening section, various verb patterns are introduced and practised within the context of hopes, ambitions, and plans. In a second grammatical focus, *going to*, *will*, and the Present Continuous for future are contrasted. There is a reading text about teenagers who are sent to a therapy camp because they are badly behaved, and the *Listening and speaking* activity exploits the song *The Voice Within* by Christina Aguilera.

Language aims

Grammar – verb patterns Students might well have come across several of the verb patterns in this unit, but they will probably not have seen them presented under the heading 'verb patterns'. It is worth explaining what a pattern is, i.e. something that repeats itself.

POSSIBLE PROBLEMS

- Mistakes of form are common with verb patterns, and it is this area that is specifically practised in the *Grammar spot* and first practice activity.

  *I'm going work as a designer. **She hopes finding a job soon.*
  *He wants have a restaurant.

- Two possible patterns with *like* are also presented, and these cause problems of form and use. With the two forms being similar, they are easily mixed up, but learners also find the conceptual difference of 'general versus specific preference' difficult to grasp.

  Common mistakes of form

  *I like play football. **I'd like having a drink.*

  Common mistakes of use

  *I'm thirsty. I like a Coke. **Do you like to come to the cinema tonight?*

  In this unit, we suggest that for a general preference, *like* + *-ing* is used. Students might come across *like* + infinitive – this use of *like* has more of an idea of 'this is how I prefer to do things' rather than 'I enjoy'.

  I like to keep my desk tidy.

  The verb patterns presented in this unit are such high frequency items (with the exception of *hope*), that once you have presented them, they will automatically be revised and practised in many classroom activities. If mistakes occur in subsequent lessons, remind students of the rules.

---

going to, will, and Present Continuous for future *Going to* is contrasted with *will* in this unit. Both items are traditionally taught in a first-year book, so the forms will not be new. In this unit *will* is used to express a future intention decided as you speak. This is in contrast with *going to*, which expresses a pre-planned intention. Students might well perceive this conceptual difference quite easily, but will often forget to apply it. Selecting appropriate future forms causes many problems for a long time. The unit also looks at using the Present Continuous form to talk about future arrangements.

Common mistakes

'Have you booked a holiday yet?' **'Yes. We'll go to Spain.'*
*What will you do tonight? **What do you do tonight?* **What you do tonight?*
'The phone's ringing.' **'OK. I answer it.'*

Students often use the base form of the verb to express a spontaneous offer or intention, rather than *will*.

*I open the door for you.

Making offers and expressing intentions are common occurrences in the day-to-day interactions of classrooms, whether students are acting in roles or just being themselves. When you hear mistakes with this use of *will*, it is worth reminding learners of the rule. They might learn it all the better for seeing the item in a real context. For example, if a student offers to help you collect in some books and says 'I collect the books for you', take the opportunity to point out to the class how *will* should be used here.

This unit deals with the modal use of *will*. *Will* as an auxiliary verb to show future time is dealt with in Unit 9.

Vocabulary The *Vocabulary and speaking* section looks at -ed and -ing adjectives.

Everyday English This section looks at vocabulary and functional language in the context of feelings.

Notes on the unit

STARTER (SB p38)

This starter activity gets students talking about themselves and previews their ability to form and use the verb patterns focused on later in the unit.

Give students a few minutes to prepare some sentences, then either put them in small groups to chat, or nominate a few people and have a brief class discussion. Don't worry about errors made with the verb patterns at this stage, but note how well students can use them.

HOPES AND AMBITIONS (SB p38)

Verb patterns

Lead in by asking students about their hopes and ambitions. If they are young, you could ask questions such as *What job do you hope to get? Would you like to go to university/college? What would you like to study? Are you going to travel?*

If they are more mature, you could ask *What do you hope to do in the next ten years? Would you like to travel? Where would you like to go?*

1 **T 5.1** [CD 2: Track 2] Ask students to look at the pictures and work in pairs to match them with the sentences. Do one as an example. When they are ready, students listen to the recording and check whether their predictions are correct.

Answers and tapescript
1 c 2 f 3 b 4 d 5 e 6 a

T 5.1

Ella
Well, I'd like to be a vet. I've got three pets – two rabbits and a kitten called Princess. I love looking after them, so I think I'll be a good vet. I asked my mum if I could have a puppy, but she said no. When I'm a vet, I want to have two dogs and a horse as well.

Joe
I can already play the piano, but now I'm learning to play the electric guitar. I love it! I'd love to be in a rock band. I want to play lead guitar. And write all the songs. I'm thinking of asking my friends if they want to start a band.

Juliet
It's an important year for me at school this year. I'm doing nine subjects. I'm going to study hard and get really good grades in all my exams, so I can go to university. But I'm still going to have fun. I'm seeing my boyfriend tonight!

Hannah
I'd like to go back to work next year. I worked in a bank before I had children, but I don't want to do that any more. I hope to go back to college and train to be a primary school teacher. I've worked part-time at Ella and Joe's school for a few years now, and I really enjoy it.

David
I've been in the same job for twenty years. I'm an accountant for a big company, and I visit all the company offices regularly. I'm thinking of changing my job, because I'm tired of travelling all the time. Actually, I'd like to start my own business.

Edie
Last year I joined a travel club for people my age. It's marvellous! I really enjoy meeting new people and seeing new places. I'm looking forward to going on a world cruise with my friend, Margaret. I met her on the last cruise. We're going to the Caribbean. I can't wait!

2   Ask students to listen again and complete the chart. You may need to pause after each section to give them time to write.

Answers

	Ambitions/Plans	Reasons
Ella	to be a vet	has got pets – 2 rabbits and a kitten and loves looking after them.
Joe	to be lead guitarist in a rock band and write all the songs	can already play the piano and is learning electric guitar
Juliet	to go to university	studying hard/wants good grades
Hannah	to go back to college and train to be a primary school teacher	has worked part-time in a school and enjoyed it
David	to change his job/start his own business	tired of travelling
Edie	going on a cruise	enjoys meeting new people and seeing new places

3 The aim of this activity is to allow students to discover verb patterns and their rules for themselves. Focus students on the example then let them underline the other examples in exercise 1. Ask them which verbs are followed by *to* + infinitive, which are followed by *-ing*, and which are followed by preposition + *-ing*. You may then wish to put students in pairs to find more examples of these patterns in the tapescript on p119.

Answers
1 I'd like to be a vet.
2 I'm going to study hard ...
3 I'm thinking of changing my job ...
4 I'm looking forward to going ...
5 I would love to be in a rock band. I want to play lead guitar.
6 I hope to go back to college and train to be ...

See underlined examples in tapescript 5.1 above.

GRAMMAR SPOT (SB p39)

1 Ask students to work in pairs to complete the sentences using the words *go abroad*. Write the sentences on the board in the feedback and point out the different verb forms.

Answers
I'd like to go abroad
I'm looking forward to going abroad
I hope to go abroad
I enjoy going abroad
I'm thinking of going abroad
I love going abroad
I'd love to go abroad

Point out that the verb *go* is in the infinitive after some verbs and *-ing* after others, and that we use *-ing* after prepositions like *of*. The *to* in *looking forward to* is a preposition. You could try drilling these sentences around the class.

2 Answer this question as a class. Try to get from students the idea that *like going* is a general, all-time preference. It applies to the past, present, and future. *Would like to go* refers to now or the (near) future. If you feel it would help your class to do so, translate these two sentences.

Refer students to Grammar Reference 5.1 on p132 and the verb patterns on p158.

PRACTICE (SB p39)

Discussing grammar

1 Ask students to work in pairs to do this exercise, or let them do it individually, then check with a partner. In the feedback, refer back to the rules if necessary, then get students to work in pairs to make correct sentences with the other verbs.

Answers
2 b, c 3 b, c 4 a, b 5 b, c 6 a, c

1 enjoy living
2 are hoping to go
3 want to go
4 I'm looking forward to seeing
5 want to learn
6 'd love to have

Making questions

2 Ask students to work in pairs to do this exercise.

T 5.2 [CD 2: Track 3] Play the recording so that students can check their answers. Ask students to think of possible answers that A could give, then put them in pairs to practise the conversations. Encourage students to use the correct stress and intonation.

Answers and tapescript
1 A I hope to go to university.
  B What do you want to study?
2 A One of my favourite hobbies is cooking.
  B What do you like making?
3 A I get terrible headaches.
  B When did you start getting them?
4 A We're planning our summer holidays at the moment.
  B Where are you thinking of going?
5 A I'm bored.
  B What would you like to do tonight?

Talking about you

3 This exercise provides some personalized free practice for students. Encourage lots of interaction but make sure students are using the verb patterns accurately. As students ask and answer in pairs, monitor and note any errors regarding the use of verb patterns.

ADDITIONAL MATERIAL

Workbook Unit 5
These exercises could be done in class to give further practice, for homework, or in a later class as revision.

Exercises 1–4 Verb patterns

Exercises 5–7 *would like (to do) or like (doing)?*
Before moving on to the next presentation of *will* and *going to*, you and your class might prefer to do some skills work. You could do the reading activity Brat Camp on p42 of the Student's Book, or the song on p41.

FUTURE INTENTIONS (SB p40)

going to, will, and Present Continuous for future

1 Ask a few questions about the pictures to set the situation, and get students talking. Ask *Where are they? What are they doing?*

Ask students to work in pairs to match a sentence with each picture.

Answers
1 d 2 f 3 a 4 b 5 e 6 c

2 Ask students to work in pairs to match the lines before and after the sentences in exercise 1 to make 3-line dialogues. Do the first as an example to get students started.

3 **T 5.3** [CD 2: Track 4] Students listen to the recording and check their answers, then practise the conversations in pairs. Make sure they try to imitate the pronunciation, stress, and intonation of the sentences on the recording.

Answers and tapescript
1 **A** Why are Peter and Jane saving all their money?
  B They're going to buy a house.
  A Really? Does that mean they're going to get married?
2 **A** Oh, no! I'm late. I'm going to miss my train.
  B I'll give you a lift to the station if you like.
  A That's great. Can we go now? It leaves at five past.
3 **A** What's Annie doing this summer?
  B She's going to travel round North America.
  A Lucky her!
4 **A** The phone's ringing.
  B It's OK. I'll answer it.
  A Well if it's Susan, say I'm not in.
5 **A** I haven't got enough money.
  B Don't worry. I'll lend you some.
  A Thanks. I'll pay you back tomorrow. I won't forget. I promise.
6 **A** What are you doing tonight?
  B I'm going to stay in and watch the football on TV.
  A Oh, of course. Arsenal are playing Chelsea, aren't they?

GRAMMAR SPOT (SB p40)

Read through the rules and answer the questions as a class.

Answers
1 The two forms used are *going to* and *will*. *Going to* means that you've already decided to do something, some time before you speak about it. *Will* means that you're deciding as you speak.
2 Point out the pronunciation of *I'll* /aɪl/ and *won't* /wəʊnt/.

---

3 Note that *What are you doing tonight?* means *what are your arrangements, what's in your diary?*

What are you going to do tonight? means *what is your intention, what have you decided?* The difference is subtle, and the two uses are often interchangeable. The uses become clearer with more black and white examples of arrangements (e.g. *I'm getting married at 2.30 on the 12th*), and intentions, (*I'm going to ask her to marry me*). At this level, there is no need to get involved in the subtleties of contrasting the two uses.

It is a good idea to remind students that the verbs *go* and *come* are not generally used with *going to* but with the Present Continuous.
Examples
I'm going to go shopping. ✗
I'm going shopping. ✓
I'm going to come to France. ✗
I'm coming to France. ✓

Refer students to Grammar Reference 5.2 on p132.

PRACTICE (SB p41)

Discussing grammar

1 Ask students to work in pairs to decide which is the correct verb form.

T 5.4 [CD 2: Track 5] Students listen to the recording and check their answers.

Answers and tapescript
1 That bag looks heavy. **I'll carry** it for you.
2 I bought some warm boots because **I'm going** skiing.
3 **A** Tony's back from holiday.
  B Is he? **I'll give** him a ring.
4 **A** What **are you doing** tonight?
  B **We're going to see** a play at the theatre.
5 You can tell me your secret. **I won't tell** anyone.
6 Congratulations! I hear **you're getting married**.
7 **A** I need to post these letters.
  B **I'm going shopping** soon. **I'll post** them for you.
8 **A** What **are we having** for lunch?
  B **I'm going to make** a lasagne.

2 **T 5.5** [CD 2: Track 6] This is a type of prompt drill which aims to help students grasp the idea of the contrasting uses of *going to* and *will* by getting them to make quick decisions as to which one to use. Play each conversation opening from the dialogues in exercise 1 and pause the recording for students to respond. Make sure all students are contributing and selecting the correct tense.

Check it

3 Ask students to work in pairs to correct the sentences.

Answers

1 'What **would** you like to drink?' '**I'll have** a coffee, please.'
2 Where are the changing rooms? **I'd like to** try on these jeans.
3 I can't go out because a friend of mine **is coming** to see me.
4 I'm looking forward to **seeing** you again soon.
5 **I'm thinking of changing** my job soon.
6 Phone me tonight. **I'll give** you my phone number.
7 **I'm seeing** the doctor tomorrow about my back.

What are you doing tonight?

4 Put students in pairs. Ask them to decide who is A, and who is B. As look at the diary on p145 of the Student's Book. Bs look at the diary on p148. Tell students to ask and answer questions until they find a day when they are both free. Model the activity with a student.

Give students a few minutes to find a time when they are both free. If students finish early, ask them to arrange other meetings. Monitor closely, and note any errors of future form usage. At the end, write errors on the board, without saying who made them, and ask the class to correct.

You could extend this activity by getting students to write their own real diary for the weekend, then putting students in pairs, and telling them to ask questions to find a good time when they could meet to do homework together.

WRITING (SB p107)

Filling in a form

The aim of this writing section is to show students how to fill in a form.

1 Ask students to give you examples of when they fill in forms. Build up a list on the board.

Sample answers

enrolling at a school or university/on a course
applying for a passport/credit card/etc.
a job application
joining a club
getting married/divorced/registering a birth

2 Ask students in pairs to match expressions and questions.

Answers

1 d 2 h 3 g 4 f 5 i 6 a 7 e 8 j 9 b 10 c

3 Model the activity for students by asking the questions, then writing your own details on the board.

Ask students to follow the instructions and write the answers. Monitor and prompt.

4 Ask students to complete the form for themselves.

5 Ask students to compare their forms in pairs or small groups.

EXTRA IDEA

Ask pairs to ask and answer questions, and fill in forms for each other.

ADDITIONAL MATERIAL

Workbook Unit 5

Exercises 8–11 *will, going to,* or Present Continuous?

LISTENING AND SPEAKING (SB p41)

Song   The voice within

ABOUT THE LISTENING

This listening exercise is a song. Songs are fun and motivating, but can also be difficult for students at this level to follow. The secret is to create lots of interest at the lead-in, deal with as much vocabulary as you can before listening, and guide students to an understanding by means of activities like the 'choosing the correct word' activity in exercise 4.

The voice within is a ballad about turning to oneself rather than depending on other people to tell you what to do. It appears on the album *Stripped* along with the other hit singles *Dirty* and *Beautiful*. Christina Aguilera, who is of Ecuadorian and Irish extraction, was born in New York in 1980. Her music has Latin and hip hop influences, and her lyrics are often about how young people should be strong and positive in difficult situations.

There is some difficult vocabulary in the song, so be prepared to pre-teach/check the following items, especially with weaker classes: *tears* (the liquid that falls when people cry), *tend to, bothers* (= makes the effort), *heartache, trust* (= believe in), *don't forsake* (= don't give up). Point out that *heartache* and *forsake* are poetic words that are not often used in general conversation. Also note the use of *will* in the song, which is used functionally to make promises and to reassure.

1 Give students time to read through the questions. Elicit a few examples of typical problems (relationships with family, relationships with friends and boyfriends or girlfriends, problems with studies, issues of identity and self-esteem, etc.) Give students time to write down their three examples. Then put students in pairs to discuss their ideas. Elicit a range of ideas from the class in a short feedback session.

2 Focus attention on the photo and ask students what they know about Christina Aguilera. Elicit a few ideas from the class. Give students time to read the questions in exercise 2. Then ask them to close their books.

T 5.6 [CD 2: Track 7] Play the recording. Give students time to compare their ideas before checking the answers with the class.

Answers
Problem: The young girl in the song is feeling sad and confused.
Who is talking: A friend to a friend.

3 Give students time to read the first verse and chorus. Deal with any vocabulary queries (see the note about pre-teaching in *About the listening* above). Put students in pairs or small groups to discuss the questions. Then check the answers with the class.

Answers
1 The person giving advice is older (the speaker says 'Young girl' and speaks from experience).
2 Her friend promises to be there when she has problems. ('I'll be right here when your world starts to fall.')
3 To trust yourself and you will find the strength to make the right decision.
4 'The voice within' is the voice inside yourself – your own judgement and ability to make choices.

4 Ask students to look at the song on p150. Give them time to read the next eight lines. Elicit the correct word for the first gap (*dream*). Students complete the song, choosing from the pairs of words in italics. Remind them to use the rhyme in the song to help them.

T 5.6 Play the recording, pausing to give students time to compare their answers with the recorded version. If students have enjoyed the song, you can play it again and get them to sing along or just listen.

Answers
dream; bothers; heartache; hide; run; tight; day; journey; choose; need; forsaking; can't; stop

Talking about you

Give students a few moments to think about their answers to the questions. Put students into small groups to discuss their ideas. Conduct a short class feedback session, but allow students to volunteer their answers in case they feel self-conscious talking about problems in front of the whole class.

Brat camp

ABOUT THE TEXT
The text is about a 'brat camp' (also known as 'wilderness camps') where parents send their difficult teenagers to improve their behaviour. In the camp, teenagers (hopefully) learn responsibility by following a tough, outdoor physical regime.

The tasks on the text get students to predict content, to read for specific information, and to interpret information in the text. There are lots of opportunities for students to discuss ideas and offer their own opinions.

Most of the difficult words are dealt with in exercise 2. You may also wish to check the following words and phrases.

brat = an annoying, badly-behaved child
difficult/troubled (teenagers) = teenagers with problems
end up in (prison) = finish (in prison) as a result of what you do
It's my fault = I am to blame
body piercings = holes in your body (nose, ears, etc.) that you put jewellery in

1 Ask the questions open class, and encourage a discussion.

2 Read through the words in the box, and drill any that are difficult to pronounce, (*truant* /truːənt/; *arguing* /ɑːgjuːɪŋ/; *swearing* /sweərɪŋ/). Then check the meaning by giving explanations and using check questions, for example *What do you call it when somebody does not attend school when they should?* (playing truant), *What do you call it when an older child frightens or hurts a younger, weaker child?* (bullying).

Put students into small groups to complete the chart. In feedback, discuss as a class any areas of disagreement.

Suggested answers	
very bad	**not very bad**
playing truant	telling lies
drinking alcohol	arguing with adults
stealing	swearing
taking drugs	
fighting and bullying	
cheating at exams	

3 Ask students to read the introduction and first part of the article, and say which activities the teenagers were guilty of.

4 Put students in pairs to discuss and answer the questions. They will need to reread parts of the text to find and check answers.

Answers

1 Because it tries to deal with and solve the behavioural problems of teenagers by being tough with them.
2 They are desperate because they don't know how to deal with their children. They hope their children will learn how to behave better in the camp.
3 She thinks he's going to end up in prison. She blames herself.
4 selfish: Emily
  negative: Ned
  sees hope: Jamie

5 Ask students to look at the pictures, and predict life in the camp. The pictures show the wilderness setting of the camp and the outdoor nature of much of the activity.

6 Ask students to read the rest of the article to check their predictions. Let students check their answers in pairs before discussing as a class.

7 Put students in pairs or small groups to discuss the questions. Have a brief class feedback.

Answers

1 They have to follow rules, do physical activity, go on hikes, sleep in tents, look after themselves, and be responsible. They have to discuss problems with a psychologist. They can't have body piercings, cigarettes, music, mobile phones, or fashionable clothes.
2 They learn to look after themselves and each other, and be responsible.
3 When the camp psychologist decides they are ready – after ten weeks on average.
4 Ned felt ill and depressed. Emily was shocked, cried and hated it. Jamie had problems following orders.
5 Ned felt better after getting off drugs, and now wants to live at home again. Emily learnt how her behaviour affects other people. She is sorry she was horrible to her mother. She wants to go back to school. Jamie enjoyed the outdoor life, and learnt self-control.
6 Ned wants to live at home again. Emily wants to go back to school and become a nurse. Jamie wants to join the army.

What do you think?

Finish the lesson by encouraging students to express their own opinions. You could do this with the whole class or in small groups. Small groups maximize students' talking time, allow you to monitor and note errors, and let shy students speak without having too many people listening to them! A good way to get feedback from groups is to have one student from each group summarize what they talked about.

VOCABULARY AND SPEAKING (SB p44)

-ed/-ing adjectives

1 Ask students which adjective best describes the picture.

Answer
frightening

Ask students in pairs to complete the sentences, using words from the box.

T 5.7 [CD 2: Track 8] Play the recording so that students can check their answers. You could get them to repeat the responses using the appropriate stress and intonation.

Answers and tapescript
1 I heard footsteps in the middle of the night.
  'That's really **frightening**.'
2 The bus was full. I had to wait for the next one, so I was late for work.
  'That's so **annoying**!'
3 I saw Andy eating a burger! I thought he was vegetarian.
  'That's very **surprising**.'
4 I was lying on the beach in the sun all day yesterday.
  'How **relaxing**!'
5 On my holiday it rained every day.
  'That's just so **depressing** (**annoying**)!'
6 I ran my first full marathon on Sunday.
  'How **exhausting**!'

2 Model the example for the class, and point out that *frightening* has changed to *frightened*. Then put students in pairs to practise the other conversations.

T 5.8 [CD 2: Track 9] Play the recording. Ask students to listen and compare their answers. You could ask students to repeat the conversations if they didn't do them very well the first time.

Answers and tapescript
1 I heard footsteps in the middle of the night. I was really frightened.
2 The bus was full. I had to wait for the next one, so I was late for work. I was so annoyed!
3 I saw Andy eating a burger! I thought he was vegetarian. I was very surprised.
4 I was lying on the beach in the sun all day yesterday. I felt so relaxed!
5 On my holiday it rained every day. I was so depressed.
6 I ran my first full marathon on Sunday. I was exhausted!

Read through the rules as a class. You could check that the students understand by doing the following activity.

Write the names of two or three recent, well-known films on the board. Tell students that they are in the cinema, watching the film. Ask *How do you feel?* Elicit sentences with *-ed* adjectives from students round the class, for example *bored, excited, interested, frightened, depressed.* Then say *Now describe the film.* Elicit sentences with *-ing* adjectives from students, for example *It's exciting, It's confusing.*

3 Students complete the sentences with words from the box, and check with their partner.

T 5.9 [CD 2: Track 10] Students listen to the recording and check their answers.

Answers and tapescript
1 **A** I watched a horror film on my own last night.
   B Were you **frightened**?
2 **A** I spent four hours going round a museum.
   B Oh, no! Was it **boring**?
   A Actually, it was really **fascinating**. I loved it.
3 **A** Did you see the way she behaved!
   B Yes, it was **shocking**. Don't invite her next time.
4 I had a second interview but I didn't get the job. I'm so **disappointed**.
5 The teacher was **annoyed** because all the students were late.
6 My daughter is very **excited** because it's her birthday tomorrow.
7 I don't know how this camera works! The instructions are really **confusing**.

4 Put students in small groups to discuss things they have seen or read recently. You could help them prepare for this activity by eliciting or writing a list of possible topics on the board first. For example, a television programme, a book, a DVD, a film at the cinema, a CD, a place you went to, a test you had, a meal you ate. Let them refer to the list as they talk together.

In feedback, ask a few individuals to tell the class about their experiences. Correct any errors with *-ed* and *-ing* adjectives.

ADDITIONAL MATERIAL

Workbook Unit 5
Exercise 12 Vocabulary – *ed/ing* adjectives

How are you feeling?

1 Set the scene by asking students to look at the pictures and say how they think the people are feeling. At this stage, you could try to elicit some expressions by asking students what they think the people are saying.

Put students in pairs to match words from the box with the pictures.

Possible answers
Picture **a**: nervous, worried	Picture **d**: ill
Picture **b**: angry	Picture **e**: excited
Picture **c**: worried	Picture **f**: fed up

Many students misunderstand the word *nervous* in English. It means 'worried that a future event (e.g. an exam, interview, performance) won't go well.' It doesn't mean the same as *stressed* or *uptight* and can't be used to describe someone's general character.

2 Ask students to work in pairs to match the phrases.

Answers
1 I feel a bit nervous.	I've got an exam today.
2 I don't feel very well.	I think I'm getting a cold.
3 I'm feeling a lot better, thanks.	Not quite back to normal, but nearly.
4 I'm so angry!	I got a parking ticket this morning. Sixty pounds!
5 I'm really excited!	I'm going on holiday to Australia tomorrow.
6 I'm fed up with this weather.	It's so wet and miserable.
7 I'm a bit worried.	My grandfather's going into hospital for tests.
8 We're really happy!	We're in love!
9 I sometimes feel a bit lonely, actually.	I don't think I have many friends.

3 Now ask them to choose a reply from a–h.

T 5.10 [CD 2: Track 11] Students listen to the conversations and check their answers. You may choose to pause the recording after each phrase so that students can repeat for pronunciation, or ask them to work in pairs to practise after each conversation. Alternatively, drill some of the phrases with particularly interesting or unusual intonation patterns. For example:

That's fantastic!

Cheer up!

Answers and tapescript

1 **A** I feel a bit nervous. I've got an exam today.
  B Good luck! Just do your best. That's all you can do.
2 **A** I don't feel very well. I think I'm getting a cold.
  B Oh dear! Why don't you go home to bed?
3 **A** I'm feeling a lot better, thanks. Not quite back to normal, but nearly.
  B That's good. I'm so pleased to hear that.
4 **A** I'm so angry! I got a parking ticket this morning. Sixty pounds!
  B Oh, no! Didn't you get one last week as well?
5 **A** I'm really excited! I'm going on holiday to Australia tomorrow!
  B Lucky you! Have a good time!
6 **A** I'm fed up with this weather. It's so wet and miserable.
  B I know. We really need some sunshine, don't we?
7 **A** I'm a bit worried. My grandfather's going into hospital for tests.
  B I'm sorry to hear that! I'm sure he'll be all right.
8 **A** We're really happy! We're in love!
  B That's fantastic! I'm so pleased for you both!
9 **A** I sometimes feel a bit lonely, actually. I don't think I have many friends.
  B Cheer up! You've got me. I'm always here for you.

MUSIC OF ENGLISH – INTONATION

1 **T 5.11** [CD 2: Track 12] Play the recording. Ask students to listen and repeat, practising the intonation patterns.

Tapescript

Cheer up!	Lucky you!
Oh, dear!	That's fantastic!
Oh, no!	Good luck!
I know.	I'm so pleased to hear that!
That's good.	

2 Refer students to p120 and tapescript 5.10. Put students in pairs and let them choose two or three conversations. If a lot of students choose the same ones, you may have to adapt their choice to ensure they cover all the conversations. If you have time in class, let students rehearse the lines until they have learnt them by heart. Monitor to help with pronunciation. Ask some students to act out their conversations to the class.

4 Pairs make more conversations using some or all of the situations. Monitor and help with preparation. Let some pairs act out their conversations to the class. Ask other students to comment on the pronunciation.

Don't forget!

Workbook Unit 5

Exercise 13 Pronunciation – Confusing vowel sounds

Exercises 14–15 Check it

Grammar Reference
Look at the exercises on SB p132–133 as a class, or set for homework. The answers are on TB p155.

Word list
Remind your students of the Word list for this unit on SB p154. They could translate the words, learn them at home, or transfer some of the words to their vocabulary notebook.

Pronunciation Book Unit 5

What ... like? • Comparatives/superlatives
Synonyms/antonyms
A city break

Introduction to the unit

The theme of this unit is describing places and things. This provides a useful context to practise the grammar for this unit, *What ... like?* and comparatives and superlatives. The text in the *Reading and speaking* section describes the multicultural diversity of London. In the *Listening and speaking* section, five people talk about the best things in life that are free.

Language aims

Grammar – *What ... like?* This question, which asks for a description, causes difficulties for students.

> **POSSIBLE PROBLEMS**
> - *Like* is used as a preposition in *What ... like?*, but students only have experience of it as a verb, as in *I like dancing*.
> - The answer to the question *What ... like?* does not contain *like* with the adjective.
>   *What's John like?*   **He's like nice.*
> - Students may find *What ... like?* a strange construction to ask for a description. In many languages the question word *how* is used to do this. In English, however, *How is John?* is an inquiry about his health, not about his character and/or looks, and the answer is *He's very well.*
>   *What ... like?* is introduced first in the unit to provide a staged approach to the practice of comparatives and superlatives in the second presentation. It is a useful question in the practising of these.

Comparatives and superlatives It is assumed that students will have a certain familiarity with these, although of course mistakes will still be made. The exercises bring together all aspects of comparatives and superlatives:

- the use of *-er/-est* with short adjectives, *-ier/-iest* with adjectives that end in *-y*, and *more/most* with longer adjectives.
- irregular adjectives such as *good/better/best* and *bad/worse/worst*.
- *as ... as* to describe similarity and *not as ... as* to describe difference.

Common mistakes

*She's more big than me.   **He's the most rich man in the world.*
*She's tallest in the class.   **It's more expensive that I thought.*
*He is as rich than the Queen.

Students experience little difficulty with the concept of these structures but experience more difficulty in producing and pronouncing the forms. One of the most common problems is that they give equal stress to every word and syllable, so that utterances sound very unnatural.

There are a lot of controlled activities which aim to practise the form, and a pronunciation drill to practise natural connected speech.

Vocabulary Adjectives are practised in the *Vocabulary and pronunciation* section, where students are asked to explore the use of synonyms and antonyms.

Everyday English This section looks at and practises the functional language involved in booking a room in a hotel.

Notes on the unit

STARTER (SB p46)

The aim of this activity is to introduce and personalize the theme of the listening task to follow. Give students two or three minutes to write answers. Then model the pairwork activity by asking the *What's your favourite…?* question to two or three students in the class. Put students in pairs to ask and answer. Encourage them to use adjectives to expand on their responses, for example:

What's your favourite town?
Venice. It's very beautiful.

MY FAVOURITE THINGS (SB p46)

What's it like?

> *What … like?* and descriptive adjectives are contextualized in this short interview with a singer.
>
> Leroy is an imaginary singer, but he is typical of black British R&B performers. *R&B* stands for rhythm and blues. However, modern R&B is much influenced by soul music and hip hop. *The Brit Awards* are music prizes awarded annually – the equivalent of Grammies in America. *Al Pacino* is a leading Hollywood actor, often cast in crime thrillers. *Arsenal* is a leading English football club based in north London. *Brave New World* is a novel by Aldous Huxley. Written in the 1930s, it predicts a world in which people are created by genetic engineering, and lead controlled lives. *Chicken satay* is an Indonesian dish, consisting of chicken in a peanut sauce.

1 Ask students to look at the photos and discuss the question in pairs.

> **Answers**
> a Arsenal   d *Brave New World*
> b Al Pacino   e chicken satay
> c soul music

2 Ask students to match the adjectives to the pictures, then check with a partner. Do the first as an example.

T 6.1 [CD 2: Track 13] Play the recording. Students listen and compare their answers.

> **Answers and tapescript**
> a (Arsenal) fantastic, exciting
> b (Al Pacino) brilliant, talented
> c (soul music) beautiful, sad
> d (*Brave New World*) amazing, funny, sad, shocking
> e (chicken satay) spicy, delicious

My favourite things
I = Interviewer   L = Leroy

I Welcome to another edition of *Favourite Things*. Today in the studio we have cool R'n'B singer, Leroy! Welcome, Leroy. Thank you for coming to talk to us about your favourite things.

L Hi there.

I So Leroy let's look at your list of favourites. Now, your first choice is the film star, Al Pacino. Can you tell us about him? Why do you like him so much?

L Well, every time I see Al Pacino in a movie I think he's brilliant, he's just a brilliant actor. He's so talented. You know he's been nominated six times for Oscars, –er but in fact, he's only won once and that was years ago, in 1993. I can't believe it!

I OK. And your next favourite thing is Arsenal, Arsenal Football Club. So you're a big football fan, then?

L Yeah, I am. I'm a London boy, you see, and I support my local team, which is Arsenal. They are fantastic players. And always exciting to watch! I still go to a match whenever I can.

I And now your number three – ah – soul music
…

L Oh yeah, I'm crazy about soul music – you know, it's the reason I wanted a career in the music business. It's beautiful music but can sometimes be very sad. It's where modern R'n'B music comes from.

I Is that right? I didn't know that. Now your number four is a food, chicken satay. I don't know that. What's it like?

L It's spicy and delicious! I just love sitting in front of the TV with a plate full of chicken satay. Mmmm!

I I must try it! And finally in your list you have *Brave New World*. I saw the film. But what's the book like?

L It's an amazing book about the future. It's funny, sad, and shocking. It's written by Aldous Huxley and it's my favourite book of all time.

GRAMMAR SPOT (SB p46)

> Before you ask students to match the questions and answers, give them the opportunity to tell you if they heard the question *What … like?* Ask *Did anyone hear the questions the interviewer asked Leroy?*
>
> Now do the matching activity as a class. The aim is to make clear the difference between the verb *to like* and the preposition *like*.
>
> > **Answers**
> > 1 Do you like soul music?   Yes, I do./No, I don't.
> >   What's soul music like?   It's sad./It's beautiful.
> > 2 The second question, *What's soul music like?*

You could ask students to read the tapescript on p120 to see the questions in context. You could ask them to underline the questions in the tapescript.

Refer students to Grammar Reference 6.1 on p134.

What's London like?

1 Ask students to do this on their own and compare their answers with a partner when they finish. They should be able to do it quite quickly.

2 **T 6.2** [CD 2: Track 14] Students listen and check their answers. Drill the questions around the class, or play and pause the recording for students to repeat. Students then practise the dialogue with a partner.

Answers and tapescript

1 **Q** What's **London** like?
   A Well, it's a really exciting city! There's so much going on all the time.

2 **Q** What's **the weather** like?
   A It's OK, and not very cold in winter, but people don't come here for the sunshine!

3 **Q** What **are the people** like?
   A They're very interesting. They come from all over the world. London's a very cosmopolitan city.

4 **Q** What **are the buildings** like?
   A Fantastic! Lots of them are historical and famous, but there are some wonderful modern ones, too.

5 **Q** What **are the restaurants** like?
   A They're great! You can find food from every country in the world.

6 **Q** What's **the night-life** like?
   A Oh, it's amazing! There are so many clubs and theatres, and, of course, the music scene is fantastic!

3 This activity allows students to practise the new structure, *What's … like?*, in a fairly controlled yet personalized way. Ask students to work in pairs, model what you want them to say, then monitor and correct errors thoroughly.

ADDITIONAL MATERIAL

Workbook Unit 6
These exercises could be done in class to give further practice, for homework, or in a later class as revision.
Exercise 2 *What is / are … like?*

GOOD, BETTER, BEST! (SB p47)

Comparatives and superlatives

It is assumed that your students will already have some familiarity with comparatives and superlatives, and so different aspects of them are brought together in this text, including the uses of *as … as* and *much* as an intensifier.

1 **T 6.3** [CD 2: Track 15] Ask students to look at the photos of the cities. Ask *Where do you think they are? What do you know about the cities? What are they like?*

Play the recording, pausing when necessary. Students work in pairs to complete the interview. Play the recording again to check their answers.

In the feedback, point out that *as* is pronounced /əz/, and that *much* is strongly stressed, and used to show a big difference when comparing.

Answers and tapescript

I Do you travel a lot, Leroy?
L Oh yeah. I sing all over the world. Last year I was in Berlin, Tokyo – oh, and of course, Detroit.
I And what are they **like**?
L Well, they're all big, busy cities. Tokyo's the biggest and the **busiest**. It's **much** bigger **than** Berlin.
I And is it **more** interesting?
L Well, they're all interesting, but, in fact, for me the **most** interesting is Detroit.
I Really? Why?
L Well, in some ways perhaps it isn't as interesting **as** the other two cities – it doesn't have historical buildings, or beautiful, old Japanese temples – but you see, Detroit is the birthplace of soul music and that's everything to me.
I I see. So Detroit's best for music. And what about food? Which is the **best** city for food?
L Ah, the food. For me there's no question, Tokyo definitely has the **most** delicious food – I just love Japanese food!
I I see. Is it even better **than** chicken satay?
L Ah, I don't know about that!

GRAMMAR SPOT (SB p48)

1 As a class, ask students to tell you the comparative and superlative of each adjective. Make sure students pronounce the comparatives accurately, particularly the weak stress /ə/ on *-er*. You may wish to do this as a repetition drill. Ask your students to work in pairs to say what the rules are.

Answers

	Adjective	Comparative	Superlative
a	old	older	(the) oldest
	new	newer	(the) newest
	(Rule: add *-er/-est* to one-syllable adjectives)		
b	big	bigger	(the) biggest
	sad	sadder	(the) saddest
	(Rule: when adjectives end consonant + one vowel + one consonant, double the consonant and add *-er/-est*)		
c	busy	busier	(the) busiest
	funny	funnier	(the) funniest
	(Rule: change *y* to *i* and add *-er/-est*)		
d	interesting	more interesting	(the) most interesting
	delicious	more delicious	(the) most delicious
	(Rule: adjectives of 3+ syllables are preceded by *more* and *most*, and do not have *-er/-est* added)		

> **Note:** Two syllable adjectives can be confusing as they sometimes take *-er*, (*cleverer, yellower*), and sometimes don't, (*more normal, more recent*). It is a question of usage.

2 Check that students know the comparative and superlative forms of these irregular adjectives. Point out the pronunciation of worse /wɜːs/ and worst /wɜːst/.

> **Answers**
>
> | good | better | (the) best |
> |------|--------|------------|
> | bad | worse | (the) worst |

3 *As … as* is used to say that two compared things are equal. Point out the weak /ə/ stress in *as … as*.

> **Answers**
> Berlin is the smallest.

Refer students to Grammar Reference 6.2 on p134.

2 Ask students to compare some cities in their country. Monitor and help with correct use of superlatives.

Pronunciation

3 **T 6.4** [CD 2: Track 16] This is a short pronunciation exercise. The aim is to practise the links between words in connected speech, and weak forms. This is something students often find difficult, but with repeated practise, you can make them see that using weak forms and connected speech actually makes it *easier* to speak English fluently, and comparatives and superlatives are a good example of this.

Play the first sentence on the recording (or model it yourself) and highlight the weak forms, *bigger* /bɪɡə/ and *than* /ðən/.

Do the same with the second sentence, pointing out the weak stresses on *as … as* and the word links which join /t/ in *isn't* to /ə/ in *as*, and /g/ in *big* to /ə/ in the second *as*.

> **Tapescript**
> Tokyo's bigger than Berlin.
> Berlin isn't as big as Tokyo.

4 Ask students to work in pairs on the next set of sentences.
T 6.5 [CD 2: Track 17] Play the sentences on the recording one by one (or model them yourself) and get the whole class to chorus them, then ask individual students to repeat them or practise them with a partner.

> **Tapescript**
> Is Peter as old as you?
> He's older than us, but younger than you.
> Their teacher's funnier than ours.
> Our lessons are more interesting than theirs.

5 **T 6.6** [CD 2: Track 18] Play the recording. Students listen and read.

Poems and rhymes are good ways of remembering irregulars and exceptions. Ask students to learn this by heart and then chant it as a class.

> **Tapescript**
> Good, better, best.
> Never, never rest
> 'til your good is better,
> and your better best.

PRACTICE (SB p48)

Test your general knowledge

These exercises provide accuracy and fluency practice of comparatives and superlatives.

1 Ask students to tell you what they can see in the photos. Check that they have heard of the buildings, places, animals, and cars mentioned.

Divide students into teams of four or five. Tell them they must compare the things in teams, and put them in order. Point out the example sentences, and model what students might say, for example *I'm not sure, but I think the Empire State building is taller than the Eiffel Tower …*

Monitor, and make sure students are using comparatives and superlatives as they compare the things.

2 **T 6.7** [CD 2: Track 19] A good way of doing the feedback is to ask each team what they thought for answer 1, then play the recording to check, pause it, and award points to teams that got the answer right before moving on to number 2.

> **Answers and tapescript**
> 1 The Empire State Building is taller than the Eiffel Tower, but the Petronas Towers are the tallest.
> 2 Monaco is smaller than Andorra, but the Vatican City is the smallest.
> 3 The Atlantic Ocean is bigger than the Arctic Ocean, but the Pacific Ocean is the biggest.
> 4 A human is faster than an elephant, but a horse is the fastest.
> 5 A Porsche is more expensive than a Rolls Royce, but a Ferrari is the most expensive.
> 6 A shark is more dangerous than a lion, but a hippopotamus is the most dangerous.

3 Ask teams to prepare one more similar general knowledge question to ask other teams. You could get them to write the question on a piece of paper then pass it to the next team. Once teams have discussed all the questions set by other teams, they must return the paper to the original team, who then reveal the correct answer.

Talking about you

4 Read through the categories as a class. You could elicit adjectives students might use to compare the things. For example,
holidays: *relaxing, interesting, exciting, expensive*
films: *funny, exciting, frightening*
music: *musical, noisy, exciting, modern, cool.*

Put students in pairs to discuss and compare the categories. In feedback, find out which types of holiday, film, and music are most popular.

Conversations

5 Read through the example as a class. Elicit alternative ways of continuing the conversation, for example … *it isn't as beautiful,* or *it's more expensive.*

Ask students to work in pairs to continue the conversations. Tell them to work through the conversations, and improvise things they could say first, then write down any good ideas they have. Give a time limit of no more than ten minutes. When students are ready, ask a few pairs to act out a conversation for the class.

Monitor and help while students are preparing their conversations. Some sample answers are given here so that you can give additional prompts to reluctant students. Make it clear to students that not every line of the conversation needs to contain examples of the structures – the idea is to broaden the context of use.

Go round and help with ideas and ask them to go back through their conversations to get them right and aim for good pronunciation. At the end, ask one or two pairs to act out their conversation to the rest of the class.

T 6.8 [CD 2: Track 20] Play the recording. Students listen and compare their answers. You could get students to repeat the last lines of each conversation.

Check it

6 Ask students to correct the sentences, then check in pairs. Monitor and help individuals with problems. In feedback, be prepared to go to the board and do some remedial teaching if students have problems or queries.

6 He isn't as intelligent **as** his sister / He isn't **more** intelligent than his sister.

7 This is **harder** than I expected.

8 Who is the **richest** man in the world?

9 Everything is **cheaper** in my country.

10 Rome was hotter **than** I expected.

ADDITIONAL MATERIAL

Workbook Unit 6

Exercise 1 Describing people, places, and things – An email from Australia

Exercises 3–6 Comparatives and superlatives

LISTENING AND SPEAKING (SB p49)

The best things in life are free

Students listen to five people of different ages talking about the things they love that are free. The tasks are listening for gist then listening for specific information.

1 Ask the question *What pleasures are there in life that don't cost anything?* open class. Elicit three or four suggestions. Then ask students to make their own list of three things, and compare it with a partner. Elicit a class list to the board.

> **Sample answers**
> Love: of a partner/parent/child/pet
> Sunny weather/snow
> Sunrise/sunset
> Natural beauty: mountains/lakes/seas
> a smile/a laugh/a kiss/a cuddle
> walking/dancing/singing/talking to a friend

2 **T 6.9** [CD 2: Track 21] Ask students to look at the photos, and describe what they can see. Play the recording. Students listen and put the photos in order.

In feedback, ask whether the people mentioned any things that the students already had in their list.

> **Answers and tapescript**
> a 2 b 3 c 1 d 6 e 4 f 5
>
> **T 6.9**
> **Ben**
> The best thing for me is my dog, Jasper. He's a black Labrador and he's great. I got him when he was a puppy, and I was nine. So we've grown up together. My uncle gave him to me for my ninth birthday, so he didn't cost anything. What's he like? Well, he's very loving. He's also a bit crazy, and great fun to play with. He's much more energetic than me. I'm always really tired after taking him for a walk!

Mary
Ooh, there are lots of things I like that don't cost anything, I'm sure. Let's see ... sunsets. That's one thing I love. My house is on a hill, and in the evening when I look out of my kitchen window, there's sometimes a beautiful sunset. It makes washing the dishes much easier! I also love getting phone calls and cards from my family. I suppose they cost something, but not to me! But actually, the best thing of all is my first grandchild. He's the most beautiful baby boy I've ever seen!

Michael
I work in the city, so the best thing for me is being in the countryside. I don't mind what the weather is like. Even if it's rainy and windy, it's great to be outside. It's much quieter than the city, so there's time to think. Actually, the countryside costs money, because I have to drive there first! OK, so the next best thing is going for a walk in the park near my flat after work. It's a lovely park with lots of trees and a small lake. It's the most relaxing way to end the day.

Laura
Em, well, I think the best thing for me is playing with my little sister, Abby. She's nearly four, so I'm much older than her. I've also got a brother, Dominic. He's six. But he doesn't like the games I like, so he isn't as much fun to play with. Abby's always waiting for me when I come home from school. She thinks I'm the best person in the whole world. We usually play hospitals or schools. I'm the doctor or teacher, of course, because I'm the biggest.

Kiera
Definitely the best thing for me is being with my boyfriend, Dan. We don't have to go out or spend money. I love just going for a walk and chatting with him. He makes me laugh all the time. He's the funniest person I know. And the nicest friend. We've been together for nearly a year, and our relationship just gets better and better. I think I'm really lucky.

3 **T 6.9** Put students in pairs to complete the chart. Play the recording again so that students can listen and check.

Answers

	What?	Why?	Is it free?
Ben, 15	Dog, Jasper	Grew up together – he's loving, crazy, fun, energetic	Yes
Mary, 55	Sunsets. Cards and calls from family Baby boy grandchild	Sunsets are beautiful – make washing up easier. Baby is beautiful	Sunsets and baby are free. Cards and calls cost something
Michael, 36	Countryside Walk in the park	Great, quieter then the city, time to think. Lovely, lots of trees, small lake	Countryside is not free because he has to drive there A walk in the park is free
Laura, 8	Playing with sister, Abby	Good to play with, always waiting for her, thinks she's the best person in the world	Yes
Kiera, 24	Boyfriend, Dan	Likes walking, chatting, makes her laugh, nicest friend, feels lucky	Yes

4 Ask students to choose their favourite free thing and write it down. Give them three minutes to bullet point as many reasons as they can think of to say why they like it. Then put students in pairs. They must take it in turns to speak about their favourite thing for one minute.

This is quite tricky to do. You may want to support students a bit more by introducing some language and modelling the activity.

Suggested language
I love/enjoy/really like ... because ...
What I love about ... is ...
The best thing about ... is ...
... makes me feel ...

READING AND SPEAKING (SB p50)

London: the world in one city

ABOUT THE TEXT
The texts are exploited by specific information tasks. The second task is a jigsaw reading task – this means that the students have to do an information gap exchange with a partner. Speaking activities allow students to express their opinions on the texts, and talk about their own cultures.

Greater London is a very large and diverse city. In many ways it is made up of lots of small towns all packed together. *Peckham*, *New Malden*, and *Stockwell* are 'towns' swallowed up in London's conurbation. *Green Lanes* is a long road that goes through places like Wood Green and Stoke Newington in north London.

Cyprus is an island in the eastern Mediterranean. It was partitioned into a Turkish-controlled north, and Greek south in 1975. Although peaceful, it is still a disputed territory. Cyprus is a former British colony, which is one reason why the Cypriot community is so large in London. *Madeira* is an island in the Atlantic, famous for its wine. The football club, *FC Porto*, is based in the city of Oporto, in northern Portugal. FC Porto won the European Champions' League in 2004.

You may wish to check the following set of words, used when describing a multicultural city:

immigrant = somebody who has come to live in a different country
vitality = liveliness
cosmopolitan = showing the influence of many cultures
diverse = very different
accepted = allowed to become part of a community
stick together = stay together/support each other

1 Ask students to write things they like and dislike about their capital city, then tell the class.

2 Ask students to take two or three minutes to prepare answers to the questions. Put students in pairs or small groups to tell each other about their capital cities.

If you have a multinational class, you could exploit this lead-in more fully. Ask individuals from different countries to stand up and make a brief presentation about their capital city. Encourage other students to ask them questions about their capital.

3 Ask students to look at the photos and the title. Ask *What do you think 'the world in one city' means?*

Give students a minute to read through the sentences. Tell them to guess which they think are true, and which false. Then ask students to read the introduction to the article and decide whether the statements are true or false. Let students check their answers in pairs before discussing as a class.

Answers

1	True	5	False
2	False	6	False
3	False	7	True
4	True		

4 Tell students that they are going to read two of the four texts on p51 and then exchange the information with a partner. Divide the class into groups of four or five. Call half of the groups A and the other half B. Get the A groups to read texts 1 and 3, and the B groups to read texts 2 and 4. Give students five or six minutes to read the extracts and discuss the answers to the questions in their groups. Monitor to help with any vocabulary queries. Be prepared to help students with the pronunciation of the names of the people/places.

5 Tell students to stand up and cross-pair so that the A students work with the B students. Once they have found a new partner, tell them to take it in turns to ask and answer the questions in exercise 4. With weaker classes, demonstrate the task by getting an A and B student to ask and answer the first question across the class. Remind students not to show each other their texts as they do the information exchange.

Check the answers with the whole class.

> **Answers**
> 1 **Text 1:** Posh Daddy. He's the manager of a West Indian and African hairdresser's. He's in the hairdresser's. He's doing a customer's hair.
> **Text 2:** They are the staff of the Asadal restaurant. They are in the kitchen of the restaurant. They're working.
> **Text 3:** They are the staff of the Yasar Halim Bakery. They are in the bakery. They are working and chatting.
> **Text 4:** They are the Portuguese football fans in the FC Porto Fan Club. They are in the bar of the fan club. They are drinking and chatting.
>
> 2 **Text 1:** Nigerian/African
> **Text 2:** Korean
> **Text 3:** Turkish
> **Text 4:** Portuguese
>
> 3 **Text 1:** Posh Daddy / Big Choice Barber's / Peckham
> **Text 2:** Young-il Park / the Asadal restaurant / New Malden
> **Text 3:** Yasar Halim / the Yasar Halim Bakery / Green Lanes
> **Text 4:** Jose Antonia Costa / the FC Porto Fan Club / Stockwell
>
> 4 **Text 1:** West Indian
> **Text 2:** English
> **Text 3:** Turkish Cypriot/Greek Cypriot
> **Text 4:** Madeiran
>
> 5 **Text 1:** Yes. The two black communities haven't always got on well.
> **Text 2:** Yes. Young-il was the first Korean in his school and people stared.
> **Text 3:** Not in London but in Cyprus there are still problems between the two communities.
> **Text 4:** Yes. The Portuguese and Madeirans are very separate groups.

> 6 **Text 1:** pepper soup and *kuku paka* (chicken with coconut which is hot and spicy)
> **Text 2:** *kimchi* (salty, spicy chilli peppers and vegetables)
> **Text 3:** *baklava* (a sweet cake make with honey and nuts)
> **Text 4:** *bacalhau* (salted cod with potatoes and onions)

What do you think?

Students work in small groups to discuss the questions. Monitor and encourage as much speaking as you can. It is a good idea to make one student in each group the discussion leader, responsible for asking the questions and making sure everybody has a chance to speak.

> **Sample answers**
> People come to London for jobs and money. It's an advantage for their children to speak English. People in London leave you alone so you are free to live your own life. The love of food in London creates a lot of jobs for new communities.
> Students' own answers to the rest of the questions.

WRITING (SB p108)

Describing a place – My home town: relative pronouns *who/that/which/where*

The aim of this writing section is to write a description of a place using relative pronouns.

1 Ask students where they were born. Give them one or two minutes to complete the sentence. Ask a few individuals to share their sentences with the class.

In feedback, point out that *where* is a relative pronoun, and *I was born* is a relative clause.

> ### GRAMMAR SPOT
>
> **1** and **2** Ask students to read the sentences in 1, and complete the rules in 2.
>
> > **Answers**
> > *Who* is for people
> > *Which* or *that* is for things
> > *Where* is for places

2 Ask students to join the sentences with relative pronouns. Let students check their answers in pairs.

> **Answers**
> 1 There's the boy **who** broke the window.
> 2 That's the palace **where** the Queen lives./That's the palace **which/that** the Queen lives **in**.
> 3 There are the policemen **who** caught the thief.

4 I bought a watch **which/that** stopped after two days.
5 Here are the letters **which/that** arrived this morning.
6 That's the hospital **where** I was born./That's the hospital **which/that** I was born **in**.

3 Ask students to look at the photos. Ask *Where is Newcastle? What do you know about Newcastle?*

ABOUT THE TEXT
Newcastle /ˈnjuːkæsəl/ is on the River Tyne /taɪn/ in the north-east of England. People there are often called *Geordies* /ˈdʒɔːdɪz/. *The Angel of the North* is a huge metal sculpture of a figure with outspread arms that look like rectangular flat wings.

Ask students to read the text and fill the gaps with relative pronouns.

Answers
1 where	6 where
2 which	7 who
3 where	8 who
4 which	9 which
5 which	10 who

Ask students to discuss the questions in pairs.

Answers
1 In the north-east of England.
2 Because a new castle was built there in the 12th century.
3 It was very industrial.
4 It has fashionable hotels, bars, and restaurants, and a number of new, culturally important places.
5 Seven.
6 Warm and friendly.
7 It is a sculpture.
8 A person who is born near the River Tyne.

4 Ask students to write brief notes about their home town under the headings. Let them compare their ideas with a partner.
Ask students to write their descriptions.

5 Ask a few students to read out their descriptions for the class.

ADDITIONAL MATERIAL

Workbook Unit 6
Exercise 7 Reading – The London Eye

Synonyms and antonyms in conversation
Synonyms
Check that your students know what synonyms are: words that are the same or similar in meaning. You could make the point by asking them to give you some examples in their own language.

1 **T 6.10** [CD 2: Track 22] Focus attention on the picture and elicit the synonyms (*lovely* and *beautiful*). Play the recording and get students to repeat. Focus attention on the stress shading. Drill the lines chorally and individually if necessary.

Tapescript
A Isn't it a lovely day!
B Yes, it's really beautiful.

2 Ask students to work in pairs to complete the conversations. They may need to use dictionaries to check the meaning of some of the words, but encourage them to try to guess first.

T 6.11 [CD 2: Track 23] Students listen to the recording to check their answers. Let students practise reading the conversations in pairs. If they have problems with the stress and intonation, play the recording again line by line and get students to repeat.

Answers and tapescript
1 A Look at all these new buildings!
  B Yes. Paris is much more **modern** than I expected.
2 A Wasn't that film brilliant?
  B Absolutely! It was **fantastic**. We loved it.
3 A Your bedroom's really untidy. Again!
  B What do you mean? It doesn't look **messy** to me.
4 A I couldn't believe it, their son was so impolite to me.
  B Don't worry. He's **rude** to everyone.
5 A Dan doesn't earn much, but he's always so kind.
  B He is, isn't he? He's one of the most **generous** people I know.
6 A I'm bored with this exercise!
  B I know. I'm **fed up** with it, too!

Antonyms

3 **T 6.12** [CD 2: Track 24] Remind students what antonyms are: words that are opposite in meaning. You could do this in the same way suggested for synonyms above.

Focus attention on the picture and elicit the antonyms (*cold* and *hot*). Play the recording and get students to repeat.

Focus attention on the stress shading. Drill the lines chorally and individually if necessary.

> **Tapescript**
> My soup's cold!
> I know, mine's not very hot either.

4 Check comprehension of the adjectives in the first column in the table. Focus attention on the examples for *bored*. Put students into pairs and get them to complete the table. Refer them back to exercise 2 for help with some of the adjectives. Allow students to use dictionaries if they have access to them. Check the answers with the class, drilling the pronunciation as necessary. (Note that there may be other possible answers but those given are likely to be known by students at this level.)

> **Answers**
>
> | Adjective | Synonym | Antonym |
> | --- | --- | --- |
> | bored | fed up | interested |
> | wonderful | brilliant | awful/terrible |
> | modern | new | old/old-fashioned |
> | impolite | rude | polite |
> | untidy | messy | tidy |
> | generous | kind | unkind/mean |
> | cold | cool | hot |
> | miserable | sad/unhappy | happy |

MUSIC OF ENGLISH

Read the notes in the box with the whole class. Elicit the examples of *not very* + antonym (*boring = not very interesting, miserable = not very happy*).

T 6.13 [CD 2: Track 25] Play the recording and get students to repeat the sentences. Focus attention on the stress shading and intonation arrows. Drill the lines chorally and individually if necessary. Stress to students that the use of *not very* + antonym is common in English and is a good way of avoiding being directly negative.

> **Tapescript**
> This film is so boring.
> I know, it isn't very interesting at all.
> You look so miserable.
> Well, I'm not very happy, it's true.

5 Elicit a polite response to number 1 as an example. Put students in pairs to complete the exercise. Monitor to check students' pronunciation.

T 6.14 [CD 2: Track 26] Play the recording and get students to check their answers.

> **Sample answers and tapescript**
> 1 A Tokyo's such an expensive city.
>   B Well, it's certainly not very cheap.
> 2 A Paul and Sue are so mean.
>   B They're not very generous, that's for sure.
> 3 A Their house is always so messy.
>   B I know, it's not very tidy, is it?
> 4 A That sales assistant was so rude!
>   B Mmm ... she wasn't very polite, was she?
> 5 A Jim looks really miserable.
>   B Yes, he's not very happy at the moment, is he?
> 6 A This exercise is so boring!
>   B Mmm, it's certainly not very exciting.

Assign the role of A or B to each student and get students to practise the conversations. Encourage good stress and intonation (the main stress is underlined in the tapescript). Drill the lines chorally and individually if necessary.

ADDITIONAL MATERIAL

Workbook Unit 6
Exercise 8 Synonyms and antonyms

EVERYDAY ENGLISH (SB p53)

A city break

Check comprehension of *city break* (a short holiday spent or based in a city). Elicit cities that are popular for city breaks in the students' own country and/or elicit examples of city breaks students have been on.

1 Focus attention on Rolf's ID card. Ask students to look at the form. Pre-teach/Check: *hostel, check in date, dorm* (= *dormitory*), *gender, male/female* (on the form shortened to *M* and *F*), *mixed* (both male and female), *booking fee, terms and conditions* (the conditions that apply to an agreement/financial transaction).

Give students time to complete the form. Check the answers with the class.

Answers

Booking details

Number of nights 3
Number of people 2

Please select a room

6 bed mixed dorm €20.00

Customer details

Last name	Jurgen
email	jurgen21@sdf.nor
Phone number	06 78 24 50 88
Gender	M
Nationality	Norwegian

Credit card details

Card holder's name	Rolf Jurgen
Total cost of rooms	€120.00
Total	€130.00

2   This exercise reviews question words and also practises the type of questions you might need to ask in a tourist office. Pre-teach/Check: *fix* (= repair), *cashpoint* (facility, often outside a bank, where you can get cash), *travel card* (a pass you can use on public transport). Focus attention on the example. Get students to match columns A and B first to form the questions. Check the answers.

Say the first question *Where can I buy a new backpack?* and elicit the leaflet that matches. Students match the rest of the questions with the leaflets. Check the answers.

Answers

Where can I buy a new backpack? (leaflet c)
What exhibitions are showing this week? (leaflet b)
Where's the nearest cashpoint? (leaflet f)
What time does the metro stop running? (leaflet d)
Where can I get something to eat? (leaflet g)
How long does the tour take? (leaflet a)
What play is on this week? (leaflet e)
How much is a travel card for a week? (leaflet d)
Where can I get a battery for my camera? (leaflet c)
Where is there a bar with live music? (leaflet g)

3   Pre-teach/Check the following vocabulary from the recording: *sights, sightseeing, backpack, to book in advance, gift shop*. With weaker classes, tell students they need to listen out for three things that Rolf and Jonas want to do/see and three problems, one connected with each activity.

T 6.15 [CD 2: Track 27] Play the recording and get students to listen out for the answers. Let students compare their answers in pairs. Play the recording again if necessary. Check the answers.

Answers and tapescript

- Rolf and Jonas want to go on a sightseeing tour. They want to go to a modern art exhibition. Jonas wants to buy a present for his mother's birthday.
- Jonas can't take his backpack onto the tour bus. They have to book in advance for the modern art exhibition. The gift shop is closed for lunch.

T 6.15

R = Rolf   J = Jonas   W = woman in tourist office

R   Excuse me. Could you help me?
W   Certainly, if I can.
R   We'd like to take a trip on one of those buses that show you all the sights. You know, where you can get off and back on where you want ...
W   Ah, yes. You want a city sightseeing tour. It stops in twenty places, and it costs twenty euros.
J   How long does the tour take?
W   Well, it depends, whether you get off or not, but if you stay on and don't get off, about an hour and a quarter.
J   Where can we buy a ticket?
W   Here, or at the bus station. But you can't go on with your backpack.
J   Sorry? What did you say?
W   Your backpack ... you know ... your bag. It's too big. You have to leave it somewhere.
J   Ah, OK! No, don't worry, I'll leave it at the hostel. Thanks Another thing, I've read that there's an exhibition of modern art on at the moment. Is that right?
W   Yes, that's right. It's on at the Studio until the end of next week.
R   How much is it to get in?
W   Twelve euros, but it's best to book a few days in advance.
R   Oh, that's a shame. We wanted to go tonight. Never mind.
J   Oh, and one more thing. I need to buy a present for my mother. It's her birthday soon. Is there a gift shop around here?
W   There's a good one just round the corner, but it's closed for lunch at the moment. It'll be open again at 2.00.
J   OK. That's great. Thanks for all your help.
R   Thanks a lot.
W   Pleasure. Bye-bye

4   **T 6.15** [CD 2: Track 27] Play the recording again, pausing at the end of each gapped line in the exercise to give students time to write their answers. Check the answers with the class.

5 Ask a pair of students to ask and answer the example question across the class. Put students in pairs and have them ask and answer the rest of the questions in exercise 2. If they don't know the exact answer to any of the questions, get them to guess or imagine a possible answer.

Planning a break

6 Before students start the personalization task, elicit the language that they might need to use and write the structures on the board:

Where to stay/eat/shop
There's a (lovely café with paintings by local artists).
There are (some good restaurants near the museum).
You'll find (the best shops in the city centre).
If you need (a hotel), ask at the (tourist office).
The best place for (souvenirs) is the (open market).

What to see/do
Remember to visit (the new art gallery in the High Street).
Don't miss (the street musicians in the main square).
You must go to (the museum) to find out about (the city's history).
If you are interested in (art), check out (the exhibition in the town hall).

How to get around
The metro starts at (6.30) and finishes at (midnight).
There's a (good bus service).
The cheapest way to get around is to (buy a travel card).
There's a taxi rank at (the station).
You can buy tickets for (public transport) at the stations or at the tourist office.

With weaker students elicit some examples of information for a tour of the city where the students are studying. With monolingual classes, put students into pairs or groups of three to do the task. In multilingual classes, students can work individually. Give them time to put the information together. Elicit some examples from the class in a feedback session. Alternatively, students can compare their ideas in pairs or small groups. If students have produced guides for different cities, ask them to exchange the information with a partner or different group. If students have written about the same city, they can also exchange the information and compare. If appropriate, you can display the guides students have written on the classroom walls.

Present Perfect • *for, since*
Word endings
Making conversation 2

Fame!

Introduction to the unit

This unit uses the theme of fame to introduce the Present Perfect. The theme naturally lends itself to talking about people's experiences, which is one of the main uses of the Present Perfect. The new structure is introduced by means of short texts about famous families. The *Reading and listening* section has a humorous magazine article about an imaginary temperamental film star, and the *Listening and speaking* section has an interview with a real rock band.

Note The *Practice* section includes a speaking activity that requires cards. If you wish to do this activity, you will need to photocopy and cut up the cards on p132 of the Teacher's Book before class.

Language aims

Grammar – Present Perfect This is the first unit in *New Headway Pre-Intermediate – the THIRD edition* where the Present Perfect is dealt with. The simple aspect is introduced and practised. In Unit 12, the simple aspect is revised, and the continuous aspect is introduced.

The Present Perfect means 'completed some time before now, but with some present relevance', and so joins past and present in a way that many other languages do not. In English, we say *I have seen the Queen* (at some indefinite time in my life), but not **I have seen the Queen yesterday*. Other languages express the same ideas, but by using either a past tense or a present tense. In many other European languages, the same form of *have* + the past participle can be used to express both indefinite (Present Perfect) and finished past (Past Simple) time.

Common mistakes

*I have watched TV last night.
*When have you been to Russia?
*Did you ever try Chinese food?

Many languages use a present tense to express unfinished past. However, English 'sees' not only the present situation, but the situation going back into the past, and uses the Present Perfect.

Common mistakes

*I live here for five years.
*She is a teacher for ten years.
*How long do you know Paul?

Students are usually introduced to the Present Perfect very gently in their first year course, so they will not be unfamiliar with the form. This unit aims to introduce students to some uses/meanings of this tense, but your class will not have mastered it by the end of the unit. It takes a long time to be assimilated.

Vocabulary This section looks at noun, verb, and adjective endings.

Everyday English This section practises short answers and extending conversations to make them more polite. There are also exercises on short answers throughout the Workbook whenever a new tense or verb form is introduced.

Notes on the unit

STARTER (SB p54)

This is a quick check that students know the Past Simple and past participle forms of these common irregular verbs. Ask students to work in pairs to help each other with the answers. They can check their answers in the irregular verbs list on p158 of the Student's Book.

Answers

Base form	Past Simple	Past participle
write	wrote	written
be	was/were	been
make	made	made
win	won	won
have	had	had
read /riːd/	read /red/	read /red/
do	did	done
get	got	got (gotten in US English)
know	knew	known
become	became	become

All the forms are irregular.

FAMOUS FAMILIES (SB p54)

Present Perfect and Past Simple

> **ABOUT THE APPROACH**
> The approach used here is to test the students' ability to recognize and use the Present Perfect. Students have to match Past Simple sentences to dead famous people, and Present Perfect sentences to their living descendants. By doing so, students should develop familiarity with the concepts of finished and unfinished past, and experiences up to now.

1   Ask students to look at the photos. Ask *What do you know about these people?* Ask students to guess how they think the people are related. You could tell them the answers, or make them wait until they do exercise 3. Follow up by asking students if they can think of other famous families.

Answers
Julian Lennon is John Lennon's son.
Sophie Dahl is Roald Dahl's granddaughter.
Bella Freud is Sigmund Freud's great-granddaughter.
Caroline is Prince Rainier's daughter.

2   Ask students to complete the sentences with the correct name. Do the first as an example, and let students check their answers in pairs.

T 7.1   [CD 2: Track 28] Play the recording so students can check their answers. At this stage you may wish to play and pause the recording to drill the sentences containing the Present Perfect around the room, paying particular attention to the contracted *has*.

Answers and tapescript
1   Sigmund Freud invented psychoanalysis to help his patients.
2   Prince Rainier of Monaco governed the tiny principality for nearly 56 years.
3   Bella Freud has made clothes for many famous people, including Madonna.
4   John Lennon was a founder member of *The Beatles*.
5   Sophie Dahl has modelled for *Vogue* and Yves Saint Laurent.
6   Julian Lennon has been in the music business since 1984.
7   Roald Dahl wrote many children's books, including *Charlie and the Chocolate Factory* and *The BFG (The Big Friendly Giant)*.
8   Princess Caroline of Monaco has been married three times and has four children.

GRAMMAR SPOT (SB p55)

1   Ask students to work in pairs to underline the examples of the Past Simple. The aim is to consolidate what is known (i.e. the Past Simple) before moving on to the new (i.e. the Present Perfect), and to reinforce the idea that the Past Simple is used to refer to finished past time.

Answers
1   invented
2   governed
4   was
7   wrote

Ask students why the Past Simple is used. Then ask them to underline examples of the other tense, the Present Perfect.

Answers
3   has made
5   has modelled
6   has been
8   has been married

In feedback, check that students understand that the Past Simple sentences refer to dead people because what they did in their lives is finished. The Present Perfect sentences refer to living people because they describe past actions that have some continuity with the present, i.e. these people can still do more of these things in their lives.

2 Ask students to answer the questions.

> **Answers**
>
> *John Lennon made a lot of records* – Past Simple, because he is dead and can make no more.
> *Julian Lennon has made a lot of records* – Present Perfect, because he is still alive, and can make more now and in the future.
> *John Lennon has played...* is wrong because we use the Present Perfect to talk about something that started in the past and has continued to now. (John Lennon last played with the Beatles in 1970.)

3 Ask students to compare the examples in pairs.

> **Answers**
>
> *for* is used with a period of time, and *since* is used with a point in time.

Refer students to Grammar Reference 7.1 and 7.2 on p135.

3 Ask students to work in pairs or small groups to put the verbs in the correct tense. Encourage them to look back at the sentences in exercise 2 to help them.

T 7.2 [CD 2: Track 29] Play the recording so that students can check their answers.

> **Answers and tapescript**
>
> 1 John Lennon **started** his first band when he was 15. His eldest son, Julian, **has been** in the music business since he was 19. He **has made** five albums. He **didn't know** his father very well.
> 2 Roald Dahl **wrote** the story *The BFG* in 1982 for his granddaughter, Sophie. It is about a little girl called Sophie. Sophie Dahl **has been** a model since she was 17, but she also likes writing. She **has written** some short stories and one novel.
> 3 Sigmund Freud **worked** in Vienna for most of his life. His great-granddaughter, Bella Freud, **was born** in London and **has worked** there since 1990. But when she was a fashion student, she **lived** in Rome.
> 4 Prince Rainier of Monaco **married** American film star Grace Kelly in 1956. Their daughter, Caroline, **has had** quite a tragic life. She **divorced** her first husband after only two years and both her mother and her second husband **died** in terrible accidents. She **has been** married to her third husband, Prince Ernst of Hanover, since 1999.

4 Do 1 and 2 as a class to establish the two question forms, one in the Present Perfect and one in the Past Simple, and drill them to establish a model. Then put students in pairs to write the questions.

T 7.3 [CD 2: Track 30] Play the recording so that students can check their answers. Drill all the questions around the room.

At this stage, ask students in pairs to ask and answer the questions. Monitor and correct.

> **Answers and tapescript**
>
> 1 When did John Lennon start his first band?
>   When he was 15.
> 2 How long has Julian Lennon been in the music business?
>   Since he was 19.
> 3 When did Roald Dahl write *The BFG*?
>   In 1982.
> 4 How many novels has Sophie Dahl written?
>   Just one.
> 5 Where did Sigmund Freud work?
>   In Vienna.
> 6 Where has Bella Freud worked since 1990?
>   In London.
> 7 Who did Prince Rainier marry?
>   The American film star, Grace Kelly.
> 8 How many times has Princess Caroline been married?
>   Three times.

PRACTICE (SB p55)

Discussing grammar

1 The aim of this exercise is to check that students have grasped the form and use of the Present Perfect. It tests some of the typical errors and confusions made by students learning this tense. Students work in pairs to choose the correct verb form.

> **Answers**
>
> 1 Have you ever been   4 was
> 2 saw   5 have bought, have made
> 3 have liked   6 have been

Speaking

2 This is a mingle activity, where students ask the same question to everyone in the class. Photocopy p132 of the Teacher's Book, and cut it up into sentences. (If you paste them onto card, you can use them again.)

Every student must have a sentence. Read the example in the Student's Book, showing that they have to turn their sentences into a question beginning *Have you ever ... ?* Make sure students don't go round the class saying 'Find someone who has been to China.'

Before you ask the class to stand up, check that everyone's question is correct. Model the activity with a strong student, asking a *Have you ever ... ?* question, and three or four follow-up questions to show that you want students to find out as much as they can.

Students stand up and ask everyone, making a note of the answers.

3 When they have finished and have sat down, allow them a minute to decide what they are going to say when they report back to the class. Ask all students to report back.

for and *since*

4 Students work in pairs to complete the time expressions with *for* and *since*. Before they start, remind students of the rule in the *Grammar spot*: *for* is used with a period of time, and *since* is used with a point in time. For example, *. . . for ten minutes* but *. . . since January 2004*.

Answers

1	for	4	since	7	for
2	since	5	since	8	since
3	for	6	for	9	for

5 Ask students to work in pairs to match the lines to make sentences. Do the first as an example to give them the idea then monitor and help.

T 7.4 [CD 2: Track 31] Play the recording so that students can compare their answers. You could play and pause and drill the sentences around the class. Get students to make similar sentences about themselves then read them out to the class.

Answers and tapescript

1 I've known my best friend for years. We met when we were 10.
2 I last went to the cinema two weeks ago. The film was terrible.
3 I've had this watch for three years. My dad gave it to me for my birthday.
4 We've used this book since the beginning of term. It's not bad. I quite like it.
5 We lived in Edinburgh from 2001 to 2005. We moved because I got a job in London.
6 We haven't had a break for an hour. I really need a cup of coffee.
7 I last had a holiday in 2003. I went camping with some friends.
8 This building has been a school since 1999. Before that it was an office.

Asking questions

6 **T 7.5** [CD 2: Track 32] Ask students to work in pairs to complete the conversation, then play the recording so they can check their answers. Ask students to tell you why the different tenses are used.

Drill the three questions round the class, paying particular attention to the intonation pattern of *Wh*-questions, then ask students to work in pairs to practise the conversation.

Answers and tapescript

A Where **do you** live, Anna? (Present Simple, because it is true now.)
B In a flat in Green Street.
A How long **have you lived** there? (Present Perfect, because it is unfinished past – starting in the past and continuing until now.)
B Only for er,... three months. Yes, since June.
A And why **did you** move? (Past Simple, because it asks about a finished past event.)
B Well, we wanted to live near the park.

7 **T 7.6** [CD 2: Track 33] This activity gives students lots of controlled speaking practice in manipulating the question forms of three different tenses. Be prepared to have to do a lot of prompting and correcting.

Model the first conversation with a confident student, then ask students to work in pairs to practise. Ideally, they should be able to do this without having to write, just using the prompts, although it may be a good idea to let them write out the first conversation for confidence. Play the recording so that students can compare their answers. Ask two or three pairs to model one of their conversations for the class at the end.

Sample answers and tapescript

1 A What do you do?
  B I work in advertising.
  A Really? How long have you done that?
  B For ... just over two years.
  A And what did you do before that?
  B I worked for a small publishing company.
2 A Have you got a car?
  B Yes, we've got a Volkswagen Golf.
  A How long have you had it?
  B Since April this year.
  A Did you pay a lot for it?
  B Not really, it was £6000.
3 A Do you know Alan Brown?
  B Yes, I do.
  A How long have you known him?
  B For a long time – about ten years.
  A Where did you meet him?
  B We met in London – at drama school.

8 This activity extends the previous two activities with some personalized speaking practice. This could be done in pairs or as a mingle activity.

ADDITIONAL MATERIAL

Workbook Unit 7
These exercises could be done in class to give further practice, for homework, or in a later class as revision.

Exercises 1–7 Present Perfect

The band *Goldrush*

ABOUT THE LISTENING

This is an interview with five young male members of a British rock band called *Goldrush*. Inspired by American country and rock music, *Goldrush* haven't had international or commercial success yet, but have had a lot of critical acclaim and 'underground' success, and have also toured the United States. The interview is exploited by a prediction task and listening for specific information exercises. Tasks also recycle and practise the Present Perfect.

You may wish to pre-teach the names of the musical instruments listed in exercise 4, as well as other language connected to rock music: *band, album, record, concert, tour, influence*

1 Talk to students about the kind of music they like. Ask the questions in the Student's Book. Focus on the last question *What questions would you like to ask your favourite bands and singers?* You could prompt with questions such as *How long have you been together? What are you doing at the moment? When are you going to make another record?* Give students time to write their questions down.

2 Ask students to look at the photos. Ask the questions.

Answers

- Students' own ideas. However, the band's appearance suggests a rock band. Hamish's shirt might also suggest a country and western influence.
- The musical instruments in the photos: electric guitar, drums, bass guitar.

3 Ask students to read the questions. Ask if any of them are similar to the questions students wrote in exercise 1. Pre-teach/check the following vocabulary from the recording: *tape machine, passionate about music, Flaming Lips* (the name of a band), *a dream come true*.

T 7.7 [CD 2: Track 34] Tell students that the recording is quite long, but that they don't need to understand every word to answer the questions. Play the recording and get students to note down their answers to the questions. Allow students to check their answers in pairs. Play the recording again if necessary. Check the answers with the class.

Answers and tapescript

1 Robin and Joe are brothers. They have played together since they were teenagers.
2 Since 2002.
3 He started when he was at school. He wrote songs in his bedroom and recorded them on a tape machine.

4 Neil Young because he's so passionate about music; a band called *The Flaming Lips*, who are amazing; Bob Dylan because he's written so many fantastic songs.
5 Because so much of the history of rock music is there.
6 Two mini-albums.
7 They're going back to play in America, and then they're going to Australia for the first time.

T 7.7

The band *Goldrush*

I = Interviewer   R = Robin   J = Joe
H = Hamish   Ga = Garo   Gr = Graham

I ... and that was *Goldrush* playing the song *Wait for the wheels* from their mini-album Ozona. And here we have the five band members in the studio! Welcome, guys!
All Hello. Hi, there. It's good to be here.
I Now, tell us a bit about yourselves. How long have you all been together as a band?
R Well, my brother Joe and I have always had a band!
J That's right. Since we were teenagers, really.
R First, we started a band called *Whispering Bob* in 1999. Then, in ... 2002 Graham and Garo joined us and we changed our name to *Goldrush*. Finally, Hamish here, joined two years ago.
I So, Robin, how did you start?
R Well, when I was at school, I started writing songs in my bedroom and recording them on a tape machine. Our first band was with our schoolfriends, wasn't it, Joe?
J Yes, but some of our first concerts were pretty bad!
R Yeah, they were!
I So in *Goldrush*, which instruments do you all play?
R We all play several instruments. I sing and play guitar and piano.
J And I play bass, violin, trumpet, keyboards, ...
R In fact, anything!
H I play bass and guitar.
Ga I play guitar as well, and drums.
Gr And I play ...drums ... and drums! (All laugh)
I And how would you describe your style of music?
J We're a rock band.
I Who has influenced you the most?
J Firstly, Neil Young, because he's so passionate about his music.
Ga And also a band called *The Flaming Lips*, who are just amazing.
Gr Yeah, and now we've recorded and toured with *The Flaming Lips*, which is just a dream come true for us.
All Yeah.
R And recently, I've become really interested in Bob Dylan. He's written so many fantastic songs for so many years.
I You've toured the US a few times. What was that like?
Ga It was an amazing experience! So much of the history of rock music is there.

H We had a great tour playing with Mark Gardener.

I Where else have you played? Which other countries have you been too?

R We've played in Spain twice, in Barcelona and Madrid. And last year we played in concerts in Azerbaijan and Uzbekistan!

J Yeah, they certainly aren't places we ever expected to play!

Ga And in Hong Kong we played with some great friends of ours, *Six by Seven*.

I Your first album *Don't bring me down* came out in 2002. How many albums have you made since then?

Gr We've made two mini-albums. One's called *Extended Play* and we've just finished another called *Ozona*. They have six songs on each of them.

I So what's coming up in the future? What are your plans?

R Well, first, we're going back to play in America, and then we're going to Australia for the first time! We're looking forward to that.

I Well, guys, good luck with everything. (Thanks.) It was great talking to you. Are you going to play us out with something?

J Yes, this song is called 'There's a world'.

I Let's hear it for *Goldrush*!

4 Let students look at the information in the table. Check comprehension of the instruments if you didn't pre-teach them (see *About the listening* above).

T 7.7 [CD 2: Track 34] Play the recording. Get students to listen to the interview and tick the correct boxes. Get students to check their answers in pairs. Then check the answers with the class.

Answers

Instruments they play	Bands/musicians they have played with	Places they have visited
✓ guitar	☐ Whispering Bob	✓ the United States
✓ piano	☐ Neil Young	☐ Poland
✓ bass	✓ The Flaming Lips	✓ Spain
✓ violin	☐ Bob Dylan	✓ Azerbaijan
✓ trumpet	✓ Mark Gardener	✓ Uzbekistan
✓ keyboards	✓ Six by Seven	✓ Hong Kong
☐ saxophone		☐ Australia
✓ drums		☐ South Africa

Ask individual students to tell you the bands the guys have played with, and the countries they have been to. This is to give further controlled practice of the Present Perfect. You could also ask about the bands they haven't played with, and the countries they haven't been to, to get practice of the negative.

Language work

5 Focus attention on the first time expression in list A and on the example. Elicit one or two more examples from list A. Then put students in pairs to complete the exercise. If students have problems remembering the information from the recording or using the time expressions in the lists, refer them to the tapescript on p121 of the Student's Book. Check the sentences with the whole class.

In the feedback, point out that the verb forms in the sentences from A are in the Present Perfect, because they refer to the past up to the present, and probably into the future. The verb forms in the sentences from B are in the Past Simple, because they refer to finished past time.

Answers

A
Robin and Joe have had a band since they were teenagers.
Robin has become interested in Bob Dylan recently.
The band have played in Spain twice so far.
They have been to the US a few times.
They have just finished (their mini-album called) *Ozona*.

B
They started a band called *Whispering Bob* in 1999.
Graham and Garo joined the band 2002.
Hamish joined the band two years ago.
Robin wrote songs/recorded songs on a tape machine when he was at school.
The band played in Uzbekistan last year.

Roleplay

6 This activity could last a short while or about an hour, depending on how you organize it, (and whether your class are motivated by it). If you allow the musicians and journalists about fifteen minutes to prepare, then have the interviews and record them, then listen to the recorded interviews for feedback, you should easily fill an hour, depending on the size of your class.

Divide the class into groups of four and refer them to the roleplay information on p151 of the Student's Book. Let students decide who are the band members and who is the journalist. Give students time to prepare their ideas – the journalists the questions he/she wants to ask, and the band members information about their profile and experiences. Feed in any new vocabulary as necessary.

With bigger classes, get students to roleplay the interview with the groups all working at the same time. With smaller classes, you can get the groups to perform the roleplay one by one. Students often enjoy the latter option as they like hearing what the other 'bands' have to say.

Davina Moody – Drama Queen

ABOUT THE TEXT

This is a humorous text, set as a gossipy article from a glossy magazine. The students have to predict and read, read for gist, and read for specific information. The follow-up activity is an out-of-class project in which students must research and present a similar article to the class.

Davina Moody is, of course, an imaginary film star. The two main areas of difficult vocabulary are character adjectives and jobs. Note also the occasional Americanism used in the text, e.g. *movie* as well as 'film', *sidewalk* (pavement). There are also phrases connected with movies: *a champagne reception* (a short party held to greet people arriving for an important event), *a premiere* (a party held on the opening night of a film or play), *the movie flopped* (the film failed at the box office).

1 The aim of the lead-in is to get students talking about the topic of film celebrities. You could bring in pictures of well-known stars and put them on the board, then ask who they are, why they are famous, then tell the class why you like them. This way, you provide a model for the activity.

Give students two or three minutes to think of examples of celebrities in the news and what they have done. Then elicit a range of examples from the class.

2 Ask students to look at the title and photographs. Ask *What is a drama queen?*

Answer

A drama queen is someone who tends to treat a particular problem as more important and serious than it really is. Drama queens are really annoying! They are similar to 'prima donnas'.

Ask students to look at the adjectives in the box. Read them out, modelling the main stress in each word. You could ask students to mark the main stress on the words, or repeat the words after your model. Check the meanings by asking students to find the words in their dictionaries and to explain them to a partner. You could ask students in pairs to divide the words into positive and negative adjectives.

Then put students in pairs to decide which words describe Davina. Have a brief class feedback. Check the answers.

Answers

temperamental, *moody*, *bad-tempered*, *spoilt* and *selfish* are likely to describe a 'drama queen'.
Davina may also be *talented*. If she is a drama queen, she is unlikely to be *easy-going*, *thoughtful*, or *kind*.
temperamental and *moody* describe a person who quickly changes from one mood to another, from being happy to being angry, for example.
spoilt is often used to describe children who expect to get everything they want, and tend to be badly-behaved.

3 Ask students to read the first part of the article and answer the questions. In feedback, check that students know what *entourage* is, (a group of people that travel with someone famous, rich, or important), and know what the jobs of the people in her entourage are.

Answers

1 By private jet.
2 Her entourage: PA, PA to the PA, hairdresser, make-up artist, manicurist, chef, dietician, masseuse, personal trainer, chauffeur, bodyguards, spaniel, and vet.
3 No, they've looked after some of the world's most famous film stars.
4 No – she was very moody.

4 Ask students to look at the paragraph headings. (You could write them on the board to stop students actually reading the paragraphs). Ask students to work in twos or threes to make guesses about what they think will happen in each paragraph, then elicit a few ideas and write them on the board.

5 Ask students to read the article quickly to check their predictions. They don't have to read every word – just enough of each paragraph to get the gist. It is a good idea to set a strict time limit of about five minutes. Establish which student(s) predicted the disasters most accurately. Elicit examples of what they predicted from the headings in the text.

6 Read through the sentences with students. Give them longer this time to find information in the text, and correct the false sentences. Let students check fully with a partner before feedback.

Answers

1 False – 17 rooms
2 True – a 'near' breakdown
3 True – she became a child star 30 years ago
4 False – she has never worn yellow
5 True – the lights were yellow
6 False – the staff were too afraid to wake her
7 False – she was too upset to attend
8 True – it flopped
9 False – the manicurist ran away with the hotel manager to start a new life

What do you think?

Ask the questions open class, and elicit opinions. You could ask students if they know of any examples of real 'drama queen' behaviour from film stars or other celebrities.

T 7.8 [CD 2: Track 35] Play the recording. Ask students to listen, then discuss the questions as a class.

Project

7   If students are particularly interested in this topic, encourage them to research an article about a celebrity from a tabloid newspaper or magazine like *Hello!* or *OK!* and present their findings in the next lesson.

A biography – Paragraphing: Two princesses

The aim of this writing section is to write a biography, organized into appropriate paragraphs.

1   Ask students in pairs to think of famous people. Elicit ideas and write them on the board.

2   Ask students what they know about Princess Caroline of Monaco. Build up facts and opinions on the board.

You could pre-teach and write the following words on the board to help students predict Caroline's life:

paparazzi (photographers who follow famous people)

accident   tragedy   playboy   divorce   heir

3   Ask students to read the text and check their predictions. Then ask students to work in pairs to put the paragraphs in order.

4   Ask students in pairs to read the facts about Princess Stephanie, and decide how to separate the facts into paragraphs.

Ask students to write the biography, using the prompts. Monitor and help.

5   Ask students to research and write a biography of a celebrity who interests them. This is best set as homework.

Word endings

1   Lead in by writing the noun endings on the board, and asking students to tell you any jobs they can think of that finish with the endings. Ask students to find jobs in the text on p59 that have these endings.

2 Put students in pairs or small groups to make jobs from the words.

T 7.9 [CD 2: Track 36] Play the recording so that students can check their answers. In feedback, make sure you point out the strong stress in the jobs.

> **Answers and tapescript**
> **ar**tist, poli**ti**cian, mu**si**cian, ac**coun**tant, **de**corator, pho**to**grapher, re**cep**tionist, in**ter**preter, **sci**entist, li**bra**rian, elec**tri**cian, **law**yer /ˈlɔːjə/

3 Ask students to work in pairs to complete the charts with endings from the box. Do one or two as examples to get students started.

> **Answers**
>
> | Noun | Verb | Noun | Adjective |
> |---|---|---|---|
> | ar'rival | ar'rive | mood | 'moody |
> | 'trainer | train | friend | 'friendly |
> | invi'tation | in'vite | fame | 'famous |
> | organi'zation | 'organize | 'patience | 'patient |
> | expla'nation | ex'plain | 'happiness | 'happy |
> | de'cision | de'cide | 'kindness | kind |
> | em'ployment | em'ploy | 'difference | 'different |
> | im'provement | im'prove | 'danger | 'dangerous |
> | dis'cussion | dis'cuss | di'saster | di'sastrous |
> | ag'reement | ag'ree | 'beauty | 'beautiful |
> | imagi'nation | i'magine | use | 'useful |
> | ad'vertisement | 'advertise | help | 'helpful |

Pronunciation – word stress

4 **T 7.10** [CD 2: Track 37] Put students in pairs to look at the examples and answer the questions.

Play the recording. Ask students to listen, check their answers, and repeat the words.

> **Answers and tapescript**
> 1 With two-syllable nouns and adjectives, the stress is on the first syllable.
> 2 With two-syllable verbs, the stress is on the second syllable.
> 3 The stress is on the syllable before -tion and –sion, e.g. invi'tation, de'cision.
> 4 The stress moves: i'magine, imagi'nation; 'advertise, ad'vertisement; 'politics, poli'tician; 'photograph, pho'tographer
>
> **T 7.10**
> 1 beauty   noisy
>   kindness   friendly
>   lawyer   famous
>   artist   different
>   difference

> 2 arrive   discuss
>   invite   employ
>   explain   agree
>   improve
>
> 3 invitation   ambition
>   explanation decision
>   information   discussion
>
> 4 imagine / imagination   advertise / advertisement
>   politics / politician   photograph / photographer

Talking about you

5 Put students in pairs to underline the correct word. Ask students to take it in turns to ask and answer the questions.

> **Answers**
> 1 patience   6 employ
> 2 patient   7 improvement
> 3 mood   8 ambition
> 4 dangerous   9 politician
> 5 difference   10 happiness

ADDITIONAL MATERIAL

Workbook Unit 7

Exercise 8 Vocabulary – Making opposites
Exercise 12 Pronunciation – Word stress

EVERYDAY ENGLISH (SB p61)

Making conversation 2 – short answers

Short answers have been practised throughout the Workbook. The aim here is to bring them all together and practise them orally, and to show students that it is more polite if you add more information to your answer.

1 **T 7.11** [CD 2: Track 38] Read the instructions as a class. Play the recording and ask the questions. Students should be able to tell you that in the second conversation the speaker uses short answers, a more animated intonation, and they give more information to be more polite.

> **Tapescript**
> **A** Do you like cooking?
> **B** Yes.
>
> **A** Do you like cooking?
> **B** Yes, I do, especially Italian food.

MUSIC OF ENGLISH – SOUNDING POLITE

1 **T 7.12** [CD 2: Track 39] Read through the rules and examples as a class. Play the recording and ask students to listen and repeat. Point out that short answers rise, then fall in intonation.

> **Tapescript**
> 'Do you like cooking?'   'Yes, I do.'
> 'Have you ever been to Venice?'   'No, I haven't.'

2 **T 7.13** [CD 2: Track 40] Ask students to listen and repeat the sentences.

> **Tapescript**
> 'Do you like cooking?' 'Yes, I do, especially Italian food.'
> 'Have you ever been to Venice?' 'No, I haven't, but I'd love to go one day.'

2 Ask students to work in pairs to complete the short answers. Do the first as an example. Remind students that we can't use *I've, they've, he's*, etc. in short answers.

T 7.14 [CD 2: Track 41] Play the recording. Ask students to listen, check their answers, and try to remember the other information. Students then choose some of the conversations and practise them with a partner.

> **Answers and tapescript**
> 1 A Are those new jeans you're wearing?
>   B No, they **aren't**. I've had them for ages.
> 2 A Have you got the time, please?
>   B No, I **haven't**. I'm sorry, my watch has stopped.
> 3 A Can you play any musical instruments?
>   B Yes, I **can** actually. I can play the violin.
> 4 A Do you like learning English?
>   B Yes, I **do**. Most of the time I like it a lot.

3 Ask students to work in pairs to complete the short answers and match the correct line to each conversation.

T 7.15 [CD 2: Track 42] Play the recording. Ask students to listen and check their answers.

Put students in pairs to choose one of the conversations, and think of ways to continue it. Ask students to act out their conversation to the class.

> **Answers and tapescript**
> 1 A Is it still raining?
>   B No, **it isn't. It's just stopped.**
> 2 A Did you see the football last night?
>   B Yes, **I did. It was a great game.**
> 3 A Have you got change for a pound?
>   B No, sorry, **I haven't. I've only got a ten-pound note.**
> 4 A Have you tried the new pizza place?
>   B Yes, **I have. I went there last weekend with Frank.**
> 5 A Are you ambitious?
>   B Yes, **I am. I want to have my own business one day.**
> 6 A Are you doing anything tonight?
>   B No, **I'm not. Why? What are *you* doing?**

4 Students work alone or in pairs to think of questions, using the prompts.

5 Ask students to stand up and mingle, asking their questions to as many different students as possible. When they answer, they should give as much information as possible to extend the conversation so that they sound more polite and natural.

Don't forget!

Workbook Unit 7

Exercise 8 Vocabulary – Word endings – adjectives

Exercises 9–10 Reading – Steven Spielberg, a Hollywood legend

Exercises 11 Pronunciation – Word stress

Exercises 12–13 Check it

Grammar Reference
Look at the exercises on SB p135–136 as a class, or set for homework. The answers are on TB p155–156.

Word list
Remind your students of the Word list for this unit on SB p155. They could translate the words, learn them at home, or transfer some of the words to their vocabulary notebook.

Pronunciation Book Unit 7

have to • should/must
Words that go together
At the doctor's

Do's and don'ts

Introduction to the unit

This unit introduces the functional language of obligation and advice. In the first presentation section 'What's his job?', students use *have to* to talk about the duties and disadvantages of different professions, and about family rules. In the second presentation section, 'Problems, problems', *should* and *must* are presented in the context of a newspaper problem page. In the *Listening and speaking* section, students listen to a father and daughter talking about how they feel about the daughter leaving home at the age of 18. The *Reading and speaking* section contains an article about jobs and gender.

(NB – The way *Do's* /duːz/ is written in *Do's and Don'ts* breaks the normal rule of not using apostrophes with plurals.)

Language aims

Grammar – *have to* This might be the first time that your class has been introduced to *have to* to express obligation. *Must* is taught to express strong advice/suggestions and strong obligation. Students may use *must* to refer to a general obligation, when *have to* sounds more natural. *Should* is more appropriate for mild obligation or advice.

Common mistakes

**You've got hiccups. You must drink a glass of water.*
**My parents must work six days a week.*

Students often find the verb *have* a problem, because it has so many different uses. In Unit 2, it was seen as a full verb with two forms, one with *got* and one with *do/does*. In Unit 7, it was seen as an auxiliary verb in the Present Perfect. In this unit, it is seen operating with another verb in the infinitive.

should/must There is an introduction to modal auxiliary verbs on p136 of the Grammar Reference. Ask students to read this before you begin the presentation of *should* and *must* to make suggestions and give advice.

Both *must* and *should* present few problems of meaning, but learners often want to put an infinitive with *to*.

Common mistakes

**You should to do your homework.*
**You must to see the doctor.*

Vocabulary Two areas of collocation are dealt with: verbs and nouns that go together, and compound nouns.

Everyday English The functional situation, *At the doctor's*, is practised. It introduces the vocabulary of illnesses and revises the language of advice.

Notes on the unit

STARTER (SB p62)

The aim of this *Starter* is to find out how well students can use *have to*. Put students in pairs to make sentences using the prompts in the lists.

WHAT'S HIS JOB? (SB p62)

have to

> **ABOUT THE LISTENING**
>
> *Have to* is presented in the context of an interview with a country vet called Tristan. In the interview, Tristan talks about his routine and the responsibilities of his job.
>
> Vocabulary you may wish to pre-teach:
>
> *night shift* – a period of work at night
>
> *(be) on call* – (be) ready to work if necessary
>
> *surgery* – the place where a doctor or vet sees patients or sick animals
>
> *emergency* – a serious event that needs immediate action
>
> *triplets* – three animals or children that are born to one mother at the same time
>
> *have your own practice* – have your own vet's business

1 **T 8.1** [CD 2: Track 43] Students listen to Tristan talking about his job, and answer the questions. Ask students to discuss the questions with a partner before you get feedback.

Answer and tapescript

Tristan is a vet. He works in the country and likes his job.

T 8.1

I = Interviewer   T = Tristan

I What hours do you work, Tristan?

T It depends. I sometimes have to work at night but I usually work about eight to ten hours a day. It's hard to be exact.

I How often do you have to work at night?

T Well, I have to be on call two nights a week.

I And do you have to work at weekends?

T Sometimes. In this job you have to work very unsocial hours because you never know if there'll be an emergency.

I Tell me about your days.

T Well, there's always variety and that's good. In the mornings I work here in the surgery but in the afternoons I have to go out on visits – often, here in the countryside, to farms.

I What's the most difficult thing about the job?

T Well, it's the night shifts really. When I'm on call at night I don't have to stay in the surgery, I can go home but I can never relax. I can't watch TV or have a drink. And when I get back home after an emergency I find it really difficult to sleep.

I I hear the training's quite hard.

T Oh yes, I had to study for five years. I was at Liverpool University, and as part of my training I came here to do work experience and when I graduated, they offered me a job. I didn't have to look for a job.

I That was lucky.

T Yes, I know, but the other students on my course have all got good jobs now.

I Are you well-paid?

T It's not too bad! When I have my own practice it'll be better.

I And what are the secrets of being good at your job?

T Well, obviously you have to love working with animals, but also you have to be sensitive to their owners – pets are important to people and sometimes you have to give bad news. You have to stay calm in emergencies. Two nights ago I helped a sheep have triplets – three's quite unusual for a sheep. The farmer was delighted. When I save an animal's life, that's fantastic, no matter what time of night it is.

I And what are your plans for the future?

T Well, as I said, eventually I'd like to have my own practice. Anyway, nice to talk to you. Er, I've got to go now. Bye.

I Thanks, and bye.

2 The aim of this exercise is to focus students on the positive, negative, question, and past forms of *have to*. Put students in pairs to complete the sentences. They may need to listen to the recording again.

Answers

I sometimes **have to** work at night.
Do you have to work at weekends?
When I'm on call, I **don't have to** stay in the surgery.
I **had to** study for five years.
I **didn't have to** look for a job.

3 Focus attention on the examples in the *he* form. Ask students to change the rest of the sentences, working individually. Then check the answers.

Answers

He sometimes **has to** work at night.
Does he have to work at weekends?
When he's on call, he **doesn't have to** stay in the surgery.
He **had to** study for five years.
He **didn't have to** look for a job.

4 Elicit the missing words for the first sentence. Students work in pairs to complete the questions and answers. Then check the answers with the class.

Answers

1 'How long **does** he have to **work**?'
2 '**Does** he **have to** work at night?
3 'How long did he **have** to study?'
4 'Because he didn't **have to** look for a job.'
5 'What other things **does** Tristan **have to** do?' 'He has to **be sensitive to owners and stay calm in emergencies.**'

GRAMMAR SPOT (SB p63)

Read through the *Grammar spot* as a class. Get students to complete the sentences in exercise 3. Point out that *have to* uses the auxiliary verb *do/did* to make the question and negative forms.

> **Answers**
> 3 What time **do** you **have to** get up?
> I **don't have to** get up early.
> Yesterday, I **had to** get up early.

Refer students to Grammar Reference 8.1 on p136.

PRACTICE (SB p63)

Pronunciation

1 **T 8.2** [CD 2: Track 44] Ask students to listen to the sentences and notice the different pronunciations.

> **Tapescript**
> 1 I have a good job.   I have to work hard.
> 2 He has a nice car.   She has to get up early.
> 3 I had a good time.   I had to take exams.

Play the recording again. There are pauses to allow your class time to repeat the sentences. Drill the sentences around the class.

Talking about jobs

2 Check comprehension of all of the jobs in the box, using the photographs at the bottom of the page to help. Drill the pronunciation of the longer words as necessary. Focus attention on the questions in the table. Point out that the questions about education and training require the past form *had to*. Model the activity by choosing a job and getting students to ask you questions. Make sure they use *have to* in some of the questions. When they have guessed your job, put students in pairs to play the game. Monitor and check for accurate use of *have to*. Feed back on any common errors at the end of the task or in the next lesson.

3 Ask students to discuss as a class the jobs they would like to do, and those they wouldn't like to do. This second question, *Why?*, should prompt examples of *have to*. Notice that students are expected to use the third person plural here, not second person singular.

Talking about you

4 Introduce the discussion by asking one or two students some of the questions or by telling students about what you had to do when you lived at home with your parents. Put students in small groups of three or four to discuss the questions. In the feedback, ask one student from each group to summarize some of the more interesting comments made.

ADDITIONAL MATERIAL

Workbook Unit 8
These exercises could be done in class to give further practice, for homework, or in a later class as revision.
Exercises 1–5 *have to*

PROBLEMS, PROBLEMS (SB p64)

should /must

Should and *must* are presented in the context of a problem page. By matching and completing sentences, students produce 3-line dialogues using the modals.

You may need to pre-teach *bully* (someone who frightens or hurts smaller, weaker people), *coward* (someone who is not brave), and *ruin* (destroy).

Lead in by writing *Problem page* on the board, and asking *Where do you find a problem page? What sort of problems do people write about? Do you ever read problem pages?*

1 Ask students to match the problems and advice, and check their answers with a partner. In feedback, ask students what other advice they would give. If any students use *should* or *must* correctly then encourage them, but the aim at this stage is to set the context and find out what they know.

> **Answers**
> 1 b   2 d   3 a   4 c

2 Ask students to complete the sentences in pairs.
T 8.3 [CD 2: Track 45] Play the recording. Students listen and check.

Drill the sentences round the class, paying particular attention to the strong stress on the modals, and the wide intonation range used when giving advice. Then put students in pairs to practise.

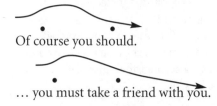

Of course you should.

… you must take a friend with you.

Answers and tapescript

1 **A** My ex-boyfriend is going to my best friend's wedding. He was horrible to me. Should I go?
  B Of course you should. But look happy and wear a fantastic dress! I think you **should** show your ex that you're fine without him.

2 **A** There's a group of bullies at school. They're making my life miserable.
  B You must tell your parents and your head teacher about this. You **shouldn't** let these cowards ruin your life.

3 **A** I've fallen in love with my boss. Should I tell him?
  B No, you shouldn't. It will only cause problems at work. I **don't think you should** have relationships with people you work with.

4 **A** I'm 16. I chat to a boy on the Internet. He wants to meet me. Should I go?
  B I don't think you should. You have no idea what he's really like. If you do go to meet him, you **must** take a friend with you. This is really important.

GRAMMAR SPOT (SB p64)

Put students in pairs to discuss the questions, then have a whole class discussion. Point out that *must* and *should* are followed by a base infinitive, without *to*, and without adding *-s* with *he* or *she*.

Answers

1 *You should go to the wedding* expresses a suggestion. *You must see a doctor* expresses a strong obligation – and, therefore, stronger advice.
2 We do not add *-s* with *he/she/it*, and we do not use *do/does* in the question and negative.

Refer students to Grammar Reference 8.2–8.4 on p136.

3 Check students understand the vocabulary used in each situation, and give them a few minutes to think of advice for each. Model the first situation by reading out the sentence and getting advice from students. Put them in groups of three to do the exercise.

Sample answers

Ankle: You should rest. / You must see a doctor.
Exams: You should relax and forget about them. / You should study hard.
Job: You should get another job. / You should try to make friends with the people.
Computer: You should buy another one. / You should take it back to the shop.
Parents: You should listen to them. / I don't think you should argue with them.
Car: You must take it to the garage. / You should get another one.

must or *should*?

1 Students work in pairs or small groups to complete the sentences. In feedback, check that the students are clear that *must* is used for strong obligation and *should* when it is the best thing to do.

Answers

1 must
2 should
3 must (in some countries seat belts may not be obligatory – in which case *should* is the best answer)
4 should
5 must

What do you think?

2 Students work in pairs or small groups to make sentences. You may wish them to write a few sentences for consolidation.

Sample answers

If you want to do well in life, you must/have to work hard.
If you want to learn English, you must/have to learn the grammar.
If you want to do well in life, you don't have to go to university.
If you want to learn English, you should buy a dictionary/ you shouldn't speak your language in class.
If you want to do well in life, you should work hard/ you should go to university.
If you want to keep fit, you should do some sport/ you shouldn't smoke.

EXTRA IDEA

Students work in groups to think of advice to give someone coming to their country for six months. Get them to make a poster with four or five *shoulds* or *musts* on it, for example *You should bring sunglasses, It's sunny*, or *You must try to learn the language*. Put the posters on the classroom walls for everybody to read.

ADDITIONAL MATERIAL

Workbook Unit 8
Exercises 6–7 *should*
Exercise 8 *have to* or *should*?
Exercise 9 *must*

Leaving home

ABOUT THE LISTENING

Students listen to a father, and then his daughter talking. The father is worried because his 18-year-old daughter has left to go to London. The daughter is concerned, and a little annoyed, because her parents worry too much and she needs to be independent. There are slight differences between what the father thinks his daughter's life is like, and the actual truth. Students must listen to both monologues intensively.

1 Divide students into small groups of four or five to discuss the questions. If you have a multinational class, try to mix nationalities within the groups so that there is a genuine information gap.

Sample answers

2 Homesickness, loneliness, shortage of money.

3 Ian Mitchell is a father and Evie Mitchell is his daughter. He's worried because she has left home and is living alone in a big city.

2 **T 8.4** [CD 2: Track 46] Ask students to look at the picture of Ian and his wife. Play the recording. Ask students to listen to Ian talking about his daughter. Set a gist question, for example *How does he feel about Evie leaving home?*

Put students in pairs to discuss the questions. You may need to play the recording again if students are unsure about some answers.

Answers and tapescript

1 She's 18. Four months ago.

2 She says she's having a great time.

3 She wanted to do a ballet course.

4 She's living in a flat.

5 She's living with her boyfriend.

6 He doesn't have a job. His name is Michael.

7 She dances in a theatre or club.

8 Because Michael has no job.

9 Sometimes – not a lot.

10 She says they should get a mobile so she can text them, and that they shouldn't worry.

T 8.4
Leaving home
Ian Mitchell

My daughter Evie is living in London now. She went there four months ago, and I'm really very worried about her. She says she's having a great time but I just think London's such a dangerous place for a young girl, and she's still only 18. She shouldn't live so far away from home. Her mother went with her to help her look for somewhere to live. But I didn't go. I

don't like London – I don't like big cities.

Why did she have to go there? I don't understand. She says she wants to be a dancer, and she's doing a sort of course, a ballet course or something. But ballet isn't a real job, and you don't earn much money being a dancer, do you? She's a clever girl. I think she should go to university.

She's living in a flat in London – with her boyfriend, I think, and I don't like that at all! We've never met the boyfriend – Michael, I think his name is. He hasn't got a job and so Evie has to earn some extra money – she works at the weekends as a dancer in a theatre or club, I think. I just hope it's a nice place.

She phones home sometimes, but not a lot, and we phone her, but so often her mobile's turned off or she doesn't answer. When I do manage to talk to her, she just tells us that we should get a mobile so she can text us. She says we shouldn't worry. How can we not worry? We're her parents, we miss her and of course we worry, sometimes I can't sleep at night. She really must come home more often.

3 **T 8.5** [CD 2: Track 47] Ask students to look at the picture of Evie. Ask *Where is she? What is she doing? Do you think she's happy? Why?*

Play the recording. Ask students to listen to Evie, and look at the questions in exercise 2. Ask students to notice which answers are different from her father's.

Put students in pairs to discuss the answers.

Answers and tapescript

1 Four months ago.

2 Yes, she loves it. There's lots to do and see.

3 Because she wants to be a dancer.

4 She's living in a small flat.

5 She's living with another dance student – Francine.

6 He is doing the same ballet course as Evie. His name is Marco.

7 She teaches children's dance classes.

8 Because London is expensive.

9 Three times a week.

10 She says they must come to London to visit her. She thinks they should get a mobile so that she can send them text messages.

T 8.5
Leaving home
Evie Mitchell

I want to be a professional dancer, so I came to London four months ago to start a course at the English National Ballet School. If you want a good dance career, you have to go to a good school and you have to start young – I'm almost 19, nearly too old! I know my parents are worried about me living in London, but it isn't dangerous. You just have to be careful, that's all. It was difficult in the beginning. I didn't know anybody, and London's such a big place. But I love it now. There's lots to do and see.

I'm living in a small flat near the ballet school with Francine, another dance student. We're good friends now. And I've also got a boyfriend! His name's Marco and he's doing the same course. He still lives with his parents, quite close to our flat. His parents are really kind, and I often spend the evenings with them. I want to take Marco home to meet my parents. But the train journey is expensive. And I haven't got much money. London's really expensive, so Francine and I have to work every weekend. We teach children's dance classes at a school nearby. It's good fun, actually!

I phone my parents three times a week! My dad always sounds so worried! He shouldn't be. I try to tell him not to worry but he doesn't listen. I love my mum and dad very much, but I can't live at home for the rest of my life. They really must come to London to visit me. And I think they should get a mobile. Then I could send them text messages, and maybe they wouldn't worry so much.

What do you think?

Put students in small groups to discuss the questions. Ask one student to lead the discussion. It is that student's responsibility to ask the questions and make sure everybody speaks. Ask another student to be prepared to summarize what the group said for the class at the end.

Roleplay

The secret of a good roleplay is plenty of preparation time, and a genuine opinion gap. Divide the class into equal numbers of A and B groups, with about four students in each group. Group A students are the 'parents' and group B students are the 'Evies'. Tell the 'parent' groups to make a list of five or six concerns that they may have. They can refer to what Ian actually said on the recording if they want to. Tell the 'Evie' group to think of five or six things they can say to reassure their parents. Give the students five minutes to prepare. Monitor and prompt. You could write the following language on the board for students to refer to if you wish:

I'm worried about …
I'm concerned that …
I don't think you should …
What will you do if …
You shouldn't worry about …
… won't be a problem
I'll be OK if …

When students are ready, tell them to find a partner from an opposite group. Alternatively, you divide them into pairs, with a parent and an Evie in each pair. Give a clear start signal. At the end, ask the 'parents' whether they feel reassured.

Letters and emails – Formal and informal expressions

The aim of this writing section is to write a formal letter and an informal email using formal and informal expressions.

1 Put students in pairs to match beginnings and endings, and discuss the questions.

> **Answers**
> 1 a/b/c/g
> 2 f
> 3 a/b/d/g
> 4 e
> 5 a/b
> 6 a/b/d/g
> 2 and 4, e and f are formal. The others are informal.
> 3 and 6, a and d would only be used in emails.

A formal letter

2 Ask students to read the formal letter. Ask some simple questions, for example *Who's written the letter? What's her address? Who is she writing to? Why is she writing?*

Ask students to complete the letter with words from the box. Let students check their answers in pairs.

> **Answers**
> 1 advertisement   6 application form
> 2 interested in   7 some information
> 3 frequently   8 to hearing
> 4 However   9 sincerely
> 5 to improve

3 Ask students in pairs to compare a formal letter in English with conventions in their own language. Elicit differences in feedback. Then summarize a few rules for students.

> **Answers (a few rules)**
> The writer's address and the date are in the top right hand corner.
> The recipient's full name and address is top left but lower than the date.
> If you know the name of the person you are writing to, use it. Just use the surname. So for a man, write *Mr Smith*, and for a woman *Ms Smith*. You can also write *Mrs Smith* for a married woman, and *Miss Smith* for an unmarried woman, but only if you know that this is how they prefer to be addressed.
> If you don't know the recipient's name, write *Dear Sir* for a man, and *Dear Madam* for a woman, or *Dear Sir or Madam* if you are not sure of their sex.
> If you start a letter with *Dear Mr/Ms Smith*, end with *Yours sincerely*, your signature, and your full name. If you start with *Dear Sir or Madam*, end with *Yours faithfully*, your signature,

and your full name. It helps if you remember that **f**aithfully is more **f**ormal (they both begin with '**f**').

Use formal language, no slang, and avoid abbreviating, so write *I would* not *I'd*.

Use standard conventions. For example, *I look forward to hearing from you.*

An informal email

4 Ask students to read the email. Ask *Why is Concetta writing to Rob?*

Ask students in pairs to match highlighted lines from the email with formal phrases in the letter.

Answers
I'm thinking of coming = I am interested in coming
use English a lot at work = use English frequently in my job
I think I need some extra lessons = I now feel that it is necessary to continue my studies
I especially want my pronunciation to be better = I would especially like to improve my pronunciation
an ad = an advertisement
Can you send me some more information about = Please could you send me further information about
I'd also love to = I would also like to
Can't wait to hear from you = I look forward to hearing from you
Love = Yours sincerely

5 Ask students in pairs to match the informal and formal phrases.

Answers
It was great to hear from you.	Thank you for your letter of 1st November.
Thanks for...	Thank you for...
I want to ask about....	I would like to enquire about...
I'm sorry about...	I apologize for...
I'm sorry to have to tell you that...	I regret to inform you that...
I'm sending you a copy of...	Please find enclosed a photocopy of...
If you need any more help,	If you require further assistance,

6 Ask students to write a letter to the language school. Give students a few minutes to prepare first. Tell them to think about how to express their address and date, and to think about their own language learning history and reasons for wanting to learn more English. Once students have written their letter, ask them to write the email.

You may wish to set these writing tasks for homework.

Jobs for the boys ... and girls

ABOUT THE TEXT
This is a jigsaw reading. In groups, students read about either a female plumber or a male nanny, then compare their text with a partner. This creates an information gap which should create lots of speaking opportunities for students.

The Equal Opportunities Commission, or EOC (/iː/ /əʊ/ /siː/), is a government-funded agency working to eliminate sex discrimination in the UK. It also fights racism, and any other form of prejudice.

You may wish to pre-teach the following phrases: *recommend a career in …* (advise someone to get a job for life in …), *cross the gender gap at work* (change to a job which is not typical for someone of your gender or sex), *ignore the prejudice* (take no notice of the unreasonable opinions against you).

1 Ask students to look at the jobs in the box. Use mime or examples to check ones they don't know, and point out difficult pronunciations, (*plumber* /ˈplʌmə/; *secretary* /ˈsekrətri/).

Put students in small groups to discuss the questions, then have a brief class feedback. Find out how 'traditional' your students' views are.

2 Ask students to read the first part of the article, and find answers to the questions. Let students compare answers in pairs before discussing as a class.

Answers
1 'Free to Choose'. It means that any individual has the right to choose to work in any job.
2 They are still recommending some careers only for boys and others for girls.
3 Students' own opinions. In Britain, science subjects are traditionally for boys, and languages are more typical for girls.
4 Childcare for girls, and building, engineering, and plumbing for boys.

3 Divide the class into equal numbers of A and B groups, with about four students in each group. Ask students to read their text quickly.

4 Ask students to discuss and answer the questions in their groups. They will need to keep looking back at the text to find the answers.

Once students have found answers to all the questions, pair As with Bs so that they can compare their texts. As the texts are quite short, you could let students read their partner's text once they have discussed the answers.

Answers

Jenny
1 Psychology
2 Plumbing. She was fascinated when watching a plumber working, and wanted to learn how to do it.
3 Male plumbers. They think it's a job for big, strong men.
4 Yes. She loves fixing things.
5 Try it, but you have to be tough.

Alex
1 Engineering
2 He's a nanny. He has always loved children.
3 Nanny agencies and some parents. They think that men can't look after children as well as women.
4 Yes. He says it's wonderful to be part of a child's development.
5 Go for it, ignore the prejudice, and show people you can do it.

What do you think?

Put students in small groups to discuss the questions. Ask one student to lead the discussion. It is that student's responsibility to ask the questions and make sure everybody speaks. Ask another student to be prepared to summarize what the group said for the class at the end.

ADDITIONAL MATERIAL

Workbook Unit 8

Exercise 11 Vocabulary – Men and women

VOCABULARY AND PRONUNCIATION (SB p68)

Words that go together – applying for a job

1 Read the introduction as a class. See if students can give you any other common verbs + complements. Put students in pairs to match the verbs and complements in the two boxes. Check all the answers as a class in the feedback.

Answers

interview somebody for a job
study hard / study engineering
earn a lot of money
take care of children
do engineering / do a lot of training
change career
work hard / work together / with somebody
spend time with someone / spend a lot of money
get on together / with somebody

2 **T 8.6** [CD 2: Track 48] Ask students to look at the photo on the page. Ask *What's the situation? What questions is she asking him? What is he saying?*

Ask students to read through the questions. Play the recording. Ask students to listen, then put students in pairs to discuss the answers to the questions.

Answers and tapescript

1 Because he loves children, and because his mother died and he had to help his father look after his younger brother and sister.
2 One year
3 One
4 How to change nappies, cook healthy meals, and how to play with children and organize their days.
5 Meet Jack and see how well Alex gets on with him.
6 Do I have to wear a uniform?

T 8.6

R = Rachel Foley (Jack's mother)   A=Alex

R Good morning, Alex. Nice to meet you. I have to say that this is a first! Interviewing a man for this job.
A I know it's, it's unusual.
R Well, certainly a man has never applied for it before. Tell me, have you always been a nanny?
A No, not at all. I was studying engineering in Stockholm, and I knew I could earn a lot of money as an engineer but it was boring, so I stopped and decided to look at other careers.
R OK, I understand that. But why a nanny? Why did you choose this career, a career in childcare?
A Well, obviously it's because I love children, but it's much more than that. You see my mother died when I was just twelve years old and I had to help my father take care of my younger brother and sister.
R Ah, I see. So you didn't have to do a lot of training to be a nanny?
A Oh yes, I did. I had to train for a year. I had to learn how to look after children properly. Actually, I was the only boy on the course – so I really enjoyed it!
R So what kind of things did you learn?
A Well, you know, how to change nappies ...
R Very important!
A How to cook healthy meals for children. How to play with them and organize their days. We worked hard and we all felt fully-qualified for the job at the end of the course.
R Well, before I offer you the job I'd like you to meet Jack and spend some time with him to see how well you two get on together.
A I'd love to.
R Well, let's go and meet him. He's adorable! Oh I forgot – do you have any questions for me?
A Just one. Do I have to wear a uniform?
R No, that's not necessary. You look just fine.
A Thank you very much.
R OK, let's ....

3 Play the recording again. Ask students to describe the interview with their partner. Monitor and make sure students are using words that go together accurately.

Compound nouns

4   Read the example of the compound noun with the class and ask students if they can think of any other examples.

T 8.7 [CD 2: Track 49] Play the recording. Ask students to listen and mark the stress on the compound nouns.

Answers and tapescript

<u>child</u>care   <u>job</u> interview   <u>training</u> course

Play the recording again. Ask students to listen and repeat. Emphasize the point that the stress is on the first word. Make sure that students exaggerate the stress pattern as their natural inclination is to give both words equal stress.

5   Students now work in pairs to match the nouns to make compound nouns. Tell students that English people have to check whether compounds are spelt as one word, two words, or hyphenated, and dictionaries sometimes disagree!

T 8.8 [CD 2: Track 50] Play the recording so that students can listen and check. Ask students to repeat the list, making sure that the stress is on the first word.

Answers and tapescript

hairdresser	flight attendant
countryside	housewife
text message	train journey
problem page	firefighter

6   On their own or in pairs, students think of sentences to define the compound nouns. Give some more examples if necessary. When students are ready, ask a few individuals to give a definition, and see if the rest of the class can guess the compound.

Some sample definitions

This is a message you send someone on their mobile phone.
This is in a newspaper – people write letters and ask for advice.
This person stays at home and looks after children.

ADDITIONAL MATERIAL

Workbook Unit 8

Exercise 10   Reading – Fired from his job

Exercise 12   Vocabulary – Job descriptions

At the doctor's

This section deals with the vocabulary and functional language of going to the doctor's. Lead in to the situation by asking students about their own experiences, without getting too personal, for example:

When did you last go to the doctor's?   What's your doctor like?

Alternatively, you could introduce the situation by writing a few of the symptoms of a cold or 'flu on the board; *a sore throat, a runny nose, a high temperature, a terrible headache*, and telling students that they are all doctors. For example, say *I've got a terrible headache, what should I do?* and elicit advice from different students. This introduces vocabulary, revises giving advice, and previews the speaking activity at the end of the section.

1   Read out the phrases in the box. Note that *diarrhoea* is pronounced /daɪəˈrɪə/. Check students understand the words.

Ask students to work in pairs to match the illnesses with the pictures.

2   Get students to read through the list of symptoms. Check comprehension of *to sneeze, to blow your nose, glands, swollen, to swallow*. Get students to complete the table with the names of the illness from exercise 1.

T 8.9 [CD 2: Track 51] Play the recording. Students listen and check their answers. Then put students in pairs to practise saying the language.

Answers and tapescript

Symptoms	Illnesses
1 I can't stop sneezing, and blowing my nose.	I've got **a cold**.
2 I keep being sick, and I've got diarrhoea.	I've got **food poisoning**.
3 It hurts when I walk.	I've **twisted my ankle**.
4 I've got stomach-ache and I keep going to the toilet.	I've got **diarrhoea**.
5 My glands are swollen, and it hurts when I swallow.	I've got a **sore throat**.
6 I've got a temperature, my whole body aches, and I feel awful.	I've got '**flu**.

3   Pre-teach/check the following vocabulary from the recording: *to eat something that disagrees with you* (= to eat something that makes you feel ill), *properly cooked* (= completely cooked), *take things easy* (= relax), *a prescription*. Give students time to read the questions.

T 8.10 [CD 2: Track 52] Play the recording. Ask students to listen and answer the questions. Let students check their answers in pairs before discussing as a class.

4 Give students time to read through the gapped sentences. Play the recording again, pausing at the end of each gapped line in the exercise to give students time to write their answers. Check the answers with the class.

5 Students look at the tapescript on p123 and practise the conversation in pairs. You could point out and drill the doctor's questions first, noting that they are mostly in the Present Perfect.

6 Ask students to imagine they feel a bit ill and write down a list of symptoms. Put them in pairs, and nominate one student to be the doctor, the other to be a patient. Students roleplay the situation. You could change pairs to give them more practice.

Don't forget!

Workbook Unit 8

Exercise 13 Pronunciation – Words that rhyme

Exercises 14–15 Check it

Grammar Reference
Look at the exercises on SB p136–137 as a class, or set for homework. The answers are on TB p156.

Word list
Remind your students of the Word list for this unit on SB p155. They could translate the words, learn them at home, or transfer some of the words to their vocabulary notebook.

Pronunciation Book Unit 8

Time clauses • *if*
Hot verbs *make/do/take/get*
Directions

Going places

Introduction to the unit

The title of this unit is 'Going places'. The future form *will* and its use in time and conditional clauses is introduced and practised in the context of two people talking about their plans for a gap year. The *Reading and speaking* text is an article about travel addicts – people who love travelling. The *Listening and speaking* is a radio programme which interviews people who *don't* like travelling.

Language aims

Grammar – *will* The use of *will* to express a future intention, or a decision made at the moment of speaking, was presented in Unit 5. In this unit we see *will* as an auxiliary of the future, where it refers to a future fact. The distinction is very subtle, and not always noticeable.

Anna will be twenty-one next year is an example of a future fact.
I'll phone you when I arrive is an example of a decision made as you speak.
I'll see you tomorrow can have elements of both meanings.

First conditional In this unit, the first conditional is presented, and in Unit 11 the second conditional is introduced. The problem with conditional sentences is that there are two clauses to get right – *will* is used in the result clause, but is not used in the condition clause, even though it too often refers to future time. In many languages, a future form is used in both clauses.

Common mistakes

*If it will rain, we'll stay at home.
*If it rains, we stay at home.

Time clauses This unit looks at clauses introduced by the time phrases *while*, *when*, *before*, *until*, *as soon as*, and *after*. These phrases are often used to refer to the future but generally they are followed by a present tense. Speakers of Germanic languages confuse *when* and *if*, as they are translated by the same word. Tense usage in time clauses presents the same problems as in the first conditional, i.e. a future verb form is not used in the time clause, even though it might refer to future time.

Common mistakes

*When it rains, we'll stay at home.
*When I will arrive, I'll phone you.
*As soon as I arrive, I phone you.

Vocabulary This looks at Hot verbs – verbs which are commonly used. It looks at common collocations of the verbs *make*, *do*, *take*, and *get*.

Everyday English Students practise the vocabulary and functional language involved in giving directions.

Notes on the unit

STARTER (SB p70)

The aim of this activity is to preview the use of *will* and *going to* in time clauses by getting students to talk about the future in a personalized activity. Ask students to work in pairs to make statements. Note how well students use the structures in the feedback.

> **Sample answers**
> If the weather is nice this weekend, I think I'll go for a walk / go to the beach.
> If the weather isn't nice this weekend, I'll probably stay at home / go to the cinema.
> When I get home tonight, I'm going to watch TV / do my homework.

A GAP YEAR (SB p70)

Time and conditional clauses

> **ABOUT THE TEXT**
> Time and conditional clauses are contextualized in two short monologues by British teenagers, who talk about their plans to travel (James) and work in an old people's home (Jessie) during their gap year.
>
> Gap years are popular in the UK. Many school-leavers take a year off between school and further studies in order to travel, do voluntary work, or get a job to save money for university or college. Increasingly, as the *Reading and speaking* text shows later, older people who feel they need a career break are taking gap years.
>
> Pre-teach the following phrases: *book a flight* (reserve a ticket on a plane), *keep in touch* (write, phone, or email to tell people you are OK), *term* (part of a school/university year)

1 Ask students to look at the photos of James and Jessie. Set the scene by asking questions, for example
   Where are they going?
   What are their plans?

2 **T 9.1** [CD 3: Track 2] Ask students to work in pairs to match the sentence halves. Play the recording so that they can check their answers.

> **Answers and tapescript**
> Before I go to university, I'm going to travel round South America.
> As soon as I have enough money, I'll book a flight to Rio de Janeiro.
> When I'm travelling around, I'll phone home twice a week.
> If I don't keep in touch, I know my parents will worry!

T 9.1
James
Well, I speak Spanish quite well, so before I go to university, I'm going to travel round South America. I've got an old school friend in Brazil and a penfriend in Guatemala, so I have some people to visit. I also want to go and see the rainforest! I'm working in a local restaurant at the moment, but as soon as I have enough money, I'll book a flight to Rio de Janeiro. I'll spend about a month in Brazil, then go on to Guatemala, I think. I'm so looking forward to going. It'll be fantastic! When I'm travelling around, I'll phone home twice a week. If I don't keep in touch, I know my parents will worry!

3 Ask students in pairs to cover the orange box, and say the sentences.

4 **T 9.2** [CD 3: Track 3] Ask students to work in pairs to match the sentence halves for Jessie. Play the recording so that they can check their answers. Then get students to cover the orange box and say the sentences.

> **Answers and tapescript**
> I'm going to work in an old people's home as soon as I finish school.
> I'll also live in the home while I'm working there.
> I'll work until I've saved enough money for a holiday.
> I'm going to Greece with some friends after the job ends.
> I won't be tired if I have a holiday before term starts!

T 9.2
Jessie
I want to do something useful before I go to college next year, so I'm going to work in an old people's home as soon as I finish school. My job is to work with the nurses and help the people get dressed, and I'll go for walks with them – things like that. The job starts in July and it's for at least nine months. I'll also live in the home while I'm working there. I'll work until I've saved enough money for a holiday. I'm going to Greece with some friends after the job ends. I'll need to relax. I won't be tired if I have a holiday before term starts!

5 **T 9.1** and **T 9.2** Play the recordings again. You could play and pause the recording for students to repeat or you could drill some of the sentences open class.

Ask students to work in pairs. Discuss each task as a class before moving on to the next one.

Answers

1 James: <u>Before</u>, <u>As soon as</u>, <u>When</u>, <u>If</u>
  Jessie: <u>after</u>, <u>as soon as</u>, <u>if</u>, <u>until</u>, <u>while</u>
2 They are present tenses (Present Simple, Present Perfect, Present Continuous) but they refer to the future. This is because in time and conditional clauses the verb after *if*, *when*, etc. stays in the present form.
3 For James, the first, second, and fourth clauses in the box use *will* to refer to future time. The third clause uses *going to* + infinitive to talk about a future intention. For Jessie, the first clause uses *going to* + infinitive to talk about a future intention, and the fourth uses the Present Continuous for a future arrangement. The other clauses use *will*.
4 The first sentence with *When* expresses something that is sure to happen. The second sentence with *If* expresses something that is possible.

Refer students to Grammar Reference 9.1–9.3 on p138.

What if...?

1 Model and drill the example sentence from the first *If* column around the class. Then ask students for suggestions as to how to make other sentences from the prompts in the first column. As you elicit each sentence, model and drill. Pay careful attention to contractions and sentence stress.

If I don't go out so much, I'll do more work.

Answers

If I do more work, I'll pass my exams.
If I pass my exams, I'll go to university.
If I go to university, I'll study medicine.
If I study medicine, I'll become a doctor.
If I become a doctor, I'll save people's lives.

Put students in pairs to do the same with the sentences on the right.

Answers

If I spend less on new clothes, I'll have more money.
If I have more money, I'll save some every week.
If I save some every week, I'll be rich when I'm thirty.
If I'm rich when I'm thirty, I'll start my own business.
If I start my own business, I'll make a lot of money.
If I make a lot of money, I'll retire when I'm fifty.

What will you do if... ?

2 Read the introduction and the ideas as a class. Do the first three or four questions and answers as a class, so students see what they have to do, then put them in pairs to improvise a dialogue. You could ask one or two pairs to act out their dialogue for the class.

T 9.3 [CD 3: Track 4] Play the recording. Students listen and compare their dialogues.

Tapescript

A I'm going on safari to Africa.
B Oh dear, what will you do if you get chased by wild animals?
A It'll be OK. I'll be in a car, so I won't get chased. But I hope I'll see lots of wild animals.
B But what if it's the rainy season?
A Don't be silly. I won't go when it's the rainy season.
B Oh, but what if there are lots of insects? You hate insects.
A I'm going to take lots of insect cream. It won't be a problem.
B And the sun – it'll be so hot. What if you get sunburnt?
A I'm going to take lots of suncream too. I'll be fine.
B But it'll be so frightening. What if you get lost in the bush?
A Look, I won't be alone. I'll have a driver and a guide.
B But what if your car breaks down?
A I'm sure it won't, and if it does, the driver will mend it.
B Ooh, but at night! What if you have to sleep in a tent?
A I'll be happy to sleep in a tent, under the stars. It'll be exciting.
B Rather you than me. All those wild animals and mosquitos – ugh!
A Well, I'll love it. I just know I will!

Refer students to the tapescript on p123. Students practise the conversation with a partner.

3 Extend the practice by getting students to make a conversation in pairs about one of the topics. Elicit a few ideas to get them started. Have one or two pairs act out their conversation for the class at the end.

Discussing grammar

4 Do the first two sentences as a class, then ask students to do the rest in pairs.

Answers

1 before	6 when / as soon as / if
2 when / as soon as	7 until
3 if	8 before
4 until	9 until
5 If	10 before / when

Talking about you

5 Do one or two examples, then give students five minutes to think of ways of completing the sentences. Put students in pairs or groups to compare their answers.

When I get to Rio . . .

6 Read the introduction as a class. Ask students to work in pairs or small groups to complete the dialogue.

T 9.4 [CD 3: Track 5] Play the recording so that students can check their answers. Then put students in pairs to practise the conversation.

Answers and tapescript

Mum Bye, my darling. Have a good flight to Rio. Remember, we're expecting a phone call from you this evening **when** you get there!

James I'll ring you **as soon as** I arrive at Diego's house.

Mum Good. What time will you get there?

James Well, the flight takes 12 hours. **If** the plane arrives on time, I'll be there about 11.30 – Rio time, of course. **If** you're asleep when I ring, I'll leave a message on the answerphone.

Mum I won't be asleep!

James OK! OK! Don't worry, Mum. I'll be fine.

Mum All right. But **when** you travel around the country, will you remember to call us regularly? Make sure you phone twice a week.

James Of course! And I'll phone you **if** I run out of money!

Mum Cheeky! But you must look after yourself, darling. Give my best wishes to Diego's parents, and don't forget to give them this present **when** you get to their house.

James Don't worry. I won't. Oh, they're calling my flight! Love you, Mum. Bye!

Mum Love you, James. Take care!

ADDITIONAL MATERIAL

Workbook Unit 9

Exercise 1 Present Simple or *will*?

Exercises 2–4 Conditional clauses

Exercises 5–8 Time clauses

VOCABULARY AND SPEAKING (SB p73)

Hot verbs – *make, do, take,* and *get*

These verbs are 'hot' because they are very common and have many different collocations. *Make* and *do* are a source of confusion for many students. We use *make* when there is an idea of creativity (*make a cake*), and *do* when there is an idea of work (*do homework*). *Take* collocates with *time, medicine,* and *photos. Get* can mean *arrive at, receive,* and *become* (when there is a sense of

change from one state to another). However, there are many exceptions, and *make,* in particular, is used in a lot of fixed metaphorical expressions.

Lead in by writing *make, do, take,* and *get* on the board and putting students in small groups to think of as many phrases as they can using these words. Give them a time limit of three or four minutes. You could give each group a different word.

Read the introduction as a class and get students to find the examples in the text on page 72.

Make and *do*

1 Elicit a word or phrase that goes with *do,* e.g. *do the washing-up.* Then ask the students to work in pairs to complete the table. Check the answers with the class.

Answers

MAKE	DO
friends	the washing-up
up your mind	a course
a fortune	me a favour
a noise	my best

2 Ask students to read sentence 1 and elicit the correct phrase from exercise 1 (*do the washing-up*). Then ask which tense students need to use and elicit the Past Simple. Elicit the correct form (*did the washing-up*). Students work individually to complete the rest of the exercise. Remind them to think about the form of the verb they need to use.

T 9.5 [CD 3: Track 6] Play the recording, pausing at the end of each sentence, to let students check their answers.

Answers and tapescript

1 I **did the washing-up** last night. It's your turn tonight.
2 Please tell the children not to **make a noise.** I'm trying to work.
3 I **did my best** but I still failed the exam.
4 I don't know if I want the chicken or the fish. I just can't **make up my mind.**
5 My sister's very popular. She **makes friends** very easily.
6 Could you **do me favour** and give me a lift to the station? Thanks.
7 My grandfather **made a fortune** in business. He's a rich man.
8 I'm going to **do a course** in Spanish before I go to Spain.

take and *get*

3 Elicit a word or phrase that goes with *get,* e.g. *get a cold.* Then ask the students to work in pairs to complete the table. Check the answers with the class.

4   Ask students to read sentence 1 and elicit the correct phrase from exercise 3 (*take a photo*). Then ask which form students need to use and elicit the infinitive. Elicit the correct form (*take a photo*). Students work individually to complete the rest of the exercise. Remind them to think about the form of the verb they need to use.

T 9.6   [CD 3: Track 7] Play the recording, pausing at the end of each sentence, to let students check their answers.

Talking about you

5   This section consolidates the hot verbs and gets students to practise them in a personalized way. Focus attention on the cartoon at the bottom of the page. Remind students that we say *do (your) homework*, not **make your homework*. Ask students to read sentence 1 and elicit the correct verbs (*take* and *get*). Then ask which form students need to use and elicit the infinitive. Elicit the correct forms (*take* and *get*). Students work individually to complete the rest of the exercise. Remind them to think about the form of the verb they need to use. With weaker classes, remind students to use *does* in sentence 6 because it's a subject question.

T 9.7   [CD 3: Track 8] Play the recording, pausing at the end of each sentence, to let students check their answers.

Get a student to ask you the first two questions in exercise 5 and give true answers. Put students into pairs and get them to ask and answer the questions. If you have time, get students to report back about their partner in a feedback session, e.g. *It takes Yuko about half an hour to get ready in the morning.*

READING AND SPEAKING (SB p74)

Travel addicts

Lead in by writing three or four interesting places that you have been to in your life on the board. Tell students to ask you questions about the places, for example *When did you go there? How many times have you been there? What did you like about the place?*

1   Ask students to write down reasons why people travel abroad. Elicit ideas from the class, then discuss the question as a class.

2   Check comprehension of *gap year*. Ask students to look at the title and read the introduction, and then discuss the questions as a class.

3   Ask students to read the article quickly to get the general idea. Set a gist question, for example *How does Ben feel about travelling?*

Then ask students to put the sentences in the right space in the article. Let students check their ideas in pairs. In feedback, ask what clues helped students fill each gap.

Answers
a 3 b 2 c 1 d 4

4   Put students into pairs. Get them to read the first sentence of Ben's summary and elicit the mistake (Ben returned six months ago). Students read the rest of the summaries, and find and correct the mistakes. Check the answers with the class (corrections are given in brackets).

Answers
BEN
Ben returned from his travels just <u>three</u> (six) months ago and now he wants to go travelling again. He spent <u>two years</u> (one/a year) travelling with his girlfriend, Jane. They visited <u>31</u> (14) countries, including Australia, Fiji and <u>Vietnam</u> (Cambodia) and <u>got married</u> (spent Ben's 31st birthday) on a beach in Thailand. It was the best time of their lives but <u>now they are happy to settle down back home</u> (coming back was awful).

SANDIE and IAN
Ben met Sandie and her boyfriend, Ian, when he was in <u>Sydney</u> (Thailand). They <u>are hoping to marry next year</u> (got married) and <u>spend</u> (spent) a year travelling <u>again</u> on their honeymoon. They both have stressful jobs as <u>lawyers</u> (IT consultants) but <u>they enjoy their work</u> (work isn't so important anymore).

REBECCA
Ben met Rebecca <u>when she was working for a computer company</u> in Australia (during her round-the-world trip). Now she's back home and <u>looking for work</u> (having trouble readjusting to life). <u>She's enjoying telling all her friends and family about her time abroad.</u> (Her parents and friends just aren't interested in her experiences.)

What do you think?

Divide students into small groups of four or five to discuss the questions. Elicit a range of opinions in a short feedback session.

Discussion

Model the activity by writing your own list of places you would like to visit on the board. Talk about them briefly.

Then give students three or four minutes to write their own lists. Put students in small groups of four or five to discuss their choices.

You could turn this activity into a series of mini-presentations. Ask individual students to stand up and tell the class where they would like to go to and why. Establish which places are most popular with the whole class in a short feedback session.

PHOTOCOPIABLE MATERIAL: EXTRA IDEA
Song **After T 9.7** [CD 3: Track 9]
***Come away with me*, TB p133**
This is intended as an informal and fun activity, which you may like to include at the end of a lesson. Photocopy the sheet on TB p133 and give a copy to each student. Work through the activities, allowing students to work in pairs wherever possible and encouraging plenty of discussion. You could do the final exercise with the whole class to round off the activity. The answers to the activities are on TB p151.

ADDITIONAL MATERIAL

Workbook Unit 9

Exercise 11 Reading – Travelling at the speed of light

LISTENING AND SPEAKING (SB p76)

Going nowhere

ABOUT THE LISTENING
Students listen to a retired couple, a worker in a vegetarian restaurant, and a French builder as they are interviewed on a radio programme about why they don't like travelling. The tasks are listening to check predictions, and listening for specific information.

The first speakers, Roger and Mary, come from Avonford, a pretty village in rural south-west England. Annabel is from Bristol, a major port and city in south-west England. Jean-Claude is from rural Provence in southern France. He mentions the Cote d'Azur, the Mediterranean coast of France.

The recording is quite long but it breaks down into three sections when the interviewer starts speaking to a new person/set of people. You might want to pre-teach the following vocabulary from the recording: *I don't see the point* (= I don't understand the purpose/use of something), *too much trouble, delay* (n), *not worth it* (= not good, useful, or enjoyable), *a mountain of mail* (= a lot of post), *a sailor, the Navy, tourist sights, to destroy, bad for the environment, to get cross* (= angry), *to put someone off something* (= to make someone not want to do something), *climate, curious, can't be bothered* (= don't want to make the effort).

1 Ask students *Do you know anyone who doesn't like travelling?* and elicit some examples. Put students into groups of three of four. Focus attention on the examples in the Student's Book and then get students to continue thinking of reasons for not travelling. Get one student to write down the reasons for their group.

Elicit a range of reasons from the class and write them on the board.

Possible answers

People with a business, for example a restaurant or hotel, don't have the time to leave.

Some people don't like foreign food.

Some people feel uncomfortable in a foreign culture, e.g. because of language problems or strange customs.

Travelling is tiring, especially for older people.

Tourist destinations are often crowded and noisy.

Travelling is expensive.

Flights get delayed.

2 Ask students to look at the photos. Ask *Where are the people? Why do you think these people dislike travelling?* If students give any new reasons in their answers, add them to the list on the board.

T 9.8 [CD 3: Track 10] Play the recording through once. Get students to compare their predictions with the reasons from exercise 1. Elicit each speaker's reason for not wanting to travel.

Answers and tapescript

1 Students' own answers.
2 Roger has already seen the world because he was in the Navy and he sailed round the world ten times.
   Annabel thinks that travel destroys tourist sights.
   Jean-Claude thinks France can give him everything he wants.

T 9.8
Going nowhere
I = Interviewer   R = Roger   M = Mary
A = Annabel   JC = Jean-Claude

I Good afternoon and welcome to this week's programme *People and Places*. Now usually we interview people who have been somewhere interesting, but today we're talking to people who prefer to stay at home! Nowadays, because travel is so cheap and easy, most people have been abroad, or are planning to go in the future. So, it seems a very strange idea to many of us not to go anywhere. So why don't some people like travelling at all? We find out why. ...

I Here I am in Roger and Mary's little cottage in the village of Avonford. Now, you're both retired, aren't you?

R Yes, that's right.

I So what's the problem?

M Well, the problem is that Roger won't go anywhere! Here we are with the time and the money to do things, and I can't get him out of the house!

R Now, that's not true, Mary. We go and visit our friends and grandchildren, and we go shopping.

M That's not what I mean, Roger!

I Why don't you like travelling, Roger?

R Well, I don't see the point. I have everything here. We live in a nice part of the world. I love my home. My friends are all in the village. I'm always busy, and I never get bored. Going away is just too much trouble. There are delays at the airport, flights are cancelled, it's just not worth it. When you get home you have a mountain of mail and the grass needs cutting. Anyway, you can see everything on TV these days.

M And we couldn't go abroad when we were younger, because we had four children and no money.

R That's right.

M But the craziest thing is that he has a travel secret.

I Oh, what's that?

M Well, when he was a teenager, he was a sailor!

R Yes, I was in the Navy for five years, and I sailed round the world ten times. So I saw the world 45 years ago. I don't need to see it again!

...

I I'm now with Annabel, who works in a vegetarian restaurant in Bristol. So, why don't you like travelling, Annabel?

A Well, I don't like some kinds of travelling, because I don't really like being a tourist and visiting famous tourist sights.

I Why not?

A There are usually lots of other tourists, you can't see anything, and you are destroying the place as well.

I What do you mean 'destroying the place'?

A Well, I've been to a lot of famous places, like the Acropolis in Greece, and the Pyramids in Egypt, and they have too many people walking on them.

I I see. What else don't you like about travelling?

A Travelling by plane – it's bad for the environment. I think there are too many people flying to too many places. It's destroying our planet. We should try to look after what we have, instead of trying to see it all before it disappears. But if I tell my boyfriend this, he gets cross – he just wants us to have a holiday somewhere nice and hot!

...

I I'm now speaking to Jean-Claude, a French builder from Provence. Tell me, Jean-Claude, what is it about foreign travel that puts you off?

JC It's because France can give me everything I want. Why should I go to another country to have food that isn't as good, wine that isn't as good, and a climate that isn't as good? France has everything. I go skiing in winter in the Alps to the best ski slopes in the world, and in summer when it is so hot I go to the Cote d'Azur and go swimming in the lovely Mediterranean. What could be better?

I But aren't you curious to see the rest of the world? Wouldn't you like to go to the United States, for example?

JC I love Europe for its history and tradition, its culture and beauty. I don't need to travel so far. And what would I eat in America? I would be hungry all the time! I have been to Italy once and Greece once. That was enough for me.

I And your wife?

JC My wife needs to be near her mother, so she agrees with me. We stay *en France*.

I So there we have it. Some like to travel, others can't be bothered. It takes all sorts to make a world! Bye-bye!

3 Elicit the speaker for the first reason (Annabel). Put students in pairs to match the statements to the speakers.

T 9.8 Play the recording a second time and let students check their answers.

Answers
A Tourism is destroying our planet.
R Going away is too much trouble … it's not worth it.
J-C I would be hungry all the time.
R You can see everything on TV these days.
A I don't like being a tourist.
R When you get home you have a mountain of mail.
J-C My country can give me everything.
A Travelling by plane is bad for the environment.
J-C I love Europe for its history and traditions.

Ask students if they agree with any of the speakers' reasons.

4 Ask students to discuss the question in pairs or small groups. Be prepared to play sections of the recording again if students can't remember all of the information. Check the answers.

Answers
1 Roger travelled round the world 45 years ago because he was in the Navy. He feels he doesn't need to see it again.
Annabel has been to the Acropolis in Greece and the Pyramids in Egypt. She felt there were too many people there.
Jean-Claude has been to Italy and Greece. He felt that was enough for him – the food, wine, and climate weren't as good as in France.
2 Roger's wife, Mary, is angry with him. They have the time and money to travel, but Roger refuses to go.
Annabel's boyfriend is cross with her because he wants to have a holiday somewhere hot.
Jean-Claude's wife agrees with him. She wants to be near her mother, so they stay in France.

What do you think?

Ask students in their pairs to discuss the questions. Elicit some opinions from the class in a short feedback session. Establish which places are the least popular travel destinations and why.

Discussing pros and cons – For and against travelling by train

The aim of this writing section is to write a discursive essay using linking words.

1 Lead in by asking students to write down their likes and dislikes about travelling by train. Ask students to share their ideas with a partner, then tell the class.

2 Ask students to read the notes, and find out if they predicted any ideas. Make sure students understand the vocabulary (*delayed* = made late; *not door to door* = with cars you walk out of your front door, get into the car, and drive to the 'door' of your destination, but when travelling by train you have to find a way to get to and from the station).

3 Ask students to read the text and discuss the purpose of each paragraph in pairs.

Answers
Paragraph 1: expresses advantages
Paragraph 2: expresses disadvantages
Paragraph 3: expresses personal view

4 Ask students in pairs to discuss where to put the linking words.

Answers (completed text)
Travelling by train has many advantages. **First of all,** there are no stressful traffic jams, and trains are fast and comfortable. **Also,** you can use the time in different ways. You can sit and read, **for example,** or just watch the world go by. **On the other hand**, you can do some work, and with a laptop and a mobile phone, the train can become your office!
However, travelling by train also has some disadvantages. **Firstly,** it is expensive and the trains are sometimes crowded and delayed. **Secondly,** you have to travel at certain times and trains cannot take you from door to door. You need a bus or a taxi, **for example,** to take you to the railway station.

Despite the disadvantages, I prefer travelling by train to travelling by car **because** I feel more relaxed when I reach my destination.

In feedback, point out the rules of form of the linking words in the text.

Answers (rules of form)

First of all, / Firstly, / Secondly, go at the start of sentences.
Also, can go at the beginning of a clause to introduce a new piece of information. When it is not used to begin a sentence, *also* generally goes between subject and verb, (*He also likes...*), or after the verb *to be*, (*Trains are also fast...*).
However, and *for example*, can go at the start or at the end of sentences. Compare the sentences in the text with *Travelling by train also has some disadvantages,* **however** *...* and *You need a bus or a taxi to take you to the railway station,* **for example** *...*
.
Because links two clauses.
You may also wish to point out the use of gerunds (*Travelling by train ...*) and the structure *I **prefer** + ing **to** + ing*, which is used for general preferences.

5 Ask students in pairs to choose one of the topics then brainstorm advantages and disadvantages together. Ask students to write their pros and cons essay individually.

EVERYDAY ENGLISH (SB p77)

Directions

The aim is to direct students in stages towards being able to understand and give directions. Students could work in pairs from the start of the lesson.

1 Ask students to look at the map and find the different things. Let them check their answers in pairs. In feedback, make sure students understand and can pronounce the words accurately.

2 Ask students to read the descriptions of the places not yet on the map, and to insert them in the correct place. The aim of this is to teach/revise the prepositions of place in italics.

Answers

1 hotel	3c greengrocer's
2a bank	4 newsagent's
2b baker's	5a The Red Lion
3a supermarket	5b The Old Shepherd
3b chemist's	

3 **T 9.9** [CD 3: Track 11] Play the recording. Ask students to listen and repeat, and notice where the voice goes up or down.

Tapescript
1 Excuse me, is there a post office near here?
  Yes. It's in Station Road.
2 Excuse me, is there a library near here?
  Yes, it's in Green Street.
3 Excuse me, where's the school?
  It's in Church Street.

4 Before you ask students to do the activity in pairs, go through the introductory example with the whole class, and then do one or two further examples yourself with individual students across the class, to check their understanding of the prepositions. Go round the class helping and correcting.

5 This is designed to teach/revise prepositions of movement. Ask students to do it on their own and then compare with a partner.
  T 9.10 [CD 3: Track 12] Play the recording. Students listen and check their answers.

Answers and tapescript
You go **down** the hill, and walk **along** the path, **past** the pond, **over** the bridge, and **through** the gate. Then you go **across** the road and take the path **through** the wood. When you come **out of** the wood, you walk **up** the path and **into** the church. It takes ten minutes.

6 Finally, personalize the activity by asking students to give directions from the school to their houses, or other places not too far from the school.

Don't forget!

Workbook Unit 9
Exercise 9 Vocabulary – Verb + preposition
Exercise 10 Vocabulary – Adjective + preposition
Exercise 12 Pronunciation – Ways of pronouncing *-ea-*
Exercises 13–14 Check it

Grammar Reference
Look at the exercises on SB p138 as a class, or set for homework. The answers are on TB p156.

Word list
Remind your students of the Word list for this unit on SB p156. They could translate the words, learn them at home, or transfer some of the words to their vocabulary notebook.

Pronunciation Book Unit 9

10

Passives
Verbs and nouns that go together
Telephoning

Things that changed the world

Introduction to the unit

The theme of the unit is 'Things that changed the world'. The stories of X-rays and paper are used to contextualize and practise passives. The *Reading and speaking* text is about the discovery of DNA and the invention of Google, the Internet search engine. In the *Listening and speaking* section, two old men complain about the modern technology that annoys them.

Note The *Everyday English* section includes a roleplay activity that requires rolecards. If you wish to do this activity, you will need to photocopy and cut up the rolecards on p134 of the Teacher's Book before class.

Language aims

Grammar – passives The unit introduces four passives: Present Simple passive, Past Simple passive, Present Perfect passive, and Future Simple passive. In the opening presentation section, they are introduced together rather than dealt with one at a time. There is a lot of emphasis on how to form the passive and when and why to use it. With this approach, students at this level can cope with studying and practising four passive tenses at one time, especially as the tense use is the same as for the active, and your students should already be familiar with this.

It is worth remembering that English generally makes more use of the passive voice than many other languages. For example, the equivalent of *one* is often used in French (*on*) and in German (*man*) instead of the passive. In English, *one* is much less common, and it can sound very formal and distant.

They is sometimes used to replace the passive in English. It is less formal.

They make good cars in Sweden. / Good cars are made in Sweden.

Vocabulary This activity is on verbs and nouns that go together (collocation).

Everyday English This section introduces useful telephone expressions and practises telephone numbers.

Notes on the unit

STARTER (SB p78)

This *Starter* introduces students to the form of the Present Simple passive in a context and use that they have probably come across before. As such, it is a good way of gently easing students into the grammatical area of the unit.

1 Ask students in pairs to make sentences from the chart. Ask for sentences open class.

> **Answers**
> Nikon cameras are made in Japan.
> Champagne is made in France.
> Ferrari cars are made in Italy.
> Whisky is made in Scotland.
> IKEA furniture is made in Sweden.

2 Ask students to work in pairs to write some sentences about what is made or grown in their own country.

A PHOTOGRAPH THAT CHANGED THE WORLD (SB p78)

Passives

> **ABOUT THE TEXT**
> This text is a natural context for passive forms, as the subject of the text, X-rays, receives rather than performs the action of the verb.
> An *X-ray* is a form of electromagnetic radiation. *The Nobel Prize* is awarded annually in Sweden to scientists and writers for outstanding achievement.
> You may wish to check the difference between the following science words: *an invention, a discovery, an experiment.*

1 To introduce the topic ask your students a few general questions about X-rays. Ask *What is an X-ray? Why is it useful? Have you ever had an X-ray? Why? When do you think X-rays were discovered?*

Ask students to read the text and decide whether the sentences are true or false. Let students check their answers in pairs before discussing as a class.

> **Answers**
> 1 ✗   4 ✓
> 2 ✗   5 ✗
> 3 ✓

GRAMMAR SPOT (SB p78)

The aim here is to check the form and establish that the passive is used when the main interest and focus is on the object of the sentence not the subject.

1 Read through the rule carefully as a class. You may wish to write the example sentences on the board, and label them to show the rule of form:

> to be + past participle
> *X-ray machines* **are used** *every day.*

2 and 3 Ask students to work in pairs to complete the table and discuss the questions.

> **Answers**
>
> | Present Simple | Past Simple | Present Perfect | will future |
> |---|---|---|---|
> | are (clearly) seen | was taken | have been used | will be used |
> | is (still) used | were discovered | have been caught | |
> | is called | were made | have been discovered | |
> | are found | was awarded | | |

3 In sentence **a**, which is active, the main interest is Wilhelm Roentgen. In sentence **b**, which is passive, the main interest is X-rays.

Refer students to Grammar Reference 10.1 on p139.

Active and passive

1 Ask your students to do this on their own, then check with a partner before feedback. Do the first as an example.

> **Answers**
> **Active**
> 1 They make Rolls Royce cars in Britain.
> 2 Over 5 million people **visit** the Eiffel Tower every year.
> 3 Alexander Graham Bell invented the telephone in 1876.
> 4 Thieves **stole** 'The Scream' by Edvard Munch in 2004.
> 5 They sold a Van Gogh painting for $82 million.
> 6 More than 2,000 people **have climbed** Mount Everest.
> 7 BMW will produce 200,000 Mini cars next year.
> 8 **Did** Leonardo da Vinci **invent** the helicopter?
> 9 Bell didn't invent television.
> **Passive**
> 1 Rolls Royce cars **are made** in Britain.
> 2 The Eiffel Tower is visited by over 5 million people every year.
> 3 The telephone **was invented** by Alexander Graham Bell in 1876.
> 4 'The Scream' by Edvard Munch was stolen in 2004.
> 5 A Van Gogh painting **has been sold** for $82 million.
> 6 Mount Everest has been climbed by more than 2,000 people.
> 7 200,000 Mini cars **will be produced** by BMW next year.
> 8 Was the helicopter invented by Leonardo da Vinci?
> 9 Television **wasn't invented** by Bell.

Active and passive

1 Put students in pairs to discuss the questions *What is paper made of?* and *Who invented it?* You could ask students to think of other questions about paper that they would like to know the answer to. Ask students to read the text to check their answers to the questions.

2 **T 10.1** [CD 3: Track 13] Ask students to read the text again and put the verbs in brackets in the correct form. Let students discuss their answers in pairs before going through them as a class. Play the recording to check the answers.

Answers and tapescript

1	is used	6	kept
2	wrote	7	was brought
3	started	8	was built
4	was invented	9	has been made
5	was made	10	uses

T 10.1

The history of paper

Today, paper **is used** for hundreds of everyday things – books and newspapers, of course, but also money, stamps, cups, bags, and even some clothes.

Long ago, before paper, people **wrote** on animal skins, bones and stones. Then in 2700 BC, the Egyptians **started** to make papyrus, which was similar to paper. But the first real paper **was invented** in AD 105 by a Chinese government official, Ts'ai Lun. It **was made** from a mixture of plants and cloth. The Chinese **kept** their invention secret for centuries.

Finally, in the 10th century, paper **was brought** to Europe by the Arabs. The first European paper mill **was built** in Spain in 1150. Since the 18th century, most paper **has been made** out of wood, because it is much stronger than cloth.

Nowadays, each person **uses** about 300kg of paper every year. That's a lot of paper.

Questions and answers

3 Ask students to match question words and answers.

Answers

When?	In AD105. In the 10th century.
Where?	In China. In Spain.
Who/by?	Ts'ai Lun
How long?	Since the 18th century.
How much?	About 300 kg.

4 **T 10.2** [CD 3: Track 14] Ask students to work in pairs to write questions using the prompts in exercise 3. They must use the passive form. Monitor and help with question forming, then play the recording for students to check. You could drill these questions for pronunciation at this stage. Write the question words on the board as prompts, model each question with a clear pronunciation, and get the class, then individuals, to repeat.

Ask students to ask and answer in pairs.

Answers and tapescript

When was paper invented?	In AD 105.
Where was the first real paper invented?	In China.
Who was it invented by?	Ts'ai Lun.
When was it brought to Europe by the Arabs?	In the 10th century.
Where was the first paper mill built?	In Spain.
How long has paper been made out of wood?	Since the 18th century.
How much paper is used by each person every year?	About 300kg.

5 **T 10.3** [CD 3: Track 15] Read through the examples with students, then let them work in pairs to complete the sentences. Play the recording so that they can check. Before letting students practise the dialogues in pairs, play the recording again, pausing after each dialogue for students to repeat.

Answers and tapescript

1 Paper is only used to make newspapers and books.
   No, it isn't. It's used to make hundreds of everyday things.
2 All clothes are made out of paper.
   No, they aren't. Only some are made out of paper.
3 Before paper, people wrote on trees.
   No, they didn't. They wrote on animal skins, bones, and stones.
4 Paper was invented by a Chinese scientist.
   No, it wasn't. It was invented by a Chinese government official.
5 The Chinese gave their invention to the world immediately.
   No, they didn't. They kept it secret for centuries.
6 They made paper out of wood.
   No, they didn't. They made it out of a mixture of plants and cloth.
7 The first paper mill in Europe was built in France.
   No, it wasn't. It was built in Spain.
8 Paper has been made out of cloth since the 18th century.
   No, it hasn't. It's been made out of wood.

Check it

6 This exercise checks the rules of form and use of passives. It could be done in class or for homework with some other exercises from the Workbook.

Answers

1 were	3 has stolen	5 don't carry	7 been eaten
2 by	4 sells	6 drunk	

ADDITIONAL MATERIAL

Workbook Unit 10
These exercises could be done in class as further practice, for homework, or in a later class as revision.

Exercises 1–5 The passive

Exercises 6–7 Active and passive

Verbs and nouns that go together

The aim of this exercise is to develop students' awareness of the collocations of some common verbs. The verbs in this exercise have been chosen because they should all be familiar to students, but they are often incorrectly used in relation to some nouns. You may wish to do it as a dictionary exercise, developing students' ability to use dictionaries to extend their vocabulary.

1 Ask your students to work in pairs to find the noun that does not go with the verb. They could do this by guessing, or by having a guess then checking in a dictionary. Tell your students to check the nouns in the dictionary first. This is more likely to tell them which verbs go with them than vice versa.

Answers
You can't say:

discover paper	make homework
tell hello	give a complaint
lose the bus	carry a watch
keep an idea	miss the way

2 Ask the same pairs of students to write sentences. Then ask several students to read aloud their sentences for the others to comment on.

3 Ask students to discuss which verbs go with the odd nouns in each group. Have a brief feedback.

Answers

invent paper	do homework
say hello	make a complaint
miss the bus	wear a watch
have an idea	lose the way

Ask students to complete the sentences with the correct verb.

Answers

1 invented	5 make
2 did	6 missed
3 wore	7 lost
4 Say	8 had

Talking about you

4 Give students a few minutes to think of answers to the questions. Then put them in pairs to ask and answer.

T 10.4 [CD 3: Track 16] Play the recording. Ask students to listen and compare their answers.

Answers and tapescript

1 Do you always wear a watch?
  Yes, all the time. Don't you?
2 Are you good at telling jokes?
  No, I'm hopeless. I can never remember the ending.
3 What was the last present you gave? Who to?
  Mmmm. I think it was when I gave some flowers to my mum for Mother's Day.
4 What was the last phone call you made? Who to? Why?
  Just before I came into class. I called a friend to ask if she's doing anything tonight.
5 Do you keep a diary?
  Yes, but I don't write very personal things in it, in case someone finds it.
6 Have you or a friend ever made a complaint in a restaurant?
  No, but my dad often complains. I find it embarrassing, but he says it's important to do it.
7 Have you ever been homesick? Did you miss your family or your friends?
  Oh, yes, when I went on an exchange to Germany when I was 16, I missed everybody.
8 What is the best advice you've ever been given?
  If you can't say anything nice, don't say anything at all.

A discovery and an invention that changed the world

ABOUT THE TEXT

This is a jigsaw reading. In groups, students read one of two different texts, and answer gist and specific information questions. Then, in an information gap task, they must share their answers with a partner who read the other text. There are opportunities for students to discuss their own opinions and experiences.

A *genome* is the complete set of genes in a living thing. *Star Trek* was an incredibly popular American sci-fi TV series, which began in the 1960s. In it, the crew of an imaginary starship visited strange new worlds in distant galaxies. Much of its imaginary technology has inspired scientists.

Difficult vocabulary from the texts is covered in the prediction task of exercise 3.

1 Ask students to look at the list, and check that they know what each invention or discovery is. Check the pronunciation of the words in the list. Ask students to tell you which are inventions, and which discoveries.

You could ask students if they know when, and by whom, the discoveries and inventions were made.

Answers
the telephone: **invented** by Alexander Graham Bell in 1876
radium (the first known radioactive element): **discovered** by Marie and Pierre Curie in 1897
penicillin (the first antibiotic): **discovered** by Alexander Fleming in 1928
television: **invented** by John Logie Baird in 1926 (many other people were involved in its development)
the Internet: **invented** by no one person – first developed in the 1970s
DNA is a discovery. Somebody found it, they didn't make it.
the atom: **discovered** by John Dalton in 1808
the electric light: **invented** by Humphrey Davy in 1800 (Thomas Edison improved on this invention and was the first to produce a long-lasting light bulb)
Google is an invention

2 Put students into groups of three or four. Elicit a few examples of important discoveries or inventions, e.g. *the computer, blood groups, aeroplanes, aspirin*. Get students to add more examples to the list in exercise 1. Ask one student to write down the examples for their group.

When the groups are ready, ask a spokesperson for each group to read their list to the class. Write the lists on the board. Find out whether there is agreement on any invention or discovery. Then ask different groups to give reasons why more contentious inventions or discoveries are important. Try to come to an agreed 'class list' of inventions and discoveries.

3 Ask students to work in pairs to research the words in their dictionaries, and do the prediction task. Monitor and help with ideas.

4 Divide students into two groups at this stage, Group A and Group B. If you have a large class, have two or three sets of each group. You don't want more than four or five students in each group. Make sure they know which text to read.

Ask students to read their text quickly and find out which words from exercise 3 are in their text. Check the answers in a brief feedback session.

Answers
DNA: structure, disease, cure, cell, contain, commit (a crime), be related to
Google: weblink, company, search engine, result, borrow, dream

5 Ask students to read their text more carefully and find answers to the questions. When they have finished reading, ask them to discuss their answers with their group. Tell them to make brief notes.

6 Tell students to stand up, walk round, and sit down with a student who read the other text. Students exchange the information in their texts and answer the questions.

Answers
DNA
1 Friedrich Miescher
2 84 years
3 Yes – other scientists thought it was too simple to be the map of human development.
4 1869 (discovered), 1953 (structure discovered), 1962 Nobel Prize), 1986 (DNA testing first used), 1990 (Human Genome Project began), 2000 (Human Genome Project completed)
5 Very. You can catch criminals with DNA testing.
6 You may be able to cure diseases, choose what babies look like, or pick the best person for a job.
Google
1 Larry Page and Sergey Brin
2 About 2 years
3 Yes – nobody would give them money.
4 1995 (Page and Brin met), 1996 (decided to make a search engine), 1998 (cheque for $100,000), 2002 (biggest search engine on Internet)
5 Very. You can find answers to questions very quickly.
6 All the world's information might be on the Internet, so that you could find everything.

What do you think?

The aim here is to round off the lesson with a personalized discussion. You could do it open class, or in groups.

> **EXTRA IDEA**
> If you have access to computers in your school (or you could set it as a homework task), you could ask students to go to the *Google* search engine, and see who can be first to find out the answer to the opening question in the *Google* text. If students type in 'common words Shakespeare', they should be able to find the answer – about 1700. Students could also research one of the discoveries and inventions in exercise 1. Set some questions, for example *When was it invented/discovered? Who invented/discovered it? Why is it useful? How many people have one/use it every year?* Ask students to present their findings to the class, or write them up for homework.

WRITING (SB p113)

A review – Books and films: referring back in a text

The aim of this writing section is to write a review of a book or film, using pronoun reference accurately.

1 Model the activity by telling students about a film you have seen recently. Ask students to complete the sentences, then talk to a partner.

2 Ask students to read the paragraph, and discuss with a partner what the words in bold refer to.

In feedback, point out that the italicized words are all pronouns. We use pronouns to replace nouns when we don't want to repeat ourselves.

Answers
It = the film
They = two friends
it = the film
That = the fact that they said the acting was terrible
it = the acting
This = the fact that his/her parents rarely go to the cinema
they = his/her parents
it = the film

3 Give students a few minutes to read the questions, and note any information they know. Ask students to discuss their ideas with a partner, then with the class. In feedback, discuss students' ideas, but don't deny or confirm any speculations at this stage.

Answers
1 *Frankenstein* is both a book and a film.
2 It is a horror story, with elements of science fiction and romance.
3 (Victor) Frankenstein is a scientist.

4 Ask students to read the review and check their predictions.

5 Ask students to read the review again and discuss what the words in bold refer to with a partner.

Answers
it = the novel *Frankenstein*
who = Victor Frankenstein
these = bones and bodies
This = making a wife for the monster
it = the monster
he = Victor Frankenstein
itself = the monster
first = the first movie
which = the character of the monster

6 Ask students to complete the review with past participles.

Answers
1 written	5 used
2 published	6 told
3 translated	7 terrified
4 said	8 made

7 Ask students in pairs to find information in the text for each heading.

Answers
Title: Frankenstein
Author: Mary Shelley
Type of book/film: horror/science fiction
Characters: Walton (an explorer), Victor Frankenstein, the monster, Frankenstein's brother, friend, and wife (Elizabeth)
Plot: Frankenstein makes a human being from dead bodies, but it is huge and ugly and scares people. Lonely, the monster wants Frankenstein to make it a wife. Frankenstein refuses, the monster kills various people, and is chased by Frankenstein. Both Frankenstein and the monster die in the end.

Ask students to choose their own book or film, prepare notes under the heading, then write a short review. Monitor and help with ideas.

Once students have completed their reviews, ask a few students to read them aloud to the class. Alternatively, pin the reviews on the wall of the classroom. Students must circulate and read the reviews, then find and ask the writers about the review they wrote.

LISTENING AND SPEAKING (SB p84)

Things that really annoy me

> **ABOUT THE LISTENING**
> Students listen to two old men complaining about automated answer phones, complicated modern machines (dishwashers, car radios, computers), how things get out-of-date so quickly, and how even something as simple as shampoo is complicated because there are so many choices. Students have to listen to check predictions and listen for specific information. There are opportunities for students to talk about their opinions and roleplay a dialogue between two people complaining.

1 Lead in by telling the class three or four things that really annoy you. Then ask students to write down three things that annoy them. Give them a minute to think, and make sure that they write on a small piece of paper that they can hand to you. Collect the pieces of paper and keep them on your desk or in a box for later in the lesson.

2 Ask students to look at the cartoons. Ask *Is the man in the cartoons young or old? Where is he? What problems is he having?* Elicit ideas from the class.

Answers
The man is in his 50s.

Cartoon 1: in a phone shop. His phone is broken, but it's out-of-date now.
Cartoon 2: on the phone. He's listening to an answerphone message for a very long time (so long that he's grown a beard!)

Cartoon 3: in the kitchen. The modern fridge has very complicated program options.
Cartoon 4: on the computer. The computer is giving him a meaningless error message before it shuts down.
Cartoon 5: in a coffee shop. There are a lot of different types of coffee to choose from.
Cartoon 6: in a camera shop: The shop assistant is using a lot of technical language.

3 **T 10.5** [CD 3: Track 17] Play the recording. Ask students to listen and note down what problems they have with the things in the list. In the feedback, ask how these problems are similar to the ones in the cartoons.

Answers and tapecript
Automated answer phones: you get a machine not a person / you don't want any of the options / you have to hold and listen to music / you get cut off. Similar to the problem in Cartoon 2.
Domestic machines: too many buttons / you don't know what to do. Similar to the problem in Cartoon 3.
Car radios: he can't find the *on/off* button / he doesn't know how to use the CD player. Similar to the problem in Cartoon 3.
Choosing a computer: he didn't understand what the shop assistant said. Similar to the problem in Cartoon 6.
Computer printers: the computer says the printer cannot be found when it is there on the desk! Similar to the problem in Cartoon 4.
Last year's technology: it gets out-of-date very quickly. Similar to the problem in Cartoon 1.
Too much choice: there are too many types of shampoo / he can't decide which one to choose. Similar to the problem in Cartoon 5.

T 10.5
Things that really annoy me
A I can't stand it when you phone someone like British Telecom, and you get a machine, not a person, and you hear 'Please choose from these options. For sales, press 1. To report a fault, press 2. To pay a bill, press 3.'
B I know. And the problem is, you don't want any of those. What you want is something completely different! So what do you press?
A And then when you do finally make a choice, you get another menu!
B And then another, and then another.
A Then you have to hold, and you get music forever!
B Until finally you hear 'Your call is very important to us, but all our operators are busy at the moment. Please call back later.' And then you're cut off!
A It drives me mad! You never actually talk to a person.
B But it's machines I can't stand.
A What do you mean? Computers and things?
B No. All machines. I can't use our dishwasher – it has too many buttons. I can't use our washing machine. What temperature do I want? What program do I want? Do I want economy? Do I use powder or one of those little bags full of liquid?

A I know what you mean. I have no idea how to use the radio in my car. I can't even find the on/off button. It has a CD player and a cassette player, but I have no idea where they are. I tried to choose a computer in a shop the other day, but I had to walk out because I didn't understand a word that the shop assistant said.
B I use my son's computer, and I can get it to work some of the time, which is a miracle. But what drives me mad is when I'm trying to print something and the computer says 'The printer cannot be found', and I'm saying 'But it's there, right next to you, you idiot. What do you mean you can't find it?'
A Another thing is the way things get out of date so quickly. I tried to buy a new battery for my camera the other day, and I was told 'Sorry sir, but these batteries aren't made any more.' So I said 'But I only bought this camera last year!' And the assistant, this boy who looked about fourteen, said 'Sorry, sir, this camera's just about ready for a museum.' What a cheek! Kids these days have no respect.
B The thing I can't stand is choice. You don't get one of anything, you get hundreds. Have you tried choosing shampoo in a supermarket? Do you want shampoo for dry hair? For greasy hair? Normal hair? Long hair? Short hair? Blond hair? Frequent use? Do you want it with fruit? With herbs? With oil? With a smell or without a smell? I can't decide! I just close my eyes and choose one.
A Now you've really got me started. Do you know how much it costs to ... ?

What do you think?

1 Give students a few minutes to work in their pairs or groups to think of complaints. Elicit ideas and write them on the board.

Possible answers
flat pack furniture: you can't open it; there are no instructions; the instructions are very confusing; the instructions are in a foreign language; there are pieces missing
people who use mobiles in public places: they don't think about other people; they shout; they talk about nothing
opening plastic packets: it's very difficult; you need a knife or scissors; the things inside go everywhere when it finally bursts open; they should be designed with a simple way of opening
people who drop litter: they're selfish; anti-social; should be made to pick it up

2 Put students in pairs or small groups to discuss the age of the people talking. Have a brief class feedback.

Suggested answers
I want a mobile ...	teenager
I've no idea how ...	older person – over 40
Me want ...	small child – under 5
Young people don't say ...	elderly person – probably over 60
I can never stay out ...	teenager

Families don't ...	older person – over 40
I really want ...	teenager or someone in their 20s

3 Read out some of the pieces of paper you collected at the start of the lesson. Students must guess who wrote which.

Roleplay

Put students in pairs to write a dialogue. Tell them to decide first who they are, and how old they are. Then tell them to make a short list of things they are going to complain about. They could use ideas from the listening, from exercises 1 and 2 of *What do you think?* or their own ideas.

Give students five or six minutes to prepare their dialogue. Monitor and help. Ask a few pairs to act out their dialogue for the class.

You could write the following useful language on the board to help students prepare:

What I really hate about ... is ...	*I can't stand it when ...*
The thing that annoys me is ...	*Another thing is ...*
What drives me mad is ...	*I know what you mean.*

EVERYDAY ENGLISH (SB p85)

Telephoning

In exercise 5 of this section, there is a roleplay that requires rolecards. Before the class, you need to photocopy enough role cards to give one to each student in your class. They are on p134 of the Teacher's Book.

At the start of the lesson, you may wish to tell students the following information about phone numbers in the UK.

ABOUT TELEPHONE NUMBERS

Telephone numbers are said one by one. We don't put two together as many languages do. 71 is seven one, not seventy-one. 0 is pronounced /əʊ/. Two numbers the same are usually said with *double*, for example, *double three*. There is a slight pause between groups of numbers when the phone number is long. For example: 020 (pause) 7927 (pause) 4863. Note that Americans say zero, not 0, and say two two, etc, not double two.

In the UK, home telephone numbers generally have six digits. For example, 633488. They are preceded by an area code. 0207 is the area code for Greater London. Numbers beginning 07 are mobile numbers.

---

1 **T 10.6** [CD 3: Track 18] Play the recording. Ask students to listen and repeat. Then ask students to practise the telephone numbers in pairs. Monitor and correct. In feedback, discuss how the numbers mentioned are expressed.

Answers and tapescript

0 = /əʊ/
00 = double /əʊ/
55, 99, 33, 88 = double 5, double 9, etc.

T 10.6

020 7927 4863	07971 800 261	061 44 501 277
01923 272 994	633488	07881 905 024

MUSIC OF ENGLISH – INTONATION WITH NUMBERS

1 **T 10.7** [CD 3: Track 19] Play the recording. Ask students to notice the falling intonation. You could read out the numbers yourself, showing the rise then fall in intonation with each set of numbers. Ask students to listen and repeat.

Tapescript

020 7927 4863
07971 800 261

2 Refer students to the stress shading and drill the sentences with the whole class. Put students in pairs to ask and answer phone numbers. You could make this a mingling activity. Students must walk round the class, and ask six people for their mobile phone numbers. (Tell students they can make up a number if they don't want to reveal their real one!)

2 **T 10.8** [CD 3: Track 20] Play the recording. Ask students to listen and answer the questions. Ask students to check their answers in pairs before feedback.

Answers

1 John is speaking to Peter.
  John wants to rearrange a meeting. He also wants Andy's phone number.
  They know each other well.
2 John is speaking to Francis, Andy's flatmate.
  John wants to speak to Andy.
  They don't know each other.
3 Darshan Gandhi is speaking to a receptionist, a secretary, and Annette Baker.
  Darshan wants to speak to Annette Baker about a job advertisement.
  They don't know each other.
4 Simon is speaking to Dawn, Annette Baker's secretary.
  Simon wants to meet up with Dawn.
  They know each other well, but haven't seen each other for a long time.

3 Ask students in pairs to complete the expressions. Monitor and help.

T 10.8 Play the recording again. Ask students to listen and check their answers.

Answers and tapescript

Conversation 1 – Pete and John

1 **P** Hello?
  J Is **that** Pete? **It's** John.

2 **J** Sorry. We were **cut** off. Listen, I'm **calling** because Jed can't **make** it on Thursday.

3 **P** I'm not sure. Can I get **back** to you later?
  J Sure. I'm going out now, give me a **ring** on my mobile.

4 **J** Oh, and can you **give** me Andy's number? I can't find it anywhere.
  P I haven't got it **on** me, sorry.

Conversation 2 – John and Andy's flatmate, Francis

1 **J** Hello. **Is that** Andy?
  F No, I'm **afraid** he's out at the **moment**. Can I take a **message**?
  J Yes please. Can you say that John **phoned**, and I'll **try** again **later**?

Conversation 3 – Darshan Gandhi, Receptionist (Dawn), Secretary (Annette Baker).

1 **R** The line's **busy**. Would you like to **hold**?

2 **R** It's **ringing** for you now.

3 **S** Who's **speaking** please?
  D **This** is Darshan Gandhi.

4 **S** Yes, I'll put you **through**.

Conversation 4 – Dawn and Simon

1 **S** **Could** I speak to Dawn Edwards, please?
  D **Speaking**.

2 **S** Great! I'll **give** you a call on Friday, then.

3 **S** OK. Speak **to** you soon. Bye for **now**!

T 10.8

Telephoning

1 **P = Pete   J = John**
  P Hello?
  J Is that Pete? It's John.
  P Hi, John. How are you?
  J Good, thanks. And you?
  P Yeah, fine, thanks.
  J Pete, I'm trying to get …
  P Hello? Hello?
  J … Sorry. We were cut off. Listen, I'm calling because Jed can't make it on Thursday.
  P Oh yeah?
  J Yeah, so are you free on Friday instead?
  P I'm not sure. Can I get back to you later?
  J Sure. I'm going out now, so give me a ring on my mobile. You've got my number.
  P Yes, it's here on my mobile!
  J Oh good! Oh, and can you give me Andy's number? I can't find it anywhere.
  P I haven't got it on me, sorry. I can give it to you when I call you back.
  J Thanks! Speak to you later, then. Bye!
  P Bye for now.

2 **F = Francis, Andy's flatmate   J = John**
  F Hello.
  J Hello. Is that Andy?
  F No, I'm afraid he's out at the moment. Can I take a message?
  J Yes, please. Can you say that John phoned, and I'll try again later? Do you know what time he'll be back?
  F In about an hour, I think.
  J Thanks. Goodbye.
  F Goodbye.

3 **R = Receptionist   DG = Darshan Gandhi**
  S = Secretary   A = Annette Baker
  R Good morning. Wells International. Gemma speaking. How can I help you?
  DG Hello, could I speak to Annette Baker, please?
  R The line's busy. Would you like to hold?
  DG Yes, please.
  R It's ringing for you now.
  DG Thank you.
  S Hello. Ms Baker's office. Dawn speaking.
  DG Hello. Can I speak to Annette Baker, please?
  S Who's speaking, please?
  DG This is Darshan Gandhi.
  S I'll just see if she's at her desk, Mr Gandhi.
      … Yes, I'll put you through.
  A Hello. Annette Baker here. How can I help you, Mr … erm … Gandhi?
  DG Hello. Well, I saw your advertisement in the Guardian newspaper, and I wondered if you could give me a little more information about …

4 **D = Dawn (secretary)   S = Simon**
  D Hello. Annette Baker's office.
  S Could I speak to Dawn Edwards, please?
  D Speaking.
  S Hey, Dawn, this is Simon!
  D Simon? Simon! How are you? I haven't heard from you in ages!
  S I know. I'm sorry, I've been away. I called your mum and she gave me your work number. Listen, do you fancy meeting up at the weekend?
  D Of course!
  S Great! I'll give you a call on Friday, then.
  D Yes, do that.
  S OK. Speak to you soon. Bye for now.
  D Bye, Simon!

4 Ask students to look at the tapescript on p124–125 of the Student's Book and practise one of the conversations in pairs.

5   There are six role cards on p134 of the Teacher's Book. Photocopy the page and cut them out, then hand them out to students. A works with B, C with D, and E with F. Make sure you get your sums right when you are deciding how many copies to make! Every A needs a B, every C needs a D, and every E needs an F. If you have an odd number of students, you will have to take a role yourself. Give out the cards and let students prepare on their own. Say you will give them a role card which tells them who they are and who's phoning who. On each one, there are decisions to be made. Ask students to think about their decisions.

When you feel students are ready, ask the As to find a B, the Cs to find a D, and the Es to find an F. Remind them that A, C, and E must start the conversation.

When they have finished, ask two or three pairs to do their roleplay again in front of the class so everyone can hear. It's a nice idea to put two chairs back to back when doing this, so students can't see each other's lips and have to rely on what they hear.

Don't forget!

Workbook Unit 10

Exercise 8 Vocabulary – Preposition + word

Exercises 9 Pronunciation - Sentence stress

Exercises 10–11 Check it

Grammar Reference
Look at the exercises on SB p139–140 as a class, or set for homework. The answers are on TB p156.

Word list
Remind your students of the Word list for this unit on SB p156. They could translate the words, learn them at home, or transfer some of the words to their vocabulary notebook.

Pronunciation Book Unit 10

11

Second conditional • *might*
Phrasal verbs
Exclamations with *so* and *such*

What if...?

Introduction to the unit

The title of this unit is '*What if…?*' and it contains two presentation sections. In the first, a text about the global village provides the context to introduce and highlight unreality in the use of the second conditional. In the second, 'Who knows?', two students, one decisive, one unsure, talk about what they are going to do after university, and this is the context used to introduce *might*.

In the *Listening and speaking* section, three people of different ages speculate about changes they face in their lives. In the *Reading and speaking* section, there is a text about the supervolcano in Yellowstone National Park and the consequences of a possible, though unlikely, eruption.

Language aims

Grammar – Second conditional The first conditional was introduced in Unit 9.

The concept of the conditionals does not seem to cause students as much difficulty as the formation. There are two common problems with this area:

1 The tenses used in the main clause and *if* clause do not seem logical.

2 The complicated structural patterns are difficult for students to manipulate and get their tongues around.

Where the second conditional is concerned, the use of a past tense in the *if* clause to express an unreal present or improbable future often strikes students as strange and illogical, especially as in many languages unreality is expressed by separate subjunctive verb forms.

Common mistake

*If I would live in the country, I would have a dog.

The subjunctive has largely disappeared from English, but one last remnant is the use of *were* in all persons of the verb *to be* in the second conditional, for example

If I were rich, I'd buy a new car.
If I were you, I'd go to the doctor.
If he were here, he'd know what to do.

However, nowadays this too seems to be disappearing, and it is equally acceptable to say

If I was rich, … etc.

The contraction of *would* to *'d* can also be a problem, not only in terms of pronunciation but also because *'d* can also be a contraction for the auxiliary *had*.

might The use of *might* is very common in English but much avoided by learners of English, who often prefer to use *maybe/perhaps + will* to express lack of certainty about the future, for example

Maybe she will come.
Perhaps I will play tennis this afternoon.

These are not incorrect, but it sounds much more natural to say

She might come.
I might play tennis this afternoon.

Vocabulary Students will already be familiar with some phrasal verbs. There are so many in English that it is impossible to study the language for even a short time and not come across some of the more common ones, for example *put on, take off* (a coat, etc.), *get on, get off* (a bus, etc.).

In the vocabulary section there is a gently-staged introduction to the different types of phrasal verbs. There are exercises which look at literal and non-literal use of these verbs.

Everyday English This section looks at the use of *so* and *such*.

Notes on the unit

STARTER (SB p86)

The aim of this starter is to get students using the second conditional in a personalized speaking activity.

1 and 2 Discuss the questions as a class or let students discuss them in small groups first. Note how competently students manipulate *would*.

THE GLOBAL VILLAGE (SB p86)

Second conditional

1 Ask questions to set the scene, for example *How many people are there in the world? What is the population of China/India/your country? What do you think the phrase 'global village' means?*

Ask students to read the text and check their predictions. Put students in pairs to complete the sentences with verbs from the box.

Answers			
2	would be	6	wouldn't know
3	would live	8	would control
5	wouldn't have	10	would die

2 Put students in pairs to ask and answer the questions.

Answers	
How many people would be women?	49
How many people would live in poor housing?	80
Would everybody have enough food?	No
Would most people have electricity?	Yes
How many people would be very rich?	5
Would most people have access to the Internet?	No

GRAMMAR SPOT (SB 87)

Go through the questions with the whole class to establish the form and use of the second conditional.

Answers

1 The first sentence describes the real world. The second is imagined. (We use the second conditional to describe unreal, imagined situations.)

2 It is acceptable to use either *was* or *were* here, although *were* is considered more correct, particularly when writing formally.

3 The first sentence, which uses the first conditional form, is more probable.
In the first sentence, the conditional clause is formed with *if* + the Present Simple tense. In the result clause, we use the auxiliary verb *will* + the infinitive without *to*. In the second sentence, the unreal conditional clause is formed with *if* + the Past Simple tense. In the result clause, we use the auxiliary verb *would* + the infinitive without *to*. *Would* is often reduced to *'d*.

Refer students to Grammar Reference 11.1 on p140.

PRACTICE (SB p87)

Discussing grammar

These are very controlled exercises to give further practice.

1 Ask students to do this orally in pairs. Ask them to make the most natural sounding sentences.

Sample answers

If I were a politician, I'd always tell the truth.
If I were you, I'd ask the teacher/I'd accept the job.
If I had the answer, I'd tell you.
If I had the time, I'd travel the world/I'd help you.
If I found a £50 note, I wouldn't keep it.
If I knew the answer, I'd tell you.
If I didn't know the answer, I'd ask the teacher.
If I didn't live in a big city, I'd be bored.

NOTE

It is important to point out to students that the sentence parts can be reversed and the main clause can equally well come before the *if* clause, for example:
I'd accept the job if I were you.
Notice that there is no comma when this happens.

2 Ask students to do this exercise on their own and then compare with a partner before you check through the exercise with the whole class.

Answers
1 If I **were** rich, I**'d travel** round the world. First I**'d go** to Canada, then I**'d go** to New York.
2 If he **worked** harder, he**'d have** more money.
3 I**'d go** to work if I **felt** better, but I feel terrible.
4 If I **could** speak perfect English, I **wouldn't be** in this classroom.
5 What **would** you **do** if a stranger **gave** you £1 million?
6 What **would** you **say** if I **asked** you to marry me?

If I were you …

3 The aim here is for some less-controlled speaking practice. Students might warm to some topics more than others. Put students into pairs or small groups to discuss the situations. The aim is to practise the result clause only, and ideally there will be a rapid exchange of ideas. Encourage students to give their real opinions.

T 11.1 [CD 3: Track 21] Play the recording. Ask students to listen and compare their ideas.

Tapescript
1 I found a wallet in the street.
  If I were you, I'd take it to the nearest police station.
2 I don't like my sister's boyfriend.
  If I were you, I wouldn't say anything.
3 I've had a row with my mother.
  If I were you, I'd buy her some flowers.
4 I never have enough money.
  If I were you, I'd stop buying so many CDs.
5 My neighbours make a lot of noise.
  If I were you, I'd move.
6 I really need to do more exercise.
  If I were you, I'd cycle to work.

PHOTOCOPIABLE MATERIAL: EXTRA IDEA
Song **After T 11.1** [CD 3: Track 22]
What if … ?, TB p135
This is intended as an informal and fun activity, which you may like to include at the end of a lesson. Photocopy the sheet on TB p135 and give a copy to each student. Work through the activities, allowing students to work in pairs wherever possible and encouraging plenty of discussion. You could do the final exercise with the whole class to round off the activity. The answers to the activities are on TB p151.

ADDITIONAL MATERIAL

Workbook Unit 11
Exercises 1–5 Second Conditional

WHO KNOWS? (SB p88)

might

Two contrasting texts, one about a teenager from Cape Town, and one about a teenager in St Petersburg, provide the context for the use of *might*. This introduction to *might* also provides a good opportunity to revise the Present Continuous and *going to* for future plans and arrangements.

Cape Town is a multi-cultural city with a mixed population. It is on the southern coast of South Africa, and overlooked by Table Mountain. Poorer people live in shanty towns or townships on the edge of the city. *St Petersburg* is a large city in northern Russia.

You may wish to pre-teach the following key vocabulary: *shanty town* (an area in or near a town where poor people live in houses made of wood, metal, and cardboard), *junk* (household rubbish such as old furniture).

---

1 Ask your students to look at the pictures of the two students. Ask the questions in the Student's Book.

2 **T 11.2** [CD 3: Track 23] Play the recording. Ask students in pairs to listen and complete the texts.

Answers and tapescript
Nisa Isaacs
I live with my parents in a shanty town outside the city. My parents collect old newspapers and junk to sell. They don't make much money, so we're poor. But I'm going to change all that. I love school. I'm studying very hard, because I**'m taking** my high school exams next year. Then I**'m going to get** a job in an office in town. But that isn't my main ambition. I really **want to go** to university. So I**'m going to work** for a while to save some money. I**'m hoping to be** an architect, then I can build my parents a proper house.

Viktor Panov
I'm studying for my certificate of Education, but I'm not sure what I want to study afterwards. I love doing art at school, so I might go to art college. That would be fun. I **might become** a designer. But I also enjoy Russian language and literature, so I **might study** that at university. I'll have to get good exam results to do that. I'd also like to try living in another country. I've got family in Germany, so I **might live** there for a while. Perhaps I could study art and design in Berlin. That would be great!

3 Ask students to discuss the questions in pairs.

Answers
1 Nisa is certain. Viktor isn't.
2 Nisa is more ambitious. She comes from a very poor background but wants to become an architect.
3 Nisa lives in a shanty town. Her parents sell newspapers and junk.
4 Art
5 Viktor
6 Nisa wants to be an architect. Viktor wants to be a designer.

4 This exercise revises future tenses in a controlled written exercise. Ask students to write sentences.

Answers
She's taking her high school exams next year.
She's going to get a job in an office in town.
She's going to university.
She's going to save some money.
She's going to be an architect.

5 This exercise checks the contrasting use of *might* to express possibilities. Ask students to write sentences. Make sure they don't try to follow *might* with *to*.

Answers
He might go to art college.
He might become a designer.
He might study Russian language and literature at university.
He might live in Germany for a while.

GRAMMAR SPOT (SB p88)

Read through the *Grammar spot* as a class.

Answers
2 We do not add *-s* with *he/she/it*. *Might*, like all modal auxiliary verbs, remains the same in all persons. We do not use *do/does* in the negative. We use *not* after the modal auxiliary verb.

Refer students to Grammar Reference 11.2 on p140.

PRACTICE (SB p89)

Discussing grammar

These exercises bring together all the grammar points in this unit.

1 You could do this as a quick oral reinforcement activity with the whole class, or you could ask your students to work on their own and underline the correct answers, then check with a partner before you conduct a feedback session.

T 11.3 [CD 3: Track 24] Play the recording. Ask students to listen and check their answers.

Answers and tapescript
1 We're having   4 I'm having
2 It'll be   5 I might
3 he might be

T 11.3
1 A What's for supper?
  B **We're having** lamb. It's in the oven.
2 A What time are we eating?
  B Don't worry. **It'll be** ready before your TV programme.
3 A Who's eating with us?
  B I've invited Jerry, but **he might be** late. It depends on the traffic.
4 I'm going into town tomorrow. **I'm having** lunch with Jo at 1.00.
5 A Are you going to have a winter holiday this year?
  B **I might**. I haven't decided yet.

Possibilities

2 This aims to give further controlled practice of *might*. You could do it as a writing exercise, but it is best as a sort of prompt drill. Do the first as an example question and answer with your students. Then put students in pairs to make conversations with the other prompts.

T 11.4 [CD 3: Track 25] Play the recording. Ask students to listen and compare their answers.

Answers and tapescript
1 A What sort of car are you going to buy?
  B Well, I'd like to buy a Mercedes or a BMW. But of course, they would be too expensive, so I might get a Fiat or a Toyota. One thing's for sure, it'll be second-hand.
2 A Where are you going on holiday this year?
  B As usual Tom and I can't agree, so we might go to Scotland, or maybe Spain. You know us, we always book at the last minute anyway!
3 A What are we having to eat tonight?
  B Well, it might be steak or it might be just a takeaway pizza. Probably the pizza – I feel too tired to cook.
4 A Who are you going to the dance with?
  B Well, I might ask Tony, but then there's also Richard. He's a great dancer, so I might ask him.
5 A What would you do if you won the lottery?
  B In my dreams! But what would I do? Well, I might just give it all away to a dogs' home. No, actually, I think I might travel the world.

3 This is a short and freer personalized activity. Students take it in turns to ask their partner questions.

Model the exchange by asking questions, for example *What are you doing/going to do after the lesson?*, and eliciting responses. Point out that if the partner is sure the answer is *I'm going to …* or *I'm … ing …*, but if the partner is not sure the answer is *I'm not sure/I don't know. I might … .*

ADDITIONAL MATERIAL

Workbook Unit 11
Exercises 6–9 *might.*

LISTENING AND SPEAKING (SB p89)

At a crossroads in life

1 In the lead-in, create interest by asking the questions in the Student's Book to the whole class.

> **Answers**
> A *crossroads* is where two roads cross over each other. *A crossroads in life* is a time when you must choose which direction to take in life.
> Examples include choosing which university to go to after school, getting a first job, choosing who to marry, moving house, changing career, having children, deciding what to do when you retire.

2 Ask students to look at the pictures of Andy, Lucy, and Maureen. Ask *How old do you think they are? What sort of 'crossroads' choices might they have to make?*

T 11.5 [**CD 3: Track 26**] Play the recording. Ask students to listen and complete the chart

> **Answers**
>
> | | What has happened? | What choices do they have? |
> |---|---|---|
> | **Andy** | Made redundant | Move to Australia or start own business |
> | **Lucy** | Boyfriend has asked her to marry him | Get married or say no and upset boyfriend |
> | **Maureen** | Her husband has died | To move to a new house on her own or live with her daughter |

3 **T 11.5** Play the recording again. Ask students to check their answers. Put students in pairs to write reasons for and against the decisions.

Answers and tapescript
Reasons for/against
Andy

Moving to Australia	For: he's always dreamed of it and has a friend there
	Against: his parents would miss him
Starting own business	For: he'd enjoy it
	Against: he'd have to work hard

Lucy

Getting married	For: it would make her boyfriend happy, she wouldn't lose him
	Against: she wants to spend money on travelling and having fun/it's too early/she might feel trapped

Maureen

Living in a flat	For: it would be safer
	Against: it would be difficult living on her own
Living with her family	For: she loves them
	Against: she would not be independent

T 11.5
At a crossroads in life
Andy

I've had some bad news about my job. I'm going to be made redundant in three months' time. It's such a shock! I've worked for the same computer company for 12 years. But I need to think what to do next.

Actually, I've always dreamed of emigrating to Australia. So I might try that! I have a friend in Melbourne, and I'm sure he would help me to find a job there. But if I went to Australia, my parents would be so sad. And they wouldn't be able to visit me very much. It's so expensive. So I would have to find a really good job, so that I could come home a lot, or pay for them to visit me. That might not be easy.

Another thing I might do is start my own business, using my redundancy money. What if I started a computer servicing company? People are always having problems with their computers. If I did that, I'd have to work really hard in the beginning. It wouldn't be easy, but I would enjoy it, I think.

Lucy

I'm so surprised! My boyfriend's just asked me to marry him! It was terrible, because I couldn't give him an answer immediately. You see, I really love my boyfriend, and I think I want to marry him sometime, but not yet.

He wants us to get married next June. That's only nine months away. I think it might be better to wait.

If we got married in June, we'd have to save all our money for the wedding and a house. But I don't want to do that. I want us to enjoy ourselves while we're young. I want to go away and travel. I'd like to learn how to ride a horse and how to scuba-dive. Oh, there's lots of things I want to do. If we waited a bit, we could do all those things.

If I got married now, I might feel trapped. That would be terrible. But what if I told him I didn't want to marry him yet? Would he understand? He might not, and I don't want to lose him. I do want to marry him. I just want to put the wedding off for a while. That's all.

Maureen

Well, my husband died three months ago, and I've got to decide what to do next. He was ill for a long time, so it wasn't a shock. But we were married for 41 years, and I can't imagine life without him.

I don't think I want to live in this house anymore. Anyway, it's so big for just one person. So I might sell it and move to a flat. I'd feel safer if I lived in a flat, because there would be other people around. I think it might be difficult living on my own. Or my daughter says I can live with her and her family. So I might do that, but I'm not sure. I love my daughter and my grandchildren very much. But if I lived with them, I wouldn't feel independent anymore. And I'm still young – I'm only 68! I'm healthy with plenty of friends. There's lots I can still do with my life, I'm sure. I just need to keep busy.

What do you think?

Put students in pairs to discuss what they would do in the different situations. In feedback, ask individuals from each pair to share one or two ideas with the class. Make sure they are using the structure *If I were (Andy), I'd …* correctly.

4 **T 11.6** [CD 3: Track 27] Play the recording. Find out which pairs had the same ideas as the speakers on the recording.

Tapescript

Andy

Well, I am now the proud owner of a new business called 'Computer Solutions'. It has been difficult, but everything's going well at the moment. In fact, my first customer was a lovely girl called Annabel, and she's now my girlfriend! And guess where she's from – that's right! – Australia! We're going there at Christmas to visit her family.

Lucy

I'm not married, but yes, I'm still with Steve. He was really upset with me at first, when I told him I didn't want to get married yet. But we talked and talked about it, and he finally agreed that we should wait. We're saving a little money every month for our future wedding. But we are also saving to go on holiday! We're going to Mexico next month. I can't wait!

Maureen

I still miss Tony every day, but life's getting a bit easier. I sold the house, and I've moved into a little flat in a retirement home. It's not too far from my daughter's house, so I see her and my grandchildren a lot. It's very nice here, and I've made some new friends. I have a special friend here called Jeff. He's on his own, too, so we do lots of things together.

Discussion – Dilemmas

Divide students into groups of four to discuss the situations on SB p151. A good way to do this is to give each student in the group one of the dilemmas. Each student must lead the discussion about their dilemma, making sure that everyone in their group has a chance to speak, and taking a few notes. In feedback, students report what their group said for the class.

EXTRA IDEA

Ask each group to think of another dilemma for the rest of the class to discuss.

WRITING (SB p114)

Writing for talking – My dreams for the future

The aim of this writing section is to write a talk, using future forms, and thinking about pauses and sentence stress.

1 Ask students to prepare a few notes under the headings, then discuss their future hopes and ambitions with a partner.

2 **T 11.13** [CD 3: Track 34] Play the recording. Ask students to read and listen, and answer the questions.

Answers

Definite plans: visit and spend Christmas with brother in Australia

Not sure about: which course to study – fashion or landscape design

Hopes, ambitions: have own business and work for herself; marry and have children

Dreams: successful gardening company; designing beautiful gardens; beautiful house; two beautiful children; successful husband

3 Ask students to read the text and underline useful expressions. In feedback, build up a list on the board.

You may wish to point out that Susannah uses *going to* for definite plans, *might* when she's not sure, and *'ll* when talking about dreams.

Possible answers

At the moment I'm …

I often dream about …

My most immediate plans are …

I'm going to …

I have to make a final decision about …

I might …

In five or ten years' time I would like to …

One day I hope to …

In my dreams I see myself …

I'll …

4 Ask students to rewrite the first paragraph, changing the information in order to talk about themselves.

5 Ask students to prepare a talk, using the useful expressions they underlined. When students are ready, ask them to mark pauses and stresses, then practise reading aloud with a partner. Ask a few individuals to read out their text for the class.

> **PRONUNCIATION HELP**
> Show students how to mark pauses and stresses by writing the following two sentences on the board, and marking it up as shown. Tell them to use a different coloured pen from the one they used when writing their talks.
>
> My most immediate plans // are holiday plans. // I'm going to visit my brother // who's working in Australia. //

READING AND SPEAKING (SB p90)

Supervolcano

> **ABOUT THE TEXT**
> The text is about the supervolcano in Yellowstone National Park, Wyoming, USA. The text is exploited by true/false questions and ordering tasks. It contextualizes the use of the second conditional.
>
> You may wish to pre-teach vocabulary around the topic of volcanoes: *active, extinct, erupt, ash, rock, lava, geyser, contaminated.*

1 Lead in by putting students in pairs to discuss the questions. Have a brief class feedback.

> **Some famous volcanoes**
> Active: Cotopaxi, Mauna Loa, Vesuvius, Mount Etna, Stromboli
> Extinct: Aconcagua, Kilimanjaro, Orizaba, Fujiyama

2 Ask students to read the first half of the article, and discuss their answers in pairs.

> **Answers**
> 1 ✗   3 ✗   5 ✗
> 2 ✓   4 ✓   6 ✓ (in the 'near' future)

3 Ask students to read the second half of the article and order the events. Check the answers as a class. Get students to read out their answers in pairs in order to practise the second conditional.

> **Answers**
> 1 87,000 people would die immediately.
> 2 there would be no summer in Europe.
> 3 only 10% of our sunlight would reach the earth.
> 4 the tropical forests would die.
> 5 Warmer countries would have famines.
> 6 Iceland might start to help feed the world.

4 Discuss the question as a class.

> **Answer**
> Because an eruption is unlikely to happen in the next few centuries.

5 Ask students in pairs to search the text, and find what the numbers refer to.

> **Answers**
> 3 million   visitors (to Yellowstone every year)
> 1960s   scientists discovered that Yellowstone was a supervolcano
> 9,000   square metres (size of the park)
> 40   number of supervolcanos
> 74,000   years ago (most recent supervolcano explosion)
> 640,000   years ago (when Yellowstone erupted)
> 250kmph   speed that ash and rock would shoot up
> 87,000   people would die if Yellowstone erupted
> 3/4   of the USA would be covered in ash
> 90%   of sunlight would be blocked by a volcanic winter

What do you think?

Divide students into small groups of four or five to discuss the questions. Ask one student to chair the discussion, making sure that everybody else has a chance to speak.

VOCABULARY AND SPEAKING (SB p92)

Students will have already met quite a few phrasal verbs because they are so common in English. These exercises are staged in such a way as to illustrate some of the different types of phrasal verbs and to show that they can have both literal and non-literal (idiomatic) meaning.

Literal phrasal verbs

1 Read through the examples with your students to make sure they have an idea what is meant by a phrasal verb. Show how literal these examples are by miming *take your coat off* and *give away money.*

2 Ask them to do this exercise on their own. Stress that the words in this exercise are used literally and, therefore, they should be able to work out the answers quite logically and easily.

Ask students to check their answers with a partner, and then go through the answers quickly with the whole class.

3 Focus students on the phrasal verbs in the box. Put them in small groups to do or mime the actions. The other students must guess which phrasal verbs they are doing or miming.

4 Ask students to complete the sentences with the correct phrasal verb.

T 11.7 [CD 3: Track 28] Play the recording. Ask students to listen and check their answers.

Answers and tapescript
1 I'm **looking for** my glasses. Have you seen them anywhere?
2 I like these jeans. Can I **try** them **on**?
3 You shouldn't drop litter on the floor! **Pick** it **up**!
4 Don't **throw away** the newspaper. I haven't read it yet.
5 If you don't feel well, go and **lie down**.
6 'Do you like my dress?' 'Let me see. **Turn round**. Yes. Very nice.'
7 Why are all these lights on? **Turn** them **off** .

Idiomatic phrasal verbs

5 Read through the introduction and make it clear that here the phrasal verbs have a non-literal, idiomatic meaning. In other words you cannot work out the meaning logically from the parts. The three examples should illustrate this.

6 Ask students to work in small groups to do or mime the actions. The other students must guess which phrasal verbs they are doing or miming. They may need to look up the verbs in a dictionary (in which case they will have to choose the correct meaning for the context), but they should try to guess the meaning from the context of the whole phrase.

7 Ask students to complete the sentences with the correct phrasal verb.

T 11.8 [CD 3: Track 29] Play the recording. Ask students to listen and check their answers.

Answers and tapescript
1 Can I **look up** this word in your dictionary?
2 I've **run out of** milk, so I can't have any cereal.
3 My boss is a great guy. I **get on** well **with** him.
4 Leave little Ela here. I'll **look after** her while you're out.
5 Oh no! Our car's **broken down**, and there isn't a garage for miles!
6 **Look out**! There's some broken glass on the floor.

Talking about you

8 Ask students to complete the sentences with the correct phrasal verbs.

T 11.9 [CD 3: Track 30] Play the recording. Ask students to listen and check their answers. Then put students in pairs to practise asking and answering the questions.

Answers and tapescript
1 How do you **get on with** your parents?
2 When did you last catch a plane? Did it **take off** on time?
3 Have you ever **looked after** a baby? Whose?
4 Do you **throw away** all your rubbish, or do you recycle some of it?
5 When did you last **try** something **on** in a clothes shop? Did you buy it?
6 When you see litter in the street, do you **pick** it **up**?
7 Have you ever **run out of** petrol? What did you do?
8 If you won a lot of money, would you **give** any of it **away**? Who to?

ADDITIONAL MATERIAL

Workbook Unit 11
Exercise 11 Vocabulary – Phrasal verbs

EVERYDAY ENGLISH (SB p93)

Ask students to look at the photos. Ask *How are the people feeling?* Elicit a range of adjectives, for example *shocked, scared, frightened, happy, excited.*

Exclamations with *so* and *such*

1 **T 11.10** [CD 3: Track 31] Play the recording. Ask students to listen and discuss the questions.

Answers and tapescript
I was scared. I was very scared. I was so scared.

So is more spoken than written. It emphasizes the adjective, and makes it stronger.

2 Put students in pairs to compare the sentences, and form the rules. Go round helping and prompting.

Answers
The rules of use are straightforward but difficult to remember.
so + adjective
such a/an + (adjective) + singular noun
such + plural or uncount noun
so many + plural noun
so much + uncountable noun

These rules are written out in Grammar Reference 11.3 on SB p141.

Put students in pairs to underline the main stress.

T 11.11 [CD 3: Track 32] Play the recording. Ask students to listen, check, and repeat the phrases.

> **Answers and tapescript**
> *So* and *such* are very strongly stressed because they are being used for emphasis.
>
> **T 11.11**
> I was <u>so</u> worried!   It's <u>such</u> a nice day!
> We had <u>so</u> much fun!

3 Ask students to complete and match the sentences. Let them check their answers.

T 11.12 [CD 3: Track 33] Play the recording. Ask students to listen and check. Ask students to practise saying the exclamations in pairs.

> **Answers and tapescript**
> 1 Their house is **such a** mess! I don't know how they live in it.
> 2 There were **so many** people at the party! There was nowhere to dance.
> 3 I'm **so** hungry! I could eat a horse.
> 4 Jane and Pete are **such** nice people! But I can't stand their kids.
> 5 I've spent **so much** money this week! I don't know where it's all gone.
> 6 A present! For me? You're **so** kind! You really didn't have to.
> 7 We've had **such a** nice time! Thank you so much for inviting us.
> 8 Molly's **such a** clever dog! She understands every word I say.

4 Put students in pairs or small groups to discuss the situations.

> **Sample answers**
> It was such a good party./We had so much fun.
> It was such a long journey./I'm so tired.
> It was so sad./It was such a good book.
> It's so lovely./That's such a nice picture.
> That was so delicious./That was such a delicious meal.
> You're so rude/stupid/annoying!

Don't forget!

Workbook Unit 11

Exercise 10 Pronunciation – Words that sound the same

Exercises 12–13 Check it

Grammar Reference
Look at the exercises on SB p141 as a class, or set for homework. The answers are on TB p156.

Word list
Remind your students of the Word list for this unit on SB p157. They could translate the words, learn them at home, or transfer some of the words to their vocabulary notebook.

Pronunciation Book Unit 11

12

Present Perfect Continuous
Hot verbs *bring/take/come/go*
Social expressions 2

Trying your best

Introduction to the unit

The title of this unit is 'Trying your best'. The story of how Al, a homeless person on the streets of New York, makes a living by selling magazines provides the context for contrasting the Present Perfect Simple and Present Perfect Continuous to talk about unfinished past. The unit also looks at the Present Perfect Continuous to express a present result of a past activity.

The *Reading and speaking* section contains a newspaper article about a 15-year-old girl who is planning a walk to the North Pole. The *Listening and speaking* section is a song called *If you come back* by the band Blue. Both the article and song provide further practice of the Present Perfect Continuous.

Language aims

Grammar – Present Perfect Simple In Unit 7 several uses of the Present Perfect Simple were presented and practised.

Your students should be familiar with the form of the Present Perfect by now, but it is most unlikely that their production of the tense is accurate. This is for the reasons mentioned in the teaching notes to Unit 7. Although a similar form of *have* + the past participle exists in many other European languages, its use in English is dictated by aspect (i.e. how the speaker sees the event), not necessarily time.

Present Perfect Continuous This tense is sometimes introduced idiomatically in first-year courses, and in this unit of *New Headway Pre-Intermediate – the THIRD edition*, it is not examined in any great depth. This is because the subtleties of it are too complex for this level. There are two aspects which students have to perceive, the perfect aspect and the continuous aspect, and it is unreasonable to expect them to be able to do this immediately. As it is a continuous verb form, there are more 'bits' for students to get wrong.

Common mistakes

*I been learning English for three years.
*I've learn English for three years.
*I've been learn English for three years.

The concepts expressed by the Present Perfect Continuous are often expressed by either a present tense verb form in other languages, or by a form of the Present Perfect Simple. Many languages manage without the need to express the ideas inherent in the continuous aspect, but English has it, and where it is possible, prefers to use it. *I've been learning English for three years* sounds much more natural than *I've learned English for three years*. But *I've lived here all my life* sounds better than *I've been living here all my life*, because of the temporariness expressed by the continuous aspect.

When the Present Perfect is used to refer to an activity with a result in the present, it can be difficult to know whether to use the simple or the continuous. *I've painted the bathroom* and *I've been painting the bathroom* refer to the same action, but mean very different things. The first refers to a completed action and the result is that the bathroom painting is finished. The second refers to a recent activity which may or may not be finished – if a 'result' is mentioned, it is not likely to be the finished bathroom, but an incidental result of the activity of painting, e.g. having paint on your clothes, being tired or stiff. If a completed quantity is stated, the Present Perfect Simple must be used, not the Continuous. This is because of the idea of activity in progress expressed by the continuous aspect and the idea of completion expressed by the simple aspect: *I've written three letters today.*

Common mistakes

I learn English for three years.
I've been knowing her for a long time.
I've been writing three letters today.
I'm hot because I've run.

Vocabulary In this section, the difference in use between *bring* and *take* and *come* and *go* are practised.

Everyday English In this section, common social expressions such as *Excuse me*, *Congratulations* and *Thank you for having me* are practised in dialogues.

Notes on the unit

STARTER (SB p94)

This is a quick question and answer session to preview the new structure introduced in this unit.

1 Students work in pairs to ask and answer the questions.
2 Answer your students' questions.

STREET LIFE (SB p94)

Present Perfect Continuous

> **ABOUT THE TEXT**
>
> The Present Perfect Continuous is contextualized in a text about a homeless person selling the magazine *Street News*. Homeless people selling magazines and newspapers are a common sight on the streets of major American and European cities. Charitable groups in several large US cities have set up organizations to help homeless people write and sell their own newspapers in order to earn some money. These newspapers campaign on behalf of the homeless and highlight the major social issues of the day. They also allow homeless people to voice their views and opinions. In Britain, homeless people sell a magazine called *The Big Issue*, the idea of which is to enable homeless people to generate income without begging, and to raise public consciousness of the issue of homelessness.
>
> You may wish to ask students to read the Grammar Reference on the Present Perfect Continuous for homework before beginning this presentation.
>
> As was explained in *Language aims*, the Present Perfect Continuous is dealt with relatively lightly in this unit. It is unrealistic to expect students to perceive all the differences of meaning between the simple and the continuous, and the perfect aspect will continue to present problems.

1 Ask students to look at the photograph of Al. Ask *Where is he? What is he doing? Why?* Elicit key vocabulary: *homeless*, *subway station*, *income*, *magazine*.

Ask students to read the text, and answer the questions.

> **Answers**
> 1 He lost his business, home, and family.
> 2 On the streets of New York
> 3 By selling the magazine *Street News*

2 **T 12.1** [CD 3: Track 35] Ask students to work in pairs to match the questions and answers. Do the first as an example. Play the recording so that they can check their answers. Ask them to complete Al's answers to question 4 in their own words.

> **Answers and tapescript**
> 1 e 2 f 3 b 4 c 5 a 6 d
>
> **T 12.1**
> 1 **How long have you been sleeping on the streets?**
>   For a year. It was very cold at first, but after a while you get used to it.
> 2 **Why did you come to New York?**
>   I came here to look for work, and I never left.
> 3 **How long have you been selling *Street News*?**
>   For six months. I'm outside the subway station seven days a week selling the magazine.
> 4 **Have you made many friends?**
>   Lots. But I get fed up with people who think I drink or take drugs. My problem is I'm homeless. I want a job, but I need somewhere to live before I can get a job. So I need money to get somewhere to live, but I can't get money because I don't have a job, and I can't get a job because I haven't got anywhere to live. I'm trapped! But now I'm trying hard to make some money by selling *Street News*.
> 5 **How many copies do you sell a day?**
>   Usually about seventy. But I've brought a hundred with me.
> 6 **How many copies have you sold today?**
>   So far, ten. But it's still early. Here, take one!

3 Drill the Present Perfect questions round the class briefly. Model the conversation with a student then put students in pairs to practise. They should take it in turns to cover the questions, then the answers, and act out the conversation.

Answer the questions as a class.

> **Answers**
> 1 Questions b and e are in the Present Perfect Continuous. The other tenses are the Present Simple (a), the Present Perfect (c and d), and the Past Simple (f).
> Point out the form of the Present Perfect Continuous at this stage:
> Question word + *have* + subject + *been* + *-ing* ... ?
> *How long* + *have* + *you* + *been* + *selling* ... ?
> 2 *How long have you been selling Street News?* asks about the activity of selling.
> *How many copies have you sold today?* asks about the number of magazines sold.
> 3 **I have been reading** this book all week.
> **I have read** two books this month.
> The first sentence refers to an unfinished activity which started in the past and continues until now.
> The second sentence refers to the number of books read during a period of time up to now.

Refer students to Grammar Reference 12.1 on p142.

4 **T 12.2** [CD 3: Track 36] Ask students to work in pairs to make questions. Do the first two as an example with the class to show students that a number of different tenses are needed. When they are ready, play the recording so that they can check and correct their questions.

> **Answers and tapescript**
> How long **have you been** trying to find a job?
> How many jobs **have you** had?
> How long **have you been** standing here today?
> How **did you** lose your business?
> How long **have you** had your dog?
> Who**'s** your best friend?
> Where **did you** meet him?
> How long **have you** known each other?

Play and pause the recording for students to repeat or drill the questions round the class. Pay close attention to the weak pronunciation of have /əv/ and been /bɪn/ in the Present Perfect questions.

5 **T 12.3** [CD 3: Track 37] Students work in pairs to ask the questions and invent Al's answers. Play the recording so that students can compare their answers.

> **Sample answers and tapescript**
> 1 How long have you been trying to find a job?
> **For over a year. It's been really hard.**
> 2 How many jobs have you had?
> **About 20, maybe more. I've done everything.**
> 3 How long have you been standing here today?
> **Since 8.00 this morning, and I'm freezing.**
> 4 How did you lose your business?
> **I had a small company, but it went out of business, and then I started having health problems. But without the job, I didn't have health insurance anymore, so things got worse.**
> 5 How long have you had your dog?
> **I've had him for about two months, that's all.**
> 6 Who's your best friend?
> **A guy named Bob, who's also from Pennsylvania, like me.**
> 7 Where did you meet him?
> **I met him here in New York.**
> 8 How long have you known each other?
> **Almost a year. I met him right after I came to New York.**

Discussing grammar

1 Students work in pairs or small groups to choose the correct verb form. Do the first one with the class as an example. Expect students to make mistakes with this exercise, and tell them not to worry. As you correct, remind them of the rules.

> **Answers**
> 1 **have you been living** (because the activity began in the past and continues to the present)
> 2 **has found** (because this is a completed activity – the action of finding doesn't last a long time)
> 3 **have been going out** (because the activity began in the past and continues to the present)
> 4 **bought** (because we have a definite time – a few months ago)
> 5 **have you had** (because *have* to express possession is a state verb, not an activity, so it cannot go into the continuous)
> 6 **has been working** (because he is still working as a postman)
> 7 **'ve been writing** (The sentence is stressing the continuous activity, not the fact that the essay is written. It may or may not be finished.)
> 8 **'ve written** (The continuous is not possible because the quantity (six) is stated.)

Talking about you

2 Ask students to work in pairs to do this exercise. Check the answers, then drill the questions. Ask the questions round the class. Finally, put students in pairs to interview each other using the questions.

> **Answers**
> 1 How long **have** you **been studying** at this school?
> 2 How long **have** you **used/have you been using** this book?
> 3 Which book **did** you **have** before this one?
> 4 How long **have** you **known** your teacher?

What have they been doing?

3 This activity practises the other use of the Present Perfect Continuous, to talk about present (incidental) results of a past activity. It differs from the similar use of the Present Perfect Simple, practised in exercise 4, which is used to talk about results of a completed past action, especially when we say *how much/many*.

Read the introduction and look at the example sentence as a class. Students work in pairs to make a sentence about the people.

> **Sample answers**
> b His back hurts because he's been digging the garden.
> c She's got paint on her clothes because she's been painting the bathroom.
> d He's got dirty hands because he's been mending his bicycle.
> e They have no money because they've been shopping.
> f They're tired because they've been playing tennis.
> g Her eyes hurt because she's been /reading/working/ studying.
> h He's wet because he's been washing the dog.
> i He's got a red face because he's been cooking/baking.

4 Students work in pairs to complete sentences. Ask them why we use the Present Perfect here (because we are talking about the completed action and we talk about *how much/many*).

> **Answers**
> 1 He's **run** five miles.
> 2 She's **painted** three walls.
> 3 They've **spent** all their money.
> 4 They've **played** six games.
> 5 He's **made** a cake and a pie.

Exchanging information

5 In this information gap activity students must ask each other questions to find out about Stelios Haji-Ioannou. In an activity of this kind the more preparation and setting up you do, the more likely it is that students will do it accurately and well.

Lead in by focusing students on the photograph of Stelios and asking them the questions in the Student's Book to find out what they know about him.

6 Divide the class into pairs and ask each pair to decide who is A and who is B. Student A should turn to page 145, Student B to page 148. Give students four or five minutes to read through their information, then prepare questions using the question word prompts. Monitor and help them prepare. When they are ready, model the activity briefly by asking one or two questions, then let students ask and answer to complete their information.

> **Answers (complete text)**
> **Stelios Haji-Ioannou**
> **The creator of easyJet airlines and the 'easy' brand**
>
> Stelios was born **in Greece** in **1967**. He was educated in **Athens** and then studied **economics** at the London School of Economics. When he was only 17, he drove a **Porsche**.
>
> He started his first business, a shipping company, when he was **25**. He sold it in **2005** for **$1.3 billion**. He now has a fortune worth at least £400 million.
>
> Stelios is best-known for creating EasyJet, which he has been running since **1995**. EasyJet is Europe's largest low-cost airline. It has over **100** jets, which fly to more than forty destinations. In its lifetime, EasyJet has carried over **150 million** passengers.
>
> Over the years, Stelios has started several businesses – **Internet cafés, travel, leisure, and personal finance**.
> Stelios supports various educational schemes. He has been helping students by **giving them money to study at the London School of Economics since 2005**. He has so far given the college over £2m.
>
> Since 2004, he has been working with 100 employees in **Camden, north London**. He also works in Athens. He travels for about four months a year, because **he is looking for new business ideas**. His motto is '**The cheaper you can make something, the more people there are who can afford it.**'

ADDITIONAL MATERIAL

Workbook Unit 12
Exercises 1–4 Present Perfect Simple
Exercises 5 and 6 Present Perfect Continuous
Exercises 7–9 Tense review

Hot verbs – *bring, take, come,* and *go*

Read through the examples as a class.

1 Ask students to work in pairs to underline the examples. Then ask the pairs to interview each other, using the questions. Ask a few individuals to summarize what their partner said for the class.

2 Ask students to look at the pictures, and point out the rules of use. You could check the students' understanding by asking them to perform simple tasks. For example, say *Maria, bring me your book. Now take it to Stefan. Come here, Alex. Now go to the window.*

3 Ask students to complete the conversations. Let them check their answers in pairs.

T 12.4 **[CD 3: Track 38]** Play the recording. Ask students to listen and check.

Answers and tapescript

1 A Goodbye, everyone! I'm **going** on holiday tomorrow.
  B Where are you **going**?
  A Australia. I'm **taking** my family to visit their cousins in Sydney.
  B Lucky you! When you **come** back, **bring** me a T-shirt!

2 A Listen, class! Please finish your work before you **go** home. And tomorrow, don't forget to **bring** in your money for the school trip. We're **going** to the Natural History Museum.
  B Oh, Miss Jones! Can't you **take** us somewhere more exciting?

3 A Daniel, you were very late last night. What time did you **come** home?
  B It was before midnight, Mum, honest. Mick **brought** me home in his car.

4 A I've been decorating my new flat. You must **come** and visit me on Saturday. And **bring** Emma and Jake with you. I'll cook you a meal.
  B Great! We'll **bring** some champagne to toast your new home!

5 (*In London*)
  A I'll miss you when I **go** back home to Spain. You must **come** and visit me at Christmas.
  B I'd love to! I want you to **take** this photo with you. It will remind you of the day we **went** to Oxford together.
  A OK. And when you visit, **bring** me some more English books to read!

6 (*In France*)
  A I'm **going** to London tomorrow, so tonight my best friend is **coming** round to my house to say goodbye. She's **bringing** a present she wants me to **take** to her sister in London.
  B Well, have a good trip!

In her father's footsteps

ABOUT THE TEXTS

The Hempleman-Adams are a real-life father and daughter. They come from Wiltshire in England. The first text was written before Alicia attempted the trip. The follow-up text reveals her success – she completed her walk across Baffin Island to the North Pole in April 2005 in temperatures that touched -50°C. The first newspaper article is exploited by a gist question and specific information questions. There are also opportunities for students to speculate and express their opinions. A tense review related to the text is incorporated.

Vocabulary related to travel may need pre-teaching: *explorer, backpack, sled, journey, trip*

1 Discuss the questions as a class.

Famous explorers

Marco Polo: first European to visit China
Christopher Columbus: discovered America
Ferdinand Magellan: sailed around the world for the first time
Roald Amundsen: first man at the South Pole
Hillary and Tensing: first men to climb Everest

2 Ask students to explain the title. Then give them three or four minutes to read the text, and check whether their explanation matches the text.

Answers

In her father's footsteps means that she is doing the same thing that her father once did. In the text, Alicia is planning to walk to the North Pole, something her father has done twice before.

3 Ask students in pairs to read the complete article and answer the questions.

Answers

1 Yes, she went there in a plane to visit her father when she was eight.
2 Four people, including her physical education teacher.
3 She's been training hard. She's been walking a lot with a heavy backpack, and practising pulling her sled long distances.
4 He's walked to the South Pole once and the North Pole twice. He's flown a balloon over the North Pole and he's climbed the highest mountains in all seven continents.
5 He's a little worried about it. He thinks the cold will be a big problem.
6 Her mother thinks that Alicia is too young to make the journey, but she's trying to stay calm about it. Her great-grandmother said 'Oh, no, not again!' when she heard about it.

4 Put students in pairs to discuss the questions. In feedback, discuss the questions as a class. The answers are the students' own ideas, so encourage a range of views.

Tense review

5 Ask students to complete the sentences. Let them check their answers in pairs.

> **Answers**
> 1 flew
> 2 hasn't walked
> 3 will start/is going to start
> 4 has been planning
> 5 has (already) made
> 6 climbed
> 7 is trying
> 8 hopes

6 Ask students to read the follow up text on page 151 of the Student's Book, and check their predictions to questions 3–5 in exercise 4.

> **Answers**
> 3 She walked up waterfalls and mountains and survived temperatures of -45°C and strong winds.
> 4 She was very successful! She finished the 200 miles in ten days, two days quicker than planned. She also finished the journey faster than her father did!
> 5 Her father feels very proud of her success – but also a bit annoyed that she took a day less than he did. His excuse is that she had much better skis than he had!

What do you think?

Have a whole class discussion on this subject. Encourage students to give reasons for their answers.

WRITING (SB p115)

Linking ideas – Words that join ideas: *and, still, just, unfortunately, ...*

The aim of this writing section is to write an autobiography using linking words.

1 Ask students to look at the example. Then ask students to join the sentences. Let them check their answers in pairs before discussing as a class.

> **Answers**
> 2 **Although** she's **only** 15 years old, she walked to the North Pole.
> 3 **Eventually**, we found someone **who** could speak Russian. / We **eventually** found someone **who** could speak Russian.
> 4 I sent you an email, **which** you didn't receive **unfortunately**. / I sent you an email, **which unfortunately** you didn't receive.
> 5 I love all ice cream **but** I **especially** love strawberry ice cream.
> 6 **When** we were having a picnic, it **suddenly** started to rain. / ... it started to rain **suddenly**.

> 7 They've **just** had a baby girl, **so of course**, they're delighted. / ... **so** they're delighted, **of course**.
> 8 He's always giving me advice. **However**, I don't **usually** follow it.

2 Ask students to read the biography and answer the questions.

> **Answers**
> He became interested in the outdoor life when he lived in a small village with his mother and loved being outside in the fresh air.
> Achievements: climbed Kilimanjaro, Everest, the highest peaks in all seven continents, and walked to the North and South Poles.
> *The impossible grand slam* is climbing the highest peaks in all seven continents, and walking to the North and South Poles.

3 Ask students to read the biography again, and put the words in the text. Let them work in pairs.

> **Answers**
> David Hempleman-Adams was born in the railway town of Swindon, Wiltshire in 1956. **Unfortunately,** when he was **just** 9 years old, his parents divorced and he had to make a big decision. Should he live with his father or move to a small village with his mother? **Eventually,** he chose to go with his mother. **Fortunately,** he loved country life and **especially** being outside in the fresh air.
> **Soon** he/He **soon** became interested in climbing. **First of all,** he climbed in the Welsh mountains, in North America, and **then** in 1981, he climbed Kilimanjaro, Africa's highest mountain. His dream was to climb Everest, and this he **eventually** did in 1993. **However,** Everest was not enough and David wanted other challenges. He wanted to climb the highest peaks in all seven continents, and to walk to the North and South Poles.
> **Although** he fell through the ice and was attacked by a polar bear, he succeeded in all his challenges. On 29 April 1998, he became the first man in history to complete the so-called 'impossible grand slam' of peaks and Poles.
> **Still** not satisfied, he took up ballooning and broke three more records. **First,** in 2000, he ballooned solo to the North Pole, **next,** in 2003, he crossed the Atlantic, and **finally** in 2004 he broke the world altitude record.
> **Also,** in 2004, David's amazing achievements were recognized worldwide in New York, **when** astronaut Buzz Aldrin presented him with the Explorer's Club medal. **At last,** he was a world hero. David married in 1992 and has three daughters. **Incredibly,** the eldest, Alicia, has followed in her father's footsteps. At **just** 15 she became the youngest person to walk to the North Pole.

4 Ask students to prepare a list of important events, and discuss them with a partner.

5 Ask students to write their autobiographies. Pass them round the class. Ask individuals to read out some of the best autobiographies.

Song – If you come back

ABOUT THE TEXT

Blue was a popular boy band, made up of four London-based singers in their twenties, Duncan, Antony, Lee, and Simon. They formed in 2000. *If you come back*, a pop classic, was their third single, released in 2001. It appears on the *All Rise* album. The band have since split up but say this is only temporary.

The difficult vocabulary is dealt with in a glossary. However, you may wish to point out that the song is full of 'pop clichés' such as 'I'll be there till the end of time' and 'we can be as one'.

Lead in by asking questions about the band and the title. Ask *What do you know about Blue? What do they usually sing about? What do you think the song, 'If you come back', will be about?*

1 **T 12.5** [CD 3: Track 39] Play the recording. Ask students to listen to the song with books closed and answer the gist questions.

Answers

The boy is singing to his girlfriend.
He is trying to persuade her to go out with him again.

2 **T 12.5** Ask students to work in pairs to complete the lines of the song. Play the song again so that students can check their answers.

Answers

loving; trying; wrong; understand; end; time; side; want; heart; phone; home; wrong; understand; end; show; lives

What do you think?

Ask students to discuss the questions in pairs or small groups, then have a class discussion. Get students to speculate on what he may have done to upset her, and on whether she will come back.

Possible answers

The boy doesn't know why she left, but he thinks he may have done 'something wrong'. Perhaps it was because he didn't know how to 'show' his love. He promises to stay by her side until the end of time, and to build their lives together.

Social Expressions 2

1 Ask students to look at the photos. Ask them what they think the people are saying in each situation. Ask students to work in pairs to complete the conversations with expressions from the boxes.

2 **T 12.6** [CD 3: Track 40] Play the dialogues and pause after each for students to check their answers. After each one ask the pairs to practise saying that dialogue together. Make sure that students use the correct stress and intonation.

Answers and tapescript

1 A **Excuse me!** Can I get past?
  B **Pardon**?
  A Can I get past, please?
  B **I'm sorry**. I didn't hear you. Yes, **of course**.
  A Thanks a lot.
2 A **I hear** you're getting married soon. **Congratulations!**
  B **That's right**, next July. July 21st. Can you come to the wedding?
  A **Oh, what a pity!** That's when we're going away on holiday.
  C **Never mind**. We'll send you some wedding cake.
  A That's very kind.
3 A **Good luck** in your exam!
  B **Same to you**. I hope we both pass.
  A Did you go out last night?
  B **No, of course not**. I went to bed early. **What about you**?
  A Me, too. **See you later** after the exam. Let's go for a drink.
  B **Good idea**.
4 A Here's my train!
  B **Don't worry**. It doesn't leave for another five minutes.
  A **Well**, I'd better get on, anyway, and find my seat. It was lovely staying with you. **Thank you for having me**.
  C **You're welcome**. It was a pleasure.
  A Goodbye, then. See you again soon, I hope.
  B+C **Bye! Safe journey!**

3 **T 12.7** [CD 3: Track 41] Ask students to listen and reply using a correct expression. A good way to do this is to play the recording and ask for choral responses, then play it again and nominate individuals to respond.

Answers and tapescript (Suggested answers in brackets)

1 Excuse me! You're sitting in my seat. (**I'm sorry**)
2 Have a great weekend! (**Thanks. Same to you**)
3 Excuse me, do you know the way ...? (**Pardon?**)
4 Thanks for all your help. (**You're welcome.**)
5 I can't come to your leaving party. (**Oh, what a pity!**)
6 Bye! I'll give you a ring when I arrive home. (**Bye! Safe journey!**)
7 Anna was so rude to everyone last Christmas. Are you going to invite her again? (**No, of course not.**)

4 Put students in pairs to make conversations. Monitor and help. Ask a few pairs to act out their conversations for the class.

EXTRA IDEA

Write expressions from the lesson on pieces of paper. Write *Excuse me, Congratulations, Can I get past please?, I'm getting married, Good luck in the test, See you soon, Thank you for having me, Let's go for a drink, Have a safe journey, See you later.* Hand out the pieces of paper so that every student has one (make duplicates), then ask students to walk round the class saying their phrase to everyone they meet. Students must respond with an appropriate phrase, and if possible continue the conversation. Monitor and participate.

Don't forget!

Workbook Unit 12

Exercise 10 Reading – The girl who reads aloud

Exercise 11 Vocabulary – Hot verbs + *go* and *come*

Exercise 12 Pronunciation – Vowel sounds and spelling

Exercises 13–14 Check it

Grammar Reference

Look at the exercises on SB p142 as a class, or set for homework. The answers are on TB p156.

Word list

Remind your students of the Word list for this unit on SB p157. They could translate the words, learn them at home, or transfer some of the words to their vocabulary notebook.

Pronunciation Book Unit 12

Photocopiable material

The following material may be photocopied freely for classroom use. It may not be adapted, printed, or sold without the permission of Oxford University Press.

Extra ideas and speaking p129

Stop and checks p136

Progress tests p144

Answer keys

Extra ideas answer keys p150

Stop and checks answer keys p152

Progress tests answer keys p153

Grammar Reference exercises answer keys p155

Extra idea Unit 3

Song Don't you want me?

1 Think of somebody who has helped you in your life. *How did he/she help you? How do you feel about that person?*

2 You are going to listen to a song called *Don't you want me?* In the song, you will hear a man singing, then a woman. Listen and decide which of the following statements are true.

He doesn't want her.
She doesn't want him.
They don't want to be with each other anymore.

3 Look at the song and complete the gaps, writing the words in brackets in the correct past tense. Listen and check.

4 Read the statements below. Decide whether they are *a fact*, *his opinion*, or *her opinion*. Discuss your ideas with a partner.

1 They met in a cocktail bar.   **a fact**
2 She became successful because of his help.
3 She became successful but it wasn't because he helped her.
4 They had a relationship for five years.
5 She still needs him.
6 She doesn't need him anymore.

5 How does the man feel? How does the woman feel? Use the words below to help you.

| angry | upset | sorry | free |

Who do you have sympathy with? Why?

Don't you want me?

You (1)_____ (work) as a waitress in a cocktail bar
When I (2)_____ (meet) you
I (3)_____ (pick) you out, I (4)_____ (shake) you up,
and (5)_____ (turn) you around,
(6)_____ (turn) you into someone new

Now five years later on you've got the world at your feet
Success has been so easy for you
But don't forget it's me who put you where you are now
And I can put you back down too

Don't, don't you want me?
You know I can't believe it when I hear that you won't see me
Don't, don't you want me?
You know I don't believe you when you say that you don't need me
It's much too late to find
You think you've changed your mind
You'd better change it back or we will both be sorry
Don't you want me baby? Don't you want me – oh?
Don't you want me baby? Don't you want me – oh?

I (7)_____ (work) as a waitress in a cocktail bar
That much is true
But even then I (8)_____ (know) I'd find a much better place
Either with or without you
The five years we have had have been such good times
I still love you
But now I think it's time I (9)_____ (live) my life on my own
I guess it's just what I must do

Don't you want me baby? Don't you want me – oh?
Don't you want me baby? Don't you want me – oh?

Ian Fleming

Student A

1 Look at the photo of Ian Fleming. Tick (✓) the adjectives that you think describe him.

sophisticated	well-dressed
kind	funny
well-educated	outgoing
good-looking	confident

2 Read the information about the first half of Ian Fleming's life. Answer the questions.

1 Where was Ian Fleming born?
2 What was his family like?
3 What happened to his father?
4 What did Ian think of school and the army?
5 What happened in the early 1930s?
6 What was Ian doing when the Second World War started?

3 Use the cues to write questions about the second half of Ian Fleming's life. Then ask your partner the questions.

1 What / he / do in his career?
   What did he do in his career?
2 Where / he / travel?
3 What / his life / like?
4 What / happen / after the war?
5 Why / 1952 / an important year?
6 How many / books / he / write / before / he / die?
   How many / he / sell?

4 Work in groups. In what ways do you think Ian Fleming was similar to James Bond?

The man behind James Bond

I AN FLEMING wrote 14 James Bond books between 1953 and 1964. But how much is the author like the hero of the books?

Ian Fleming was born in Mayfair, London, on May 28th, 1908. He had three brothers and they were the children of a rich family. His grandfather was a millionaire banker and his father was a Member of Parliament. Ian didn't know his father well because he died in the First World War, when Ian was only nine years old.

Ian was quite close to his brothers but he was very different from them. They all went to Eton, a very expensive private school in the south of England. The brothers enjoyed school, but Ian hated it. He left before graduation. He also hated being in the army and did not want a career as a soldier.

In 1930, Ian went to Geneva to continue his education. Then the next year he wanted to join the Foreign Office, but he didn't pass the exams. He went back to England and he was living with his mother, feeling very bored, when he got a job as a journalist. He worked in London, Berlin, and Moscow.

After that, he became a stockbroker. He was doing this job when the Second World War started. Then his life changed.

...

© Oxford University Press   **Photocopiable**

Ian Fleming

Student B

1 Look at the photo of Ian Fleming. Tick (✓) the adjectives that you think describe him.

sophisticated	well-dressed
kind	funny
well-educated	outgoing
good-looking	confident

2 Read the information about the second half of Ian Fleming's life. Answer the questions.

1 What did he do in his career?
2 Where did he travel?
3 What was his life like?
4 What happened after the war?
5 Why was 1952 an important year?
6 How many books did he write before he died?
  How many did he sell?

3 Use the cues to write questions about the first half of Fleming's life. Then ask your partner the questions.

1 Where / Ian Fleming / born?
  Where was Ian Fleming born?
2 What / his family / like?
3 What / happen / to his father?
4 What / Ian / think of school and the army?
5 What / happen / in the early 1930s?
6 What / he / do / when the Second World War start?

4 Work in groups. In what ways do you think Ian Fleming was similar to James Bond?

The man behind James Bond

I AN FLEMING wrote 14 James Bond books between 1953 and 1964. But how much is the author like the hero of the books?

> ...

He joined Naval Intelligence and had contact with MI5 and the Secret Service. He started working in the world of spies and went on secret missions in North Africa, Lisbon, and the USA. When he wasn't working, he enjoyed an expensive lifestyle. He was good-looking, always well-dressed, and he had a lot of girlfriends. He drank a lot and smoked about 60 cigarettes a day. This created health problems for him later in life.

After the war, he went to Jamaica, bought some land and decided to build a house. He called it *Goldeneye*, a name he also used for one of his books. In 1952, three important things happened – he got married, he had a son, and he started writing the James Bond stories. His first book was *Casino Royale*, then he wrote *Live and Let Die* in 1954.

Fleming wrote the other 12 books in the following 10 years. He continued to enjoy a life of travel, good food, and smart clothes. His last full James Bond novel was *The Man with the Golden Gun*, but Ian Fleming died before its publication. At the time of his death in 1964, his books were incredibly popular with 40 million copies sold around the world.

Find someone who ... (SB p55)

Find someone who has been to China.	Find someone who has been to Portugal.	Find someone who has written a love letter.
Find someone who has been to Australia.	Find someone who has been skiing.	Find someone who has had a party for more than thirty people.
Find someone who has tried Thai food.	Find someone who has flown in a balloon.	Find someone who has been horse riding.
Find someone who has climbed a mountain.	Find someone who has won a competition.	Find someone who has been sailing.
Find someone who has read a book by a British author.	Find someone who has broken a bone.	Find someone who has been windsurfing.
Find someone who has had an adventure holiday.	Find someone who has been to university.	Find someone who has lost something important.
Find someone who has been to Ireland.	Find someone who has worked on a farm.	Find someone who has never failed an exam.

Extra idea Unit 9

Song Come away with me

1 In your opinion, which of the following are the most romantic things for a couple to do?

> Writing a poem or song for the other person
> Running into the sea hand in hand
> Walking across fields of knee-high grass together
> Having a meal in a candle-lit restaurant
> Standing together on top of a mountain
> Watching a film together
> Listening to the rain falling on the roof
> Holding hands while walking in the park
> Travelling far away on a bus

What's the most romantic thing you have ever done?

2 Listen to a song called *Come away with me.* Which of the romantic things in exercise 1 would the singer like to do?

3 Look at the song and choose the best word in *italics* to fill each gap. Listen and check.

4 Look at this extract from the song. Then use your imagination, and discuss the questions with a partner.

> Come away with *me* on a bus
> Come away where *they* can't tempt *us*
> With *their lies*…

Who is *me*, and who is *us*?
How old are they? How do they feel?
Why do they need to go on a bus?
Where are they going? Why?
Who are *they*? What are *their lies*?
What is the story behind the song?
What do you think will happen?

Come away with me

Come away with me *tonight/in the night*
Come away with me
And I will *write/sing* you a song

Come away with me on a *bus/train*
Come away where they can't tempt us
With their *smiles/lies*

I want to walk with you
On a *cloudy/frosty* day
In fields where the *yellow/green* grass grows knee-high
So won't you try to come

Come away with me and we'll *sit/kiss*
On a mountaintop
Come away with me
And I'll never stop *loving/holding* you

And I want to *wake up/get up* with the rain
Falling on a *window/tin* roof
While I'm safe there in your arms
So all I ask is for you
To come away with me *tonight/in the night*
Come away with me

Speaking Unit 10

Student A

- You're at home. It's 7.00 p.m. You've done your English homework, exercises 1, 2, and 3 from page 9 of *Headway Pre-Intermediate Workbook*. You are now watching TV.

- Decide what you are going to do for the rest of the night. Go out, stay in, watch TV, go to bed early …?

- The phone rings. It's your friend **Student B** from your English class. Answer the phone by saying your number: *322 4987*.

Student B

- You're at home. It's 7.00 p.m. You want to start your English homework but you have left your workbook in class.

- You need to contact **Student A** from your English class to find out what the homework is, and when you can go round to his/her house to borrow a workbook.

- Phone your friend **Student A**, who will start the conversation. Ask *How are you?* and have a short chat. Then find out what the homework was. Say *I've forgotten what the English homework was. Do you know?* Ask to go round to borrow **Student A**'s workbook.

Student C

- You're at home in London at 22 Hill Road. Your house is 10 minutes' walk from Highgate tube station (on the Northern Line). It's 7.00 p.m. On Wednesday, **Student D**, from France, comes to stay with you while he/she does a one-month English course.

- You don't know how **Student D** is travelling from France – by plane or by train? Decide whether you will meet him/her at the airport, train station, or at the tube station.

- The phone rings. It's **Student D**. Answer the phone by saying your number: *899 0452*. Ask *How are you?* and have a short chat. Then find out how he/she is travelling and make arrangements for meeting him/her. End the conversation by saying *We're looking /forward to meeting you. Goodbye.*

Student D

- You are French, from Paris. On Wednesday you are going to London, England, for a one-month English course. You are staying with **Student C** in Highgate, London. You need to contact **Student C** to find out his/her address and to make arrangements for getting to his/her house.

- Decide how you are travelling to England. By plane or by train? What time do you arrive in London? Do you want **Student C** to meet you at the airport or train station, or will you take the tube to their house?

- Phone your host **Student C**, who will start the conversation. Find out his/her address, tell him/her how you are travelling, and give your arrival time. Ask *Please would you come and meet me at … (the airport/train station/tube station,)?*, or, *Which is the nearest tube station?*

Student E

- You're at home in your flat. It's 7.00 p.m. Your flatmate, Mary, is out.

- Do you know what she is doing tonight or not? Decide (or guess) what time she will be back.

- The phone rings. It's **Student F**. Answer the phone by saying your number: *622 9087*. It's for Mary. Say *I'm sorry, but Mary's … .* Ask *Can I take a message?* Write down the message for Mary. Do not give her mobile number.

Student F

- It's 7.00 pm. You are still at the office. You've found a fantastic second-hand car that you think your friend Mary would like to buy, but the owner says that somebody else is interested in buying it too.

- You need to speak to Mary urgently. If she isn't at home, leave a message for her to call you as soon as she can. Decide where she can reach you later and leave your contact numbers (at the office, at home, or out). Try to get her mobile number.

- Phone Mary. Her flatmate, **Student E**, picks up the phone and starts the conversation. Say *Hi, can I speak to Mary, please?*

Extra idea Unit 11

Song What if...?

1 We use *What if…?* when we speculate about unusual or impossible situations. In pairs, ask and answer the *What if…?* questions below.

What if there was no light?   **We wouldn't be able to see.**
What if there was no time?   **We …**
What if everybody lived forever?

2 Think of your own *What if…?* question. Ask other people in the class. Tell the class any imaginative responses.

3 Listen to a song called *What if…?* by *Coldplay*, and decide which of the following is true.

The singer is worried that there will be no light or time.
The singer is hoping that the girl will decide to have a relationship with him.
The singer is worried about making a mistake and losing his girlfriend.

4 Read the song and decide what the missing words are. The missing word usually rhymes with the word at the end of the line before it.

Listen again and check your answers.

5 Which statement best describes the message of the song?

1 *If you decide not to go out with me, I won't mind.*
2 *If you don't take a chance, you won't know whether our relationship can work.*
3 *If you want to be happy in love, you mustn't take too many risks.*

6 Do you agree with the singer? Do you think that you should take risks in life, and not worry about things going wrong? Can you think of any situations where you have taken a risk? Was it successful or not?

What if...?

What if there was no light?
Nothing wrong, nothing (1)_____
What if there was no time
And no reason or (2)_____?

What if you should decide
That you don't want me there by your (3)_____
That you don't want me there in your life?

What if I got it wrong
And no poem or (4)_____
Could put right what I got wrong
Or make you feel I belong?

And what if you should decide
That you don't want me there by your (5)_____
That you don't want me there in your life?

Oooh, let's try
Let's take a breath jump over the side
Oooh, let's try
How can you know it if you don't even try?
Oooh, let's try

Every step that you take
Could be your biggest (6)_____
It could bend or it could break
But that's the risk that you (7)_____

What if you should decide
That you don't want me there in your life
That you don't want me there by your (8)_____?

Oooh, let's try
Let's take a breath jump over the side
Oooh, let's try
How can you know it when you don't even try?
Oooh, let's try

Ohhhhh

Oooh, let's try
Let's take a breath jump over the side
Oooh, let's try
You know that darkness always turns into light
Oooh, let's try

Stop and check 1

Questions

Make questions about the missing information.

Example: She lives in _____. **Where does she live?**

1 Laura can speak _____ languages. (Two? Three?)
_____

2 The gym costs _____ a month.
_____

3 We drove _____ car. (Joe's? Sue's?)
_____

4 The bank opens at _____.
_____

5 She went to the police station because _____.
_____

6 I'm going to buy Andy a _____ for his birthday.
_____

| | 6 |

Present tenses

Complete the sentences with the correct form of the verbs in brackets. Use the Present Simple or Present Continuous.

1 We _____ (not play) in the World Cup this year.

2 This is Kasia. She _____ (come) from Warsaw.

3 We _____ (have) a barbecue tonight.

4 I _____ (wait) for an important parcel to arrive.

5 He _____ (not like) wearing a tie.

6 _____ she _____ (have) a very busy social life?

| | 6 |

have/have got

Underline the correct form in each sentence.

1 He *doesn't have / doesn't have got* a girlfriend.

2 I *have / have got* a shower at 7.30 am.

3 She *hasn't / hasn't got* a car.

4 *Do you have got / Have you got* a dog?

5 He *often has / has often got* breakfast at work.

6 *He's / He has* two brothers.

| | 6 |

Past tense forms

What is the past tense of the following verbs? Some are irregular and some are regular?

say	_____	can	_____	make	_____
phone	_____	tell	_____	shine	_____
live	_____	begin	_____	give	_____
try	_____	throw	_____	think	_____

| | 6 |

Past tenses

Complete the sentences. Use the Past Simple and Past Continuous.

1 When I saw Kevin on Saturday, he _____ (buy) a new stereo.

2 When _____ you _____ (get) back from your holiday?

3 She _____ (graduate) from Yale University in 2006.

4 I _____ just _____ (put) in my contact lenses when you phoned.

5 He _____ (get) excellent marks in his law exam.

6 She _____ (forget) to send me a birthday card.

7 I _____ (work) in New York when I met Tom.

8 We were quiet because the baby _____ (sleep).

| | 8 |

Prepositions

Complete the sentences with the correct preposition. If *no* preposition is necessary, write *nothing*.

1 I listened to the radio _____ last night.

2 I'll see you _____ 9.00 _____ the morning

3 What did you do _____ yesterday afternoon?

4 She arrived in England _____ two years ago.

5 My sister's coming to stay _____ 19 December.

6 They sold the company _____ 2003.

7 His new job starts _____ Monday.

8 We're going to Bath _____ the weekend.

9 They're getting married _____ March.

| | 10 |

© Oxford University Press   **Photocopiable**

Expressions of quantity

1 Complete the sentences with *some* or *any*.

1 I'd like _____ tea, but I don't want _____ biscuits.
2 Is there _____ sugar? I can't see _____.
3 I bought _____ bread yesterday.
4 I didn't buy _____ coffee, because I thought we had _____.
5 We need _____ milk. I'll get it later.

[ ] 8

2 There is one mistake in each of the following sentences. Find it and correct it.

1 How many money have you got?
2 I only have a little potatoes.
3 I don't have many time, so I can't help you. Sorry.
4 In the summer there are a lot tourists.
5 Close your eyes. I've got anything for you.
6 John lives anywhere near Bournemouth.
7 Anybody told me you're getting married. Is it true?
8 The security guard didn't find something unusual in her bag.

[ ] 8

Articles

Complete the sentences with *a*, *an*, *the*, or *nothing*.

1 Marina is ____ youngest student in _____ class.
2 I usually come to ____ school by _____ bus.
3 Do you like _____ Thai food?
4 She comes from _____ village in _____ south of Italy.

[ ] 7

Spelling

Correct the spelling mistake in each sentence.

1 She left her job becuase she was unhappy.
2 He's a wonderfull teacher.
3 They're haveing a lot of problems.
4 He tryed to save the ball.
5 Look it up in the dictionery.

[ ] 5

Parts of speech

Complete the table with words from the box.

advice ~~awful~~ ~~book~~ delicious destroy ~~slowly~~ ~~enjoy~~ exercise global just ~~relationship~~ ring sadly

verb	noun	verb and noun	adjective	adverb
enjoy	relationship	book	awful	slowly

[ ] 8

Verb phrases

Write a phrase from the box with each of the following verbs.

my hair   sorry   my wallet   make-up the party   a printer   the police   a sandwich

1 put on _____
2 make _____
3 miss _____
4 call _____
5 mend _____
6 say _____
7 wash _____
8 lose _____

[ ] 8

Adverbs and adjectives

Complete the sentences with an adverb or adjective from the box.

possible   possibly   near   sudden   suddenly   straight

1 I'm going to the airport _____ after work.
2 It's not _____ to enter the building without a key.
3 It _____ started to pour with rain.
4 She lives quite _____ to the train station.
5 There was a _____ noise and then everything went quiet.
6 Could you _____ lend me your pen?

[ ] 6

Shopping

Where would you buy or find these items? Write chemist's, café, post office, or clothes shop.

1 tissues _____
2 stamps _____
3 a doughnut _____
4 a tie _____
5 deodorant _____
6 envelopes _____
7 a parcel _____
8 a sandwich _____

[ ] 8

TOTAL [100]

Stop and check 2

Verb patterns

Put the verb in brackets in the infinitive or -ing form.

> John Frantz is American. He has a wonderful lifestyle and he
> wants (1)_____ (share) it with an English girl. He enjoys
> (2)_____ (go) on exotic holidays, but he wouldn't
> like (3)_____ (live) outside the United States. He hopes
> (4)_____ (find) an English wife through the Internet dating
> agency, English Rose. He'd like (5)_____ (meet) someone
> who likes (6)_____ (travel) .

| | 6 |

Future forms

1 Cross out the incorrect form. Tick (✓) if both forms
are correct.

Example
We*'re having* / ~~have~~ pasta for dinner this evening.

1 *Are you doing* / *Will you do* anything special this
weekend?
2 I'm *visiting* / *going to visit* my aunt this evening.
3 My cousins from Australia *will come* / *are coming*
to stay next month.
4 There's someone at the door. *I'll get* / *I'm getting* it.
5 We're not *buying* / *going to buy* a new car this year.

| | 5 |

2 Complete the sentences with a form of *going to* or *will*.

1 'Why have you got so much food?'
'Because I _____ (cook) a meal for ten people.'

2 'Someone told me you've got a place at university.'
'That's right. I _____ (study) psychology.'

3 'My car isn't working.'
'Ask Joe to look at it. He _____ (help) you.'

4 'I passed my driving test!'
'That's great! I _____ (buy) some champagne
to celebrate!'

5 'Why have you got your old clothes on?'
'Because I _____ (paint) the bathroom.'

| | 5 |

What ... like?

Put the words in the correct order to make a question
and then match the questions with a response a–f.

Example
What's / car / like / new / your ?
What's your new car like?   *e*

1 weather / the / what's / like?
_____ _____

2 Anne / like / what's?
_____ _____

3 the / was / what / like / film?
_____ _____

4 does / what / like / doing / she?
_____ _____

5 her / what / are / parents / like?
_____ _____

a Horse riding.
b They're a bit strict.
c It was really funny.
d It's quite hot.
e ~~It's red, and very fast.~~
f She's very nice.

| | 10 |

Comparative and superlative adjectives

1 Write the comparative and superlative form of the
adjective.

funny   _____ _____
rich   _____ _____
hot   _____ _____
interesting _____ _____
bad   _____ _____

| | 5 |

2 Write comparative or superlative sentences.

Example
My new phone / small / old one.
My new phone is smaller than my old one.

It's / funny / programme on TV
It's the funniest programme on TV.

1 It's / good / song on the CD.
_____

2 Yesterday was / long / day of the year.
_____

3 Today's exam was / difficult / yesterday's.
_____

4 Indian food / spicy / English food.
_____

5 My father speaks / bad English / my mother.
_____

6 He's / talented player / in the team.
_____

☐ 6

Past Simple and past participle

Write the Past Simple and past participle of the following verbs.

make   _____   _____
drink   _____   _____
see   _____   _____
travel   _____   _____
act   _____   _____
try   _____   _____
eat   _____   _____
break   _____   _____
know   _____   _____
spend   _____   _____
have   _____   _____
read   _____   _____
write   _____   _____
speak   _____   _____

☐ 7

Present Perfect or Past Simple?

1 Complete the sentences with the correct form of the verb in brackets: the Present Perfect or Past Simple.

1 Philip Pullman _____ (write) a lot of books. He _____ (write) his first in 1972.

2 _____ you ever _____ (try) Malaysian food?

3 I _____ never _____ (go) to Russia.

4 When _____ you _____ (break) your leg?

5 I _____ (live) in London for eight years and I don't want to move.

6 We _____ (meet) Charlotte and Dave three years ago. How long _____ you _____ (know) them?

☐ 8

2 Complete the sentences with *ever, never, for,* or *since.*

1 He's worked there _____ many years, _____ 1988, I believe.

2 I have _____ read that book.

3 We've known Paul _____ two years. Have you _____ met him?

4 I've known him _____ we went to school together, but I've _____ met his parents.

5 How are you? I haven't seen you _____ ages.

☐ 8

3 Use the verbs in the box to make questions in the Present Perfect or Past Simple.

book	cost	drink	go	live	make

1 How long _____ you _____ in your house?

2 _____ you ever _____ Irish whiskey?

3 When _____ she _____ the holiday?

4 How many films _____ he _____?

5 Where _____ you _____ for a picnic?

6 How much _____ the champagne _____?

☐ 6

have to and *should*

The following sentences are all about visiting America.
Complete them with *have to*, *don't have to*, or *should*.

When you go to America,
1 you _____ book a hotel room before you go. You
   can find one when you get there.
2 you _____ get a work permit if you want to work
   there.
3 you _____ visit San Francisco – it's beautiful!
4 you _____ change your money before you go,
   because there are a lot of 24-hour banks there.
5 you _____ hire a car, because it's the easiest way
   to travel.

$\boxed{5}$

-ed / -ing adjectives

Underline the correct adjective.

1 Did you watch the football match last night? It was
   really *excited / exciting*.
2 She was a bit *disappointed / disappointing* with her
   test result.
3 I read a *fascinated / fascinating* magazine article about
   sharks.
4 The students felt very *confused / confusing* after their
   maths lesson.
5 I'm looking forward to a *relaxed / relaxing* weekend.
6 I feel *depressed / depressing* if I don't do any exercise.
7 Some people find cricket rather *bored / boring*.
8 She has a full-time job and four young children. She's
   exhausted / exhausting!

$\boxed{8}$

Antonyms

Write the antonyms of the following adjectives.

Example
brilliant ≠ **terrible**
1 messy ≠ _____
2 generous ≠ _____
3 dry ≠ _____
4 rude ≠ _____
5 bored ≠ _____

$\boxed{5}$

Word endings

Complete the sentences. Use a *noun* from the box in the
correct form: *adjective* or *verb*.

| advertisement | beauty | decision | disaster |
| friend | improvement | invitation | use |

1 Did you _____ Sarah to the party?
2 We had a _____ holiday last year. Everybody
   got ill and it rained every day.
3 They _____ the job in the national newspapers.
4 What can I do to _____ my pronunciation?
5 He's _____ to wait a year before he goes to
   university.
6 The postman is not very _____. He never says
   'Good Morning'!
7 You should buy a bilingual dictionary. They're very
   _____.
8 She was wearing a _____ diamond ring.

$\boxed{8}$

Words that go together

Match the verbs in A with phrases in B.

A	B
give	your nose
apply	a noise
twist	your job
blow	awful
stay	advice
make	in bed
change	your ankle
feel	for a job

$\boxed{8}$

| TOTAL | **100** |

Stop and check 3

Time and conditional clauses

1 Complete the sentences with *will* + the correct form of the verb in brackets, or the Present Simple.

1 If you _____ (eat) another doughnut, you _____ (be) sick.

2 You _____ (fail) your exam if you _____ (not study) hard.

3 What _____ you _____ (do), if you _____ (fail)?

4 Our children and grandchildren _____ (suffer) if we _____ (not look after) our planet.

5 I _____ (do) my homework, as soon as this programme _____ (finish).

6 When she _____ (read) my letter, she _____ (understand) my problem.

7 Where _____ he _____ (stay) when he _____ (go) to Berlin?

8 We _____ (stay) in the classroom until the teacher _____ (tell) us to leave.

☐ 8

2 Match a line in **A** with a line in **B**.

A	**B**
1 If I pass my driving test, ☐	a will you pay for the meal?
2 You'll learn English more easily if ☐	b we find somewhere to live.
3 Will you give her these when ☐	c you study a little every day.
4 If they don't give him the job, ☐	d you don't water them.
5 I'll marry you as soon as ☐	e we'll send them to you.
6 Your plants won't grow well if ☐	f I'll buy a car.
7 As soon as we get the tickets, ☐	g I don't know what he'll do.
8 If I buy the champagne, ☐	h you see her?

☐ 8

3 Choose the correct answer, a, b, or c.

1 I'll wait here _____ you are ready.
  a while   b before   c until

2 I think I'll have a shower _____ I have dinner.
  a while   b before   c until.

3 _____ I don't have time to call you today, I'll call you tomorrow.
  a If   b When   c As soon as

4 Shall we go for a coffee _____ the class finishes?
  a if   b while   c after

5 He wants to buy a motorbike _____ he's old enough.
  a before   b as soon as   c if

6 _____ it rains, we'll have to cancel the barbecue.
  a While   b After   c If

7 He's having a driving lesson … he gets home from school.
  a until   b when   c while

8 I'll wait downstairs … you put on your make-up.
  a while   b if   c as soon as

☐ 8

Passives

1 Underline the correct verb form: active or passive.

1 Walt Disney *created / was created* the character of Mickey Mouse about eighty years ago.

2 Mickey *calls / is called* 'Topolino' in Italian and 'Mi Lo Shu' in Chinese.

3 At first he *called / was called* Mortimer Mouse.

4 He *gave / was given* the name Mickey by Walt Disney's wife, Lillian.

5 Disney *made / was made* the first full-length cartoon, 'Snow White', in 1937.

6 Mickey Mouse cartoons have *translated / have been translated* into at least sixty languages.

7 Since 1928, about 120 cartoons have *made / have been made*.

☐ 7

2 Put the verbs in brackets in the correct tense. They are all in the passive.

1 Credit cards _____ (not accept) here, I'm afraid.

2 We saw *Romeo and Juliet* last Saturday. It _____ (perform) by the Royal Shakespeare Company.

3 The offices _____ (paint) next month.

4 My car _____ (steal) three times since January.

5 The streets _____ (clean) every day.

6 The letter _____ (send) more than a week ago.

7 It's freezing in here – _____ the heating _____ (turn off)?

8 If you park your car here, it _____ (take) away.

☐ 8

Second conditional

1 Complete the sentences with the correct from of the verbs in brackets: A past tense or *would* + infinitive.

1 If I _____ (live) in the country, I _____ (have) a dog.

2 If I _____ (have) a lot of money, I _____ (buy) a speed boat.

3 I _____ (go) to the party if I _____ (be) free that evening.

4 What _____ you _____ (do) if you _____ (offer) a million pounds?

5 If I _____ (be) you, I _____ (look) for another job.

6 If I _____ (live) near to you, I _____ (come) to visit more often.

☐ 6

2 Rewrite the following sentences using the second conditional.

Example
I'm not rich, so I don't live in a big house.
If I were rich, I'd live in a big house.

1 She spends a lot of money, so she's poor.
_____

2 She smokes forty cigarettes a day, so she coughs a lot.
_____

3 He doesn't understand Portuguese, so he won't work in Brazil.
_____

4 They don't have a garden, so they don't grow vegetables.
_____

5 I don't have a boat, so I won't sail around the world.
_____

6 He loves Italy, so he always goes there on holiday.
_____

☐ 6

might

Complete the sentences with *might* and a verb from the box.

arrive	be	buy	find	leave	not like
~~rain~~	not understand	win			

Example
Take your umbrella. It **might rain** later.

1 Chris isn't here today. He _____ ill.

2 The food's very spicy. You _____ it.

3 He's seen a suit that he really likes. He _____ it.

4 Her pronunciation isn't very good at all. You _____ her.

5 The team have been playing very well. They _____ the championship.

6 The traffic is very bad on the motorway. We _____ late.

7 I'm feeling very tired. I _____ the party early.

8 Don't buy that camera yet. You _____ a cheaper one on the Internet.

☐ 8

© Oxford University Press **Photocopiable**

Present Perfect Simple and Continuous

Complete the sentences with the Present Perfect or Present Perfect Continuous form of the verb in brackets.

1 Wait a minute. I _____ (not finish) yet!

2 _____ they _____ (book) their holiday yet?

3 Anne _____ (study) for five hours.

4 We _____ already _____ (order) the champagne.

5 How long _____ he _____ (speak) on the phone?

6 I _____ just _____ (see) Jim.

7 We _____ (help) Ellie since five o'clock.

8 They _____ (not speak) to each other for five years.

9 Nobody _____ (send) me a letter for a very long time.

10 _____ he _____ (work) too hard? He seems very stressed at the moment.

[ ] 10

Hot verbs

Complete the story with the correct tense of *take*, *get*, *do*, or *make*.

A happy ending

Last Friday Pablo had a job interview. On Friday morning he (1) _____ up very early. It (2) _____ him an hour to (3) _____ ready for his interview, because he couldn't (4) _____ up his mind what to wear. When he left the house he was worried, because he couldn't remember if he had locked the door so he had to go home and (5) _____ sure. He left his house again and this time he (6) _____ lost.

When he finally arrived at the interview, he was two hours late. Then he was shocked to find that his interview was in English. He (7) _____ his best but he (8) _____ a lot of mistakes. On the way home it started to rain heavily and Pablo (9) _____ completely wet. When he got home he felt ill. He was starting to (10) _____ a cold, so he (11) _____ some tablets and lay down on the sofa, feeling very depressed. Later that evening he got a phone call – he'd (12) _____ the job!

[ ] 12

Verbs and nouns

Complete the sentences using the verbs in the box.

| make | tell | give | lose | keep | miss |

1 Don't tell Sue. She can't _____ a secret.

2 Anne _____ me a lift to the party.

3 Arsenal _____ the match 2-0.

4 Sorry I'm late. I _____ the bus.

5 Martyn _____ a very funny joke.

6 Hang on! I have to _____ a quick phone call

[ ] 6

Phrasal verbs

Match A and B to make sentences with phrasal verbs.

1 [ ] Oh no! We've run   a with your sister?
2 [ ] Do you get on   b on these trousers.
3 [ ] My car broke   c up in the dictionary.
4 [ ] I'd like to try   d Jenny's dog while she's away
5 [ ] I'll look it   e a brown leather belt.
6 [ ] We look after   f out of petrol.
7 [ ] I'm looking for   g down on the way to work.

[ ] 7

So and *such*

Find and correct the sentences that are wrong. Tick (✔) the ones that are correct.

1 We had so a brilliant time in Amsterdam last year that we've decided to go back.

2 You've grown so much since I last saw you!

3 I've got a such lot of work to do that I don't know where to begin!

4 Her parents are so nice people.

5 I didn't realise that the exam was so much difficult.

6 The queue for the restaurant was so long that we decided to go somewhere else.

[ ] 6

| TOTAL | 100 |

Progress test 1

UNITS 1–6

Exercise 1 Questions and verb forms

Put the words in the right order to make a question.

Example
job / learning / for / English / your / you / are?
Are you learning English for your job?

1 English / you / start / did / learning / when?

_____

2 tennis / often / play / how / does / she?

_____

3 do / doing / what / at / you / like / weekend / the?

_____

4 weekend / do / what / you / would / to / this / like?

_____

5 dictionary / why / got / you / haven't / a?

_____

6 much / put / my / coffee / sugar / how / did / in / you?

_____

7 phoned / doing / John / when / what / you / were?

_____

8 sandwiches / make / is / who / to / going / the?

_____

9 radio / listening / does / enjoy / to / mother / the / your?

_____

10 live / Anna / where / was / child / a / did / when / she?

_____

| 10 |

Exercise 2 Questions and tenses

Look at the chart.

Name	Xavier	Mr and Mrs Ramsey
Nationality	French	Australian
Town	London	Melbourne
Age	26	In their sixties
Family	one younger brother	no children
Occupation	chef	retired
Holiday last year	home to Paris for two weeks	two months in Scotland – visiting relatives
Holiday next year	drive to Morocco with friends	tour New Zealand for two weeks

Use the information in the chart and write the correct questions to the following answers.

Example
Where does Xavier come from?
He comes from France.

1 _____
They come from Australia.

2 _____
They live in Melbourne.

3 _____
He's 26.

4 _____
Yes, he does. He has one younger brother.

5 _____
No, they haven't got any.

6 _____
He's a chef.

7 _____
He went home to Paris for two weeks.

8 _____
They stayed there for two months.

9 _____
They're going to tour New Zealand.

10 _____
He's going to drive to Morocco.

| 10 |

Exercise 3 Tenses and verb forms

Put the verb in brackets into the correct tense or verb form.

Example

A Why _did_ you _go_ (go) to the seaside last weekend?

B Because we like ___sailing___ (sail).

A (1)_____ you _____ (know) Brian Bailey?

B Yes, I (2)_____ (meet) him two years ago while I (3)_____ (work) in Germany. (4)_____ he still _____ (live) there?

A Yes, he does. He (5)_____ (live) in Frankfurt. He (6)_____ (have got) a good job there but at the moment he (7)_____ (work) in London. He's here for a few days and I'd like (8)_____ (invite) him and you for dinner. Can you (9)_____ (come)?

B Yes, I hope so. I'd love (10)_____ (see) Brian again! When I was in Germany we (11)_____ (see) each other quite often because his office was near the school where I (12)_____ (teach) and so we sometimes (13)_____ (have) lunch together. I always enjoyed (14)_____ (talk) to him. I wanted (15)_____ (write) to him but he moved and I (16)_____ (not have) his new address.

A Well, what about dinner on Friday?

B That's fine. What time?

A Is 8 o'clock OK? I (17)_____ (ring) Brian yesterday to check the day, and I (18)_____ (ring) him again tomorrow to check the time.

B Well, 8 o'clock is fine for me. I (19)_____ (come) at about 8 and I (20)_____ (bring) a bottle of wine.

A See you on Friday then!

| | 20 |

Exercise 4 Irregular past tenses

Here are twenty verbs. Ten are regular and ten are irregular. Write the past tense form of the *irregular* verbs only.

buy	put
cook	speak
do	start
happen	take
have	talk
hear	visit
laugh	wait
leave	watch
listen	whisper
make	write

| | 10 |

Exercise 5 Count and uncount nouns

Underline the uncount noun in the following pairs of words.

Example
cheese/egg

money/pound   rice/potato   meat/hamburger

flower/flour   loaf/bread   song/music

job/homework   luggage/suitcase   food/meal

furniture/desk

| | 5 |

Exercise 6 Articles

Complete the text with *a, an, the* or nothing.

Example
I had _____ dinner with _the_ Queen.

My Aunt Vanessa is (1)_____ artist. She lives in (2)_____ beautiful old cottage by (3)_____ sea and she paints (4)_____ small pictures of wild flowers and birds. She doesn't like leaving (5)_____ cottage, but once (6)_____ year she travels by (7)_____ train to London and has (8)_____ tea with me at (9)_____ Savoy Hotel. At the moment I'm quite worried about her because she's in (10)_____ hospital, but I'm sure she'll be better soon. I'm going to visit her next week.

| | 10 |

Exercise 7 Expressions of quantity

Tick (✓) the correct sentence.

1 Is there any milk? I can't see one.
   Is there any milk? I can't see any.

2 There's some potatoes, but only few.
   There are some potatoes, but only a few.

3 There are a lot of cars parked in the street.
   There are lots cars parked in the street.

4 Have you got much unemployment in your town?
   Have you got much unemployed people in your town?

5 Only a little people believes his story.
   Only a few people believe his story.

6 How much homeworks do you have tonight?
   How much homework do you have tonight?

7 There isn't much rice and there isn't any eggs.
   There isn't much rice and there aren't any eggs.

8 There was much snow last winter.
   There was some snow last winter but not much.

9 How lovely! Somebody gave you some flowers.
   How lovely! Somebody gave you any flowers.

10 I went anywhere interesting for my holiday.
   I didn't go anywhere interesting for my holiday.

10

Exercise 8 Descriptions

Complete the dialogues with words from the box.

| worst | latest | more | as (×2) | funniest | funnier | than |
| friendlier | tastier | like | was | what | the | most |

1 A I started a new job today, working in an office.
   B What are the other people (1)_____?
   A They're very nice. They seem (2)_____ than
      the people in my old job, and the job is much
      (3)_____ interesting.
   B You worked in a shop before, didn't you?
   A Yes. Working in an office is better (4)_____
      working in a shop, I'll tell you! That was the
      (5)_____ job I've ever had. I hated it.

2 C We went out for a meal to Luigi's last night – you
      know, that new Italian restaurant.
   D Mm, I know. What (6)_____ it like?
   C It was (7)_____ best Italian meal I've ever
      had, and it wasn't as expensive (8)_____
      Giovanni's.

   D Yes. Giovanni's used to be the (9)_____
      popular restaurant around here, but then it started
      getting very expensive.
   C And the service isn't (10)_____ good as it
      used to be.
   D What did you have?
   C Paul and I both had veal, but mine was cooked in
      wine and herbs, and it was (11)_____ than
      Paul's. But *he* liked it.

3 E Have your read John Harrison's (12)_____
      book, *Going Round the World*?
   F No. (13) _____'s it like?
   E I think it's the (14) _____ book he's written.
      I laughed out loud all the way through.
   F I didn't like *The Truth and the Light*, the one that
      came out last year.
   E Neither did I. This one's much (15)_____.

15

Exercise 9 Vocabulary

Complete the sentences.

1 I'm really _____ up with this weather. It hasn't
   stopped raining for three days.

2 Lisa's _____ on her make-up.

3 'Thank you very much.'
   'Not at all. Don't _____ it.'

4 'Hello, the Continental Hotel. Can I help you?'
   'Good morning. I'd like to make a _____ for the
   27th December, please.'

5 Your room is so _____. Tidy it up now, please!

6 'I'm sorry I broke your pen.'
   'It doesn't _____. Don't worry about it.'

7 I've got four _____: two dogs, a parrot, and a
   goldfish.

8 Did you watch the tennis yesterday?
   'No, I _____ it, unfortunately Who won?'

9 Could you buy me a _____ of bread when
   you're at the shop, please?

10 I'd like a book of first class _____, please.

10

TOTAL | 100

Progress test 2

Exercise 1 Tenses

Complete the text with the correct form of the verbs in brackets: the Present Simple, the Past Simple, or the Present Perfect.

Example
I *got* (get) up at 7.00 this morning.

Carla Brown has a job in advertising. It's a good job, and she (1)_____ (earn) over £30,000 a year. She (2)_____ (study) marketing at college, and then (3)_____ (find) a job with a small advertising agency in Manchester. Since then she (4)_____ (change) her job several times. Now she (5)_____ (work) for Jerome and Jerome, which is a big company with offices all over the world. She (6)_____ (be) with the company for three years.

The company has clients in America, and she (7)_____ (be) there several times on business. Last year she (8)_____ (spend) six months there.

| 8 |

Exercise 2 Correct the mistakes

Tick (✓) the correct sentence.

Example
I have watched TV last night.
I watched TV last night. ✓

1 I have lived in Chesswood for five years.
   I live in Chesswood for five years.
2 We moved here after my daughter was born.
   We have moved here after my daughter was born.
3 Before that we have lived in London.
   Before that we lived in London.
4 I am a teacher since I left university.
   I have been a teacher since I left university.
5 I went to Bristol University in 1994.
   I have been to Bristol University in 1994.
6 We have studied English since three years.
   We have studied English for three years.
7 I never went to Russia, but I'd like to go.
   I have never been to Russia, but I'd like to go.

| 7 |

Exercise 3 *have to* or *should*?

Complete the sentences with a form of *have to*, *don't have to*, *should*, or *shouldn't*.

Example
If you feel ill, you __should__ go to bed.

1 You _____ book in advance if you want cheap tickets.
2 When you catch a plane, you _____ check in before you board the plane.
3 You _____ have too much hand luggage.
4 You _____ wear comfortable clothing.
5 A pilot _____ train for many years.
6 You _____ wear your seat belt all the time. You can take it off.
7 But you _____ wear it at take-off and landing.
8 You _____ drink too much alcohol because you might be ill
9 There is often a film on a long flight, but you _____ watch it. You can go to sleep.
10 When you've got your luggage, you _____ go through Customs.

| 10 |

Exercise 4 Time clauses

Put the words in the right order.

Example
bath / I / when / home / will / get / have / a / I
I will have a bath when I get home.

1 hear / if / I / news / any / you / I / phone / will
   _____
2 pay / as / you / I / back / soon / can / I / as / will
   _____
3 you / feel / stop / better / if / will / you / smoking
   _____
4 car / Peter / enough / when / he / buy / a / has / will / money
   _____
5 problem / help / I / you / have / you / a / will / if
   _____

| 5 |

Exercise 5 Tenses

Complete the sentences with the correct form of the verbs in brackets: the Present Simple or the *will* future.

1 I _____ (call) you when lunch _____ (be) ready.

2 If you _____ (be) late, I _____ (go) without you.

3 If she _____ (pass) her driving test, she _____ (buy) a car.

4 I _____ (go) home as soon as I _____ (finish) work.

5 If my neighbours _____ (not stop) making a noise, I _____ (go) round and complain.

| 10 |

Exercise 6 Irregular past tenses

Here are twenty verbs. Ten are regular and ten are irregular. Write in the Past Simple and Past Participle for the irregular verbs only.

	Past Simple	Past participle
appear	_____	_____
bring	_____	_____
climb	_____	_____
fall	_____	_____
feel	_____	_____
forget	_____	_____
improve	_____	_____
invent	_____	_____
know	_____	_____
let	_____	_____
lose	_____	_____
manage	_____	_____
pass	_____	_____
pick	_____	_____
speak	_____	_____
start	_____	_____
tell	_____	_____
understand	_____	_____
use	_____	_____
want	_____	_____

| 10 |

Exercise 7 Active or passive?

Underline the correct verb form.

Example
Portuguese *speaks/is spoken* in Brazil.

1 That's the third time he *has failed/has been failed* the exam.
2 'Hot lips' *wrote/was written* by Celia Young.
3 A lot of trees *cut down/were cut down* to build that house.
4 They *don't grow/aren't grown* bananas in Scotland.
5 Some pictures *have taken/have been taken* from the museum.

| 5 |

Exercise 8 Passives

Put the words in the correct order.

1 world / is / English / the / all / spoken / over
   _____

2 since / has / nylon / 1932 / made / been
   _____

3 Mary's / invited / I / to / wasn't / party / why?
   _____

4 will / when / be / new / the / bridge / built?
   _____

5 asked / car / design / were / they / to / new / a
   _____

| 5 |

Exercise 9 Second conditional

Make five sentences from the chart. Use each verb in **B** once only.

A	B	C	D	E
	lived	a dictionary		go to see her.
	earned	you	I'd	look up the word.
If I	knew	in Brazil		marry George.
	had	more money	I wouldn't	learn Portuguese.
	were	Maria's address		save it.

_____

_____

_____

_____

| 5 |

Exercise 10 Second conditional and *might*

Read the text about Jane. Then complete the sentences.

> Jane's unhappy at home and unhappy at work. She has a boring job and she doesn't earn much money. Her boss says that he will perhaps give her a pay rise next month, but he isn't sure yet. She doesn't have a car and she goes to work on crowded buses every day. She doesn't have a flat, she lives in a small room above a noisy restaurant in the centre of town. She finds it difficult to sleep because the restaurant doesn't close until after midnight. She thinks that she will perhaps go and live with her friend Wendy but she isn't sure yet because she likes living on her own.

Example
Jane **wouldn't be** unhappy if she lived in a quiet flat.

1 Jane _____ happier if she _____ a more interesting job.
2 Her boss might _____ .
3 If she _____ a car, she _____ to work by bus.
4 If she _____ live above a restaurant, she _____ it easier to sleep.
5 She might _____ her friend Wendy.

[ ] 5

Exercise 11 Present Perfect Simple and Continuous

Tick (✓) the correct sentence.

1 I saw her five minutes ago.
  I've seen her five minutes ago.
2 We are here since last Saturday.
  We've been here since last Saturday.
3 How long have you known Wendy?
  How long have you been knowing Wendy?
4 We haven't made coffee yet.
  We didn't make coffee yet.
5 He is waiting to see the doctor since nine o'clock.
  He has been waiting to see the doctor since nine o'clock.
6 When did you buy your new car?
  When have you bought your new car?
7 Mary isn't home. She's been to work.
  Mary isn't home. She's gone to work.
8 I've run in the park, so I'm tired.
  I've been running in the park, so I'm tired.
9 I've run round the park three times.
  I've been running round the park three times.
10 They already had their dinner.
  They've already had their dinner.

[ ] 10

Exercise 12 Present Perfect Continuous

Ask questions to find out *How long … ?*

Example: 'I'm learning English.'
'How long have you been learning English?'

1 'I'm waiting for a bus.'
  '_____?'
2 'Tom's saving up to buy a boat.'
  '_____?'
3 I'm having driving lessons.'
  '_____?'
4 'Alice is working in the library.'
  '_____?'
5 'The Greens are trying to sell their house.'
  '_____?'

[ ] 5

Exercise 13 Phrasal verbs

Complete the sentences with the correct preposition.

1 You should look the word ____ in the dictionary.
2 He gave _____ his job because it was boring.
3 Oh, no! The printer's run _____ of ink.
4 Look ____! There's a scorpion near your foot.
5 The plane has taken ____ five minutes early.
6 Can you look _____ the baby for a while?
7 Tom gets ____ well with most people.
8 I'm going upstairs to lie ____ for a while.

[ ] 8

Exercise 14 Vocabulary

Complete the sentences.

1 I don't want any cake, I'm trying to _____ weight.
2 I've got a _____ throat and a headache.
3 I'd love to _____ more time with my children.
4 He's _____ for a job at the hospital.
5 I'd like to _____ a complaint about the food.
6 Could you give me a _____ to the station.
7 I never _____ a watch when I'm on holiday.

[ ] 7

TOTAL [100]

Answer keys

Extra idea Unit 3

Song – Don't you want me?

Don't you want me? was a huge international hit for the British band *Human League* in 1981. It was written by lead singer Phil Oakey, based on a 'true life' story he read in an American magazine, and released on the *Dare* album.

Answers
2 She doesn't want him.
3 See tapescript.
4 1 a fact   4 a fact
   2 his opinion   5 his opinion
   3 her opinion   6 her opinion
5 The man feels angry and upset. The woman is sorry, and says she still loves him, but feels free and wants to be independent.

Answers and tapescript [CD 1: Track 34]
You **were working** as a waitress in a cocktail bar
When I **met** you
I **picked** you out, I **shook** you up, and **turned** you around,
    turned you into someone new

Now five years later on you've got the world at your feet
Success has been so easy for you
But don't forget it's me who put you where you are now
And I can put you back down too
Don't, don't you want me?
You know I can't believe it when I hear that you won't see me
Don't, don't you want me?
You know I don't believe you when you say that you don't need me
It's much too late to find
You think you've changed your mind
You'd better change it back or we will both be sorry
Don't you want me baby? Don't you want me – oh
Don't you want me baby? Don't you want me – oh

I **was working** as a waitress in a cocktail bar
That much is true
But even then I **knew** I'd find a much better place
Either with or without you
The five years we have had have been such good times
I still love you
But now I think it's time I **lived** my life on my own
I guess it's just what I must do

Don't you want me baby? Don't you want me – oh
Don't you want me baby? Don't you want me – oh

Extra idea Unit 3

Ian Fleming

About the task

This is an information gap activity based on a short biography of Ian Fleming's life.

Eton = a very prestigious private school
the Foreign Office = the British government department that deals with the UK's political relationship with other countries
Naval Intelligence = a group of people who gather secret information related to defence at sea
the Secret Service = a government organization that tries to get secret information about other countries
MI5 = the section of the British Secret Service which operates mainly in the UK
Before the lesson, make one copy of the worksheet for each pair of students. Cut the worksheets in half.

1 Ask students what they know about Ian Fleming and elicit any ideas. Put students in A/B pairs and hand out the relevant half of the worksheet. Check comprehension of the adjectives in the box. Ask students which they think can describe Ian Fleming.

2 Tell students they are going to read about part of Ian Fleming's life – the A students the first part, and the B students the second. Put the A students together in groups of three or four in one half of the room, and the B students together in the other. Give students time to read through the text and check any vocabulary. Allow them to use dictionaries if appropriate. Students then answer the questions, working in their groups. Monitor to help as necessary.

3 Focus attention on the first set of cues and the example question on each half of the worksheet. Students continue writing the questions in full. Monitor to check for accurate use of tenses and question formation.
Get students to work with a partner from the other group. The A students ask their questions and the B students answer; then get them to swap roles. Remind students not to show each other their worksheets when they are exchanging the information.

Answers 2 and 3
Student A
  1 He was born in Mayfair, London, in 1908.
  2 His family was rich. His grandfather was a millionaire banker and his father was a Member of Parliament.
  3 His father died in the First World War and so Ian didn't know him well.
  4 Ian didn't like school or the army. He left school before graduation. He didn't want a career as a soldier.
  5 In the early 1930s Ian went to Geneva to study. He wanted to join the Foreign Office but he didn't pass the exams. He went back to England and he worked as a journalist.
  6 When the Second World War started, he was working as a stockbroker.

Student B
  1 He joined Naval Intelligence and had contact with MI5 and the Secret Service. He started working in the world of spies.
  2 He went on secret missions in North Africa, Lisbon, and the USA.
  3 He enjoyed an expensive lifestyle. He was good-looking, always well-dressed, and he had a lot of girlfriends. He drank a lot and smoked about 60 cigarettes a day
  4 After the war he went to Jamaica, bought some land and decided to build a house. He called it *Goldeneye*, a name he also used for one of his books.
  5 In 1952 he got married, he had a son, and he started writing the James Bond stories.

6 He wrote the other 12 books in the following 10 years. He sold 40 million copies around the world.

4 Put students into groups of three or four to discuss the question. Elicit a range of opinions in a short feedback session.

Sample answers

Ian Fleming was rich and James Bond also appears to be rich. They both travelled a lot and they both worked in the world of spies. They were both good-looking and well-dressed, and they both had a lot of girlfriends. They both drank and smoked.

Extra idea Unit 9

Song – Come away with me

Come away with me was written by American singer-songwriter Norah Jones in 2002, and released on her debut album of the same name.

Answers

2 The singer mentions:
Writing a poem or song for the person you love
Walking across fields of knee-high grass together
Kissing on top of a mountain
Listening to the rain falling on the roof
Travelling far away on a bus

3 See tapescript

4 Students' own ideas. However, one possible interpretation is that two young lovers are being kept apart by the 'lies' of their families or friends, and the singer is trying to persuade her lover to run away with her.

Answers and tapescript [CD 3: Track 9]

Come away with me **in the night**
Come away with me
And I will **write** you a song

Come away with me on a **bus**
Come away where they can't tempt us
With their **lies**

I want to walk with you
On a **cloudy** day
In fields where the **yellow** grass grows knee-high
So won't you try to come

Come away with me and we'll **kiss**
On a mountaintop
Come away with me
And I'll never stop **loving** you

And I want to **wake up** with the rain
Falling on a **tin** roof
While I'm safe there in your arms
So all I ask is for you
To come away with me **in the night**
Come away with me

Extra idea Unit 11

Song – What if … ?

What if…? was written by the British band Coldplay. It appears on the X & Y album, their third album. It was released in 2005.

Answers

1 (sample answers)
What if there was no light? Life would be much less colourful./Life would be more dangerous./We would need to make artificial light.
What if there was no time? We wouldn't need clocks and watches. / We wouldn't have a routine./We wouldn't care about age.
What if everybody lived forever? The population would be huge./We would need a new planet to live on./We would never miss people who had died.

2 (sample questions)
What if all nationalities spoke the same language?
What if people could travel in time?
What if animals ruled the world?
What if there was life on other planets?
What if we didn't have plants?

3 Students can give their own opinions on which one they feel is the case: *The singer is hoping that the girl will decide to have a relationship with him* or *The singer is worried about making a mistake and losing his girlfriend.*

4 See tapescript.

5 2

Answers and tapescript [CD 3: Track 22]

What if there was no light?
Nothing wrong, nothing **right**
What if there was no time?
And no reason or **rhyme**
What if you should decide
That you don't want me there by your **side**
That you don't want me there in your life
What if I got it wrong
And no poem or **song**
Could put right what I got wrong
Or make you feel I belong?
And what if you should decide
That you don't want me there by your **side**
That you don't want me there in your life?
Oooh, let's try
Let's take a breath jump over the side
Oooh, let's try
How can you know it if you don't even try
Oooh, let's try
Every step that you take
Could be your biggest **mistake**
It could bend or it could break
But that's the risk that you **take**
What if you should decide
That you don't want me there in your life.
That you don't want me there by your **side**?
Oooh, let's try
Let's take a breath jump over the side
Oooh, let's try
How can you know it when you don't even try
Oooh, let's try
Ohhhhh
Oooh, let's try
Let's take a breath jump over the side
Oooh, let's try
You know that darkness always turns into light
Oooh, let's try

Stop and check 1

Questions
1 How many languages can Laura speak?
2 How much does the gym cost a month?
3 Whose car did you drive?
4 What time does the bank open?
5 Why did she go to the police station?
6 What are you going to buy Andy for his birthday?

Present tenses
1 aren't playing
2 comes
3 're having
4 'm waiting
5 doesn't like
6 Does … have

have/have got
1 doesn't have
2 have
3 hasn't got
4 Have you got
5 often has
6 He has

Past tense forms
said   could   made
phoned   told   shone
lived   began   gave
tried   threw   thought

Past tenses
1 was buying
2 did … get
3 graduated
4 was … putting
5 got
6 forgot
7 was working
8 was sleeping

Prepositions
1 nothing
2 at … in
3 nothing
4 nothing
5 on
6 in
7 on
8 at
9 in

Expressions of quantity
1 1 some   any
   2 any   any
   3 some
   4 any   some
   5 some
2 1 How much money
   2 a few potatoes
   3 much time
   4 a lot of tourists
   5 something for you
   6 somewhere near
   7 Someone/Somebody told me
   8 anything unusual

Articles
1 the   the
2 nothing   nothing
3 nothing
4 a   the

Spelling
1 because
2 wonderful
3 having
4 tried
5 dictionary

Parts of speech

verb	noun	verb and noun	adjective	adverb
destroy	advice	exercise	global	sadly
		ring	delicious	just

Verb phrases
1 put on make-up
2 make a sandwich
3 miss the party
4 call the police
5 mend a printer
6 say sorry
7 wash my hair
8 lose my wallet

Adverbs and adjectives
1 straight
2 possible
3 suddenly
4 near
5 sudden
6 possibly

Shopping
1 chemist's
2 post office
3 café
4 clothes shop
5 chemist's
6 post office
7 post office
8 café

Stop and check 2

Verb patterns
1 to share
2 going
3 to live
4 to find
5 to meet
6 travelling

Future forms
1 1 Are you doing
   2 ✓
   3 are coming
   4 I'll get
   5 ✓
2 1 I'm going to cook
   2 I'm going to study
   3 He'll help
   4 I'll buy
   5 I'm going to paint

What … like
1 What's the weather like? – d It's quite hot.
2 What's Anne like? – e She's very nice.
3 What was the film like? – c It was really funny.
4 What does she like doing? – a Horse-riding.
5 What are her parents like? – b They're a bit strict.

Comparative and superlative adjectives
1 funnier / funniest
   richer / richest
   hotter / hottest
   more interesting / most interesting
   worse / worst

2 1 It's the best song on the CD.
   2 Yesterday was the longest day of the year.
   3 Today's exam was more difficult than yesterday's.
   4 Indian food is spicier than English food.
   5 My father speaks worse English than my mother.
   6 He's the most talented player in the team.

Past Simple and past participle
made   made
drank   drunk
saw   seen
travelled travelled
acted   acted
tried   tried
ate   eaten
broke   broken
knew   known
spent   spent
had   had
read   read
wrote   written
spoke   spoken

Present Perfect or Past Simple?
1 1 has written wrote
   2 Have … tried
   3 've … been
   4 did … break
   5 've lived
   6 met   have … known
2 1 for since   3 for ever
   2 never   4 since never   5 for
3 1 have … lived   4 has … made
   2 Have … drunk 5 did … go
   3 did … book   6 did … cost

have to and should
1 don't have to
2 have to
3 should
4 don't have to
5 should

ed / -ing adjectives
1 exciting
2 disappointed
3 fascinating
4 confused
5 relaxing
6 depressed
7 boring
8 exhausted

Antonyms
1 tidy   3 wet   5 interested
2 mean   4 polite

Word endings
1 invite
2 disastrous
3 advertised
4 improve
5 decided
6 friendly
7 useful
8 beautiful

Words that go together

give advice — stay in bed
apply for a job — make a noise
twist your ankle — change your job
blow your nose — feel awful

Stop and check 3

Time and conditional clauses

1 1 eat   'll be
   2 'll fail   don't study
   3 will ... do   fail
   4 will suffer   don't look after
   5 'll do   finishes
   6 reads   'll understand
   7 will ... stay   goes
   8 'll stay   tells

2 1 If I pass my driving test, I'll buy a car.
   2 You'll learn English more easily if you study a little every day.
   3 Will you give her these when you see her?
   4 If they don't give him the job, I don't know what he'll do.
   5 I'll marry you as soon as we find somewhere to live.
   6 Your plants won't grow well if you don't water them.
   7 As soon as we get the tickets, we'll send them to you.
   8 If I buy the champagne, will you pay for the meal?

3 1 c   2 b   3 a   4 c   5 b   6 c   7 b   8 a

Passives

1 1 created   5 made
   2 is called   6 have been translated
   3 was called   7 have been made
   4 was given

2 1 aren't accepted
   2 was performed
   3 will be painted
   4 has been stolen
   5 are cleaned
   6 was sent
   7 Has ... been turned off
   8 will be taken

Second conditional

1 1 lived   would have
   2 had   would buy
   3 'd go   was/were
   4 would ... do   were offered
   5 was/were   'd look
   6 lived   would come

2 1 She wouldn't be poor if she didn't spend a lot of money./If she didn't spend a lot of money, she wouldn't be poor.
   2 She wouldn't cough a lot if she didn't smoke forty cigarettes a day./If she didn't smoke forty cigarettes a day, she wouldn't cough a lot.
   3 If he understood Portuguese, he'd work in Brazil./He'd work in Brazil if he understood Portuguese.
   4 If they had a garden, they'd grow vegetables./They'd grow vegetables if they had a garden.
   5 If I had a boat, I'd sail around the world./I'd sail around the world if I had a boat.
   6 If he didn't love Italy, he wouldn't always go there on holiday.

might

1 might be   5 might win
2 might not like   6 might arrive
3 might buy   7 might leave
4 might not understand   8 might find

Present Perfect Simple and Continuous

1 haven't finished
2 Have ... booked
3 has been studying
4 've ... ordered
5 has ... been speaking
6 've ... seen
7 've been helping
8 haven't spoken
9 has sent
10 Has ... been working

Hot verbs

1 got   7 did
2 took   8 made
3 get   9 got
4 make   10 get
5 make   11 took
6 got   12 got

Verbs and nouns

1 keep   4 missed
2 gave   5 told
3 lost   6 make

Phrasal verbs

1 f   2 a   3 g   4 b   5 c   6 d   7 e

So and such

1 such a   4 such nice
2 ✓   5 so difficult
3 such a lot   6 ✓

Progress test 1

Exercise 1

1 When did you start learning English?
2 How often does she play tennis?
3 What do you like doing at the weekend?
4 What would you like to do this weekend?
5 Why haven't you got a dictionary?
6 How much sugar did you put in my coffee?
7 What were you doing when John phoned?
8 Who is going to make the sandwiches?
9 Does your mother enjoy listening to the radio?
10 Where did Anna live when she was a child?

Exercise 2

1 Where do Mr and Mrs Ramsey come from?
2 Where do they live?
3 How old is Xavier?
4 Does he have/Has he got any brothers or sisters?
5 Have Mr and Mrs Ramsey got/Do Mr and Mrs Ramsey have any children?
6 What does Xavier do/What's Xavier's job?
7 Where did he go on holiday last year?
8 How long did Mr and Mrs Ramsey stay in Scotland?
9 What are they going to do on holiday next year?
10 What is Xavier going to do on holiday next year?

Exercise 3

1 Do ... know
2 met
3 was working
4 Does ... live
5 lives
6 has got
7 is working
8 to invite
9 come
10 to see
11 saw
12 was teaching
13 had
14 talking
15 to write
16 don't have
17 rang
18 am going to ring/will ring
19 'll come
20 'll bring

Exercise 4

bought   made
did   put
had   spoke
heard   took
left   wrote

Exercise 5

Uncount nouns

money	bread
flour	luggage
homework	meat
furniture	music
rice	food

Exercise 6

1	an	6	a
2	a	7	nothing
3	the	8	nothing
4	nothing	9	the
5	the	10	nothing

Exercise 7

Correct sentences

1 Is there any milk? I can't see any.
2 There are some potatoes, but only a few.
3 There are a lot of cars parked in the street.
4 Have you got much unemployment in your town?
5 Only a few people believe his story.
6 How much homework do you have tonight?
7 There isn't much rice and there aren't any eggs.
8 There was some snow last winter but not much.
9 How lovely! Somebody gave you some flowers.
10 I didn't go anywhere interesting for my holiday.

Exercise 8

1	like	9	most
2	friendlier	10	as
3	more	11	tastier
4	than	12	latest
5	worst	13	What
6	was	14	funniest
7	the	15	funnier
8	as		

Exercise 9

1	fed	6	matter
2	putting	7	pets
3	mention	8	missed
4	reservation	9	loaf
5	messy/untidy	10	stamps

Progress test 2

Exercise 1

1	earns	5	works
2	studied	6	has been
3	found	7	has been
4	has changed	8	spent

Exercise 2

Correct sentences

1 I have lived in Chesswood for five years.
2 We moved here after my daughter was born.
3 Before that we lived in London.
4 I have been a teacher since I left university.
5 I went to Bristol University in 1994.
6 We have studied English for three years.
7 I have never been to Russia, but I'd like to go.

Exercise 3

1	have to	6	don't have to
2	have to	7	have to
3	shouldn't	8	shouldn't
4	should	9	don't have to
5	has to	10	have to

Exercise 4

1 If I hear any news, I will phone you./I will phone you if I hear any news.
2 I will pay you back as soon as I can.
3 You will feel better if you stop smoking./If you stop smoking, you will feel better.
4 Peter will buy a car when he has enough money.
5 I will help you if you have a problem./If you have a problem, I will help you.

Exercise 5

1	'll call ... is	4	'll go ... finish
2	are late ... 'll go	5	don't stop ... 'll go
3	passes ... 'll buy		

Exercise 6

1 brought	brought
2 fell	fallen
3 felt	felt
4 forgot	forgotten
5 knew	known
6 let	let
7 lost	lost
8 spoke	spoken
9 told	told
10 understood	understood

Exercise 7

Correct forms

1	has failed	4	don't grow
2	was written	5	have been taken
3	were cut down		

Exercise 8

1 English is spoken all over the world.
2 Nylon has been made since 1932.
3 Why wasn't I invited to Mary's party?
4 When will the new bridge be built?
5 They were asked to design a new car.

Exercise 9

1 If I lived in Brazil, I'd/I wouldn't learn Portuguese.
2 If I earned more money, I'd/I wouldn't save it.
3 If I knew Maria's address, I'd/I wouldn't go to see her.
4 If I had a dictionary, I'd/I wouldn't look up a word.
5 If I were you, I'd/I wouldn't marry George.

Exercise 10

1 would be ... had
2 give her a pay rise next month.
3 had ... wouldn't go
4 didn't live ... would find
5 go and live with

Exercise 11

Correct sentences

1 I saw her five minutes ago.
2 We've been here since last Saturday.
3 How long have you known Wendy?
4 We haven't made coffee yet.
5 He has been waiting to see the doctor since nine o'clock.
6 When did you buy your new car?
7 Mary isn't home. She's gone to work.
8 I've been running in the park, so I'm tired.
9 I've run round the park three times.
10 They've already had their dinner.

Exercise 12

1 How long have you been waiting for a bus?
2 How long has he been saving up to buy a boat?
3 How long have you been having driving lessons?
4 How long has she been working in the library?
5 How long have they been trying to sell their house?

Exercise 13

1	up	5	off
2	up	6	after
3	out	7	on
4	out	8	down

Exercise 14

1	lose	5	make
2	sore	6	lift
3	spend	7	wear
4	applied/applying		

Grammar Reference exercises

Unit 1

1 1 lives   6 didn't see
   2 visited   7 Do (you) know
   3 Did (you) go   8 're arriving
   4 speaks   9 enjoys
   5 're wearing   10 don't like

2 1 'm   5 doesn't
   2 Do   6 aren't
   3 didn't   7 don't
   4 's   8 aren't

3 1 Where   5 Whose
   2 Why   6 Who
   3 What   7 Which
   4 How   8 When

4 (Sample answers)
   1 What are they watching?
   2 When did James arrive?
   3 Where does she live?
   4 Where does Joanna come from?
   5 Can you drive?
   6 What music do you like?
   7 How much does this/it cost?
   8 Did he enjoy the film?
   9 When are they coming?

Unit 2

1 1 lives   5 doesn't eat
   2 don't speak   6 go
   3 forgets   7 plays
   4 finishes   8 have

2 1 's/is studying
   2 aren't/are not going
   3 isn't/is not enjoying
   4 Are (you) seeing
   5 are (you) going
   6 are (they) laughing
   7 's/is having
   8 aren't/are not listening

3 1 Mario comes from Italy.
   2 We usually go by bus.
   3 He speaks Mandarin and Japanese.
   4 What a great meal! Everyone's enjoying it.
   5 I love coffee ice cream.
   6 What are you doing tonight?

4 1 goes   5 looks
   2 think   6 Are (you)
   3 're/are meeting   coming
   4 are (you) doing

5 1 I've/have got six cousins.
   2 Have we got any milk? / Do we have any milk?
   3 He hasn't got a car. / He doesn't have a car.
   4 My car has got a CD player. / My car has a CD player.

Unit 3

1 1 stopped   7 fixed
   2 worked   8 had
   3 didn't see   9 did (the prog-
   4 Did (they) go   ramme) finish
   5 left   10 organized
   6 did (you) arrive

2 1 Jack lost his job a month ago.
   2 We didn't have a holiday last year.
   3 We took a picnic to the park yesterday lunchtime.
   4 I sent an email but you didn't reply.
   5 Why did you go to bed so late last night?

3 1 I left when they were playing in the garden.
   2 I was just leaving home when the phone range.
   3 Why were you laughing at me?
   4 My computer wasn't working so I couldn't send emails.

4 1 was blowing   6 fell
   2 were making   7 was coming
   3 heard   8 was
   4 started   9 arrived
   5 was running

5 1 in   2 at   3 in   4 in   5 at   6 in
   7 at   8 on   9 in   10 On

Unit 4

1 1 U   2 U   3 U   4 C   5 C   6 U
   7 C   8 U

2 1 How much   4 many
   2 much   5 How many
   3 How many

3 1 a little   5 a lot of
   2 lots of   6 something
   3 a few   7 a lot of
   4 anything   8 anybody

4 1 someone/somebody, anybody/anyone, anybody/anyone, nobody/no one
   2 somewhere, anywhere
   3 anything, something
   4 nowhere
   5 nothing, Everything

5 2 My brother's an architect in a big company in London.
   3 Tokyo is the capital city of Japan.
   4 I bought a pair of sunglasses on Oxford Street.
   5 I live in a small village in the mountains in Switzerland.
   6 What a beautiful new coat you're wearing!
   7 I'm reading an interesting book at the moment.
   8 Life is wonderful when the sun is shining.

Unit 5

1 1 to go   4 changing
   2 dancing   5 hearing
   3 to see

2 (Sample Answers)
   2 I'll make one for you. / I'll make you one.
   3 I'll have cheese/ham please.
   4 I'll give it to you (now).
   5 I'll do it (for you).

3 1 I'm going to be   6 I'll help
   2 I'll answer   7 I'm going to
   3 I'm seeing   sneeze.
   4 I'm going to get   8 I'll take
   5 She's going to have

4 1 I'm going to New York on business.
   2 How long are you going to stay with Suzy?
   3 You are going to be very surprised.
   4 She isn't going to have a holiday this year.
   5 I think it's going to rain.

5 1 'm having
   2 'm going to buy
   3 will help
   4 's going to be
   5 're going

Unit 6

1 1 c   2 b   3 a

2 2 more expensive, most expensive
   3 further, furthest
   4 sadder, saddest
   5 more interesting, most interesting
   6 bigger, biggest
   7 better, best
   8 funnier, funniest

3 1 cheaper, the most delicious
   2 most popular
   3 better, most talented
   4 quickest
   5 more generous
   6 happier, happiest

4 1 as fast as   5 as difficult as
   2 as hot as   6 as high as
   3 as long as   7 as spicy as
   4 as quiet as   8 as exciting as

Unit 7

1 2 Have you seen Sarah?
   3 Have you made a decision yet?
   4 How long have you known Jamie?
   5 She's been to Sweden twice.
   6 Their plane has just landed.
   7 Where have you been?
   8 What have you done to your hair?

2 1 Have you ever been to Brazil?
   2 Have you ever seen an elephant?
   3 Have you ever won any money?

3 2 He's eaten everything.
   3 She's lost her bag.
   4 She's broken her leg.
   5 Our team have won the match.
   6 I've spent all my money.
4 1 I've been here since last week
   2 Kevin has had his new job for nine months. He loves it.
   3 I have lived here for ten years but I'm going to move soon.
   4 Bridgit has known Philip for a year and a half.
   5 We went to China in 2005.
   6 How long have you had your dog?
   7 They have known each other for three days.
   8 She's had a sore throat since this morning.
   9 Jane has been a vet for thirty years and she still enjoys it.
  10 How long have you lived in this city?
5 1 Have you ever heard   5 I've never heard
   2 I've never been   6 Did you see
   3 He never met   7 I've never won
   4 Did you talk   8 Have you ever dreamt

Unit 8

1 1 have to wear   4 Do you have to leave
   2 don't have to
   3 did you have to go to   5 had to
     6 didn't have to work
2 1 Can you drive a car?
   2 I'm afraid we must go now.
   3 She can sing very well.
   4 She must go to the dentist this afternoon.
   5 You shouldn't drink and drive.
   6 It won't rain tomorrow.
   7 Could you help me?
   8 I wouldn't like to be a policeman.
3 1 Could   5 mustn't/can't
   2 shouldn't   6 must
   3 might / may   7 can't
   4 Can   8 should
4 1 have to
   2 I don't think you should
   3 should
   4 should
   5 musn't
   6 must
   7 doesn't have to
   8 mustn't

Unit 9

1 1 A 2 B 3 A 4 A
2 1 b 2 b, c 3 a 4 c 5 a 6 b 7 c 8 a
3 1 'll/will go   4 'll/will get
   2 will (you) do 5 lies
   3 don't leave
4 2 will David/he do 5 will you do
   3 there aren't   6 he doesn't reply
   4 will Alice do

Unit 10

1 1 Tickets are sold at the box office.
   2 Stonehenge was built thousands of years ago.
   3 My car has been serviced.
   4 Three new hospitals were opened last year.
2 1 was stolen   6 will be made
   2 was invented   7 will be invited
   3 are given   8 are employed
   4 were (accidentally) 9 was written discovered   10 was painted
   5 have been built
3 2 The football match was cancelled because of heavy rain.
   3 We were told not to walk on the grass.
   4 How are chopsticks used?
   5 The kitchen is cleaned every morning.
   6 The escaped prisoner was arrested late last night.
   7 How was DNA discovered?
4 1 The money was stolen from the shop.
   2 correct
   3 correct
   4 Spanish is spoken in Latin America.
   5 correct

Unit 11

1 1 didn't 2 took 3 I'd help
   4 were you 5 won
2 1 e 2 a 3 d 4 c 5 b
3 1 'll/will, might, 'll/will
   2 might not, might, 'll/will, 'll/will/might, 'll/will
   3 won't, 'll/will, 'll/will, 'll/will
4 1 such   6 so many
   2 so   7 such, so
   3 so much   8 so much
   4 so   9 so much
   5 such   10 so, such

Unit 12

1 1 I've understood 5 been swimming
   2 been training   6 had
   3 been doing   7 believed
   4 bought   8 been looking
2 1 I've been practising a lot recently.
   2 We've been working hard this week
   3 I've been learning it for eight years.
   4 What have you been painting?
   5 We've been sunbathing at the beach.
3 1 1 have you done
    2 've/have been playing
    3 've/have hurt
   2 1 've/have decorated
    2 've/have been painting
    3 've/have only painted
    4 've/have finished
   3 1 haven't seen
    2 have you been doing
    3 've/have been travelling
    4 have you been
    5 've/have been
    6 Have you ever been
    7 've/have wanted
   4 1 Have you had
    2 've/have been shopping
    3 haven't spent/'ve spent
    4 've/have bought
    5 haven't bought
    6 've/have been trying
    7 haven't found

OXFORD
UNIVERSITY PRESS

Great Clarendon Street, Oxford OX2 6DP

Oxford University Press is a department of the University of Oxford.
It furthers the University's objective of excellence in research, scholarship,
and education by publishing worldwide in

Oxford New York

Auckland Cape Town Dar es Salaam Hong Kong Karachi
Kuala Lumpur Madrid Melbourne Mexico City Nairobi
New Delhi Shanghai Taipei Toronto

With offices in

Argentina Austria Brazil Chile Czech Republic France Greece
Guatemala Hungary Italy Japan Poland Portugal Singapore
South Korea Switzerland Thailand Turkey Ukraine Vietnam

OXFORD and OXFORD ENGLISH are registered trade marks of
Oxford University Press in the UK and in certain other countries

ISBN: 978 0 19 471588 1

Printed in China

This book is printed on paper from certified and well-managed sources.

ACKNOWLEDGEMENTS

*The authors and publisher are grateful to those who have given permission to reproduce
the following extracts and adaptations of copyright material:* pp129, 149 *Don't You
Want Me* Words and Music by John Callis, Philip Oakey and Adrian Wright
© 1981 Virgin Music Publishing Ltd and V2 Music Publishing (66.66%)EMI
Virgin Music Ltd, London WC2H 0QY Reproduced by permission of
International Music Publications Ltd. All rights reserved.
pp132, 150 *Come Away With Me* Words and Music by Norah Jones © 2001
Muthajones Music and EMI Blackwood Music Inc, USA EMI Music Publishing
Ltd, London WC2H 0QY Reproduced by permission of International Music
Publications Ltd. All rights reserved.
pp134, 150 *What If* written and composed by Berryman/Buckland/Champion/
Martin. Published by BMG Music Publishing Ltd. Used by permission. All
rights reserved.

Illustrations by: Stephen Conlin p100.

*We would also like to thank those who have given permission to reproduce the following
photographs:* Getty Images pp124 (couple at bar/Mark C O'Flaherty Photography/
Photonica), 128 (wedding couple/Justin Pumfrey/Taxi); PunchStock p126
(silhouetted couple/Photodisc); Rex Features/Everett Collection pp130–131
(Ian Fleming).